The Police We Deserve (with P. J. Stead ed.): Wolfe (1973)
Policing Freedom: Macdonald and Evans (1979)

Law and Disorder

John Alderson

HAMISH HAMILTON
LONDON

To
E R

First published in Great Britain 1984
by Hamish Hamilton Ltd
Garden House 57–59 Long Acre London WC2E 9JZ

British Library Cataloguing in Publication Data

Alderson, John
  Law and disorder.
  1. Police—Great Britain—History—20th century
  2. Police—Social aspects—Great Britain
  I. Title
  363.2'0941   HV8195.A2

  ISBN 0–241–11259–1

Printed in Great Britain by Richard Clay
The Chaucer Press, Bungay

Contents

v

APPENDICES

Acknowledgements

My thanks to the Warden and Fellows of Nuffield College, Oxford, who in their generosity awarded me a Gwilym Gibbon Fellowship in 1982–3 and time and opportunity to reflect on and discuss some of the intricacies of an illusive topic. My special thanks to Professor A. H. Halsey for his encouragement and to Carley Brown for her invaluable help in checking the manuscript. None of those to whom I extend my gratitude bear any responsibility for the shortcomings which may emerge in what follows.

J. A.

*Corruptissima republica
plurimae leges*

Tacitus

Preface

Specialists tend to write their books for other specialists. In *Law and Disorder* I have tried to provide some insight into policing and the social order for the interested lay-person as well.

It hardly needs to be stressed that the subject of policing is currently surrounded by controversy which, by the very nature of modern western society, is likely to continue. Change in society provides a constant challenge to those whose work and interests commit them to progress in this aspect of the human drama.

Prologue

British society towards the end of the twentieth century finds itself in some ways moribund. Crime and disorder pose threats to the social fabric. The institutions of state, including Parliament itself, fail to generate confidence of being able to cope adequately and in time with the problems posed by economic and other changes. The call is often heard for retreat to the older and more familiar ground of the past which people believe was more stable, where right and wrong were more clearly defined and agreed upon, and where crime and anti-social behaviour were restricted to manageable proportions. Apart altogether from the fact that the past was never so good as it appears in hindsight, there can never be any going back unless the British people have lost the will to build a new society on the foundations of the old.

Mistaken Ideas

Britain, along with many other Western societies, will experience increases in crime and disorder. Governments do not seem to have the answers to the problem or they would have applied them long ago. The government elected in 1979 both promised and planned to control crime and disorder. I did not believe that it would or could. In the event, crime rose to heights unprecedented since records were maintained and disorder and rioting were the most serious in living memory.

But a political philosophy which harbours and generates the idea that crime and disorder can be significantly rolled back by repression is in grave error. It is but a catalogue of despair to hold out that—by creating more criminal offences, increasing penal severity, restoring the death penalty, increasing police powers, applying more force, including

3

potentially lethal force, and repatriating coloured immigrants—'England's green and pleasant land' would be purged of the immorality and misbehaviour of its criminal tendency. What a programme and what a mistake! Such a catalogue of responses to social problems would, if combined, turn Britain, within a decade or so, into a more criminogenic and violent society than anything yet witnessed in modern times. A country of 'law and disorder'.

But what are the alternative responses? That is what this book is about.

People Don't Change—Social Orders Do

The ultimate thrust of my book is to proclaim that the people of Britain are no more dishonest or honest, no more peace-loving or violent, than they ever were. If there is more crime, more fear of crime, more disorder or apprehension of it, it is not because there is a shortage of criminal laws or enforcers of those laws, for both have multiplied beyond levels envisaged even 25 years ago. The search for a rational, objective explanation of the criminal and anti-social dilemma has to be carried out by examination of the social order itself. There will always be dishonesty and violence, for such things are in the nature of man, though when these things become morbid other explanations have to be pursued.

Show me the party political manifesto which proclaims that it will approach the reduction of crime and disorder through increases in democratic activity, for example, and I might begin to see a brighter light at the end of the tunnel. There is a rhetoric about freedom and democracy, and there is also the reality. Words like 'freedom' and 'democracy' fall easily from the lips of political orators, but in truth Britain is a stunted democracy.

Left, Right and Centre

At grass roots level, in neighbourhoods and communities there is a marked absence of democratic participation. As for local government, it has gone—it is no longer local, using the term in its ordinary meaning. The reforms of the early 1970s have created regional government, but by calling it 'local' an

4

illusion is created. Furthermore, in recent times it has been challenged and weakened by the central government. Ironically for a country which in the past prided itself on its local democracy, we have now to set about *recreating* local government.

At parliamentary level no-one, apart from the myopic or prejudiced, pretends any longer that the power of the people is democratically represented in the House of Commons. The present system of elections and parliamentary representation confers upon us a strong government, its apologists aver. Precisely—strong, but not democratic. Not democratic in the sense that the immense power of the modern bureaucratic executive arm of government is directly influenced by all shades of political opinion in reasonable proportions. The system serves power quite well but democracy less so. As for the House of Lords, whatever its many virtues, it makes no pretence to be democratic. Well, you may ask, what has all this to do with social order and disorder? Quite a lot!

Government by minority as in Britain, particularly when such governments are radical, is unstable government— elected dictatorships of Left or Right. There are always prospects of disorder, even of violence, in such circumstances.

If we are to seek the cause of most disorder and violence in Britain over the last 15 years, and there has been a lot, we must not look for 'a criminal fraternity'. Instead we have to look to the political divide and the related industrial divide. These are the social fissures which have largely preoccupied the police, the courts and official inquiries. The historic antagonism between those old adversaries socialism and conservatism contains the seeds of criminal violence and social and industrial damage. In these circumstances the politics of the Centre become important indeed.

The barely concealed conspiracy by the old adversaries to keep out emerging new political forces is not only to fly in the face of democracy, but also to render government less stable. It is a potential threat to a stable social order.

Participation

I am concerned that unless more democratic participation is developed at small community level, more confidence engendered in 'local' government, and more democratic representation in Parliament, Britain will in future run the risk of becoming more disorderly, unattractive, and unfair. Such a society cannot expect to possess the foundations for public peace and tranquillity. There are other clouds on the horizon too. Political extremism is one and it is related to the weakness already pointed out.

Extremism

It is well documented that the extreme Left would wish to change the social order through violence if necessary, and the Special Branch and the Security Service have long been preoccupied with keeping a watchful eye on them. And since the police are regarded as a stumbling block in their path to create chaos as a prelude to change, the two forces have long been at loggerheads.

I first experienced serious movements of the extreme Right in the early 1970s when, because of industrial chaos and violence, moves were made to set up private armies. One such movement was initiated by General Walter Walker, who no doubt hated Communism and all its works. He sent two of his lieutenants to see me. I had spoken out against the scheme.

I was put under some pressure to support the movement and given a clear impression that they believed the working classes were about to rise up in some kind of revolutionary fervour. Petrograd was mentioned and parallels were drawn with the Bolshevik uprising in Czarist Russia! I was assured that the General's movement was gathering pace and many hundreds of volunteers had already enrolled to assist the police. Reminisinces of the 1926 general strike! I refused to have any truck with the idea.

Meanwhile the extreme Right has switched its paranoia to ethnic minorities, including their much persecuted target, the Jews. Now, in order to cloak their extremism under political respectability, they have moved to infiltrate the Conservative Party.

Race

Britain today is a racist society in many ways and such

6

sentiments are not confined to the extreme Right. Even the police, prison service, and trade unions have been found to contain racists and to harbour antipathetic views. There are some seeds here for communal violence too. I have spoken out against racism in the police before. I know that it is not yet widespread. It should be rooted out with the same fervour we have always applied to the rooting out of corruption.

Recording Subversion

I came under fire from Rightist political factions for reporting that the records being amassed through Special Branch activities contained too many instances of legitimate pressure groups, protest movements, and individuals who were active in public affairs. I believed that in any case some 50% of the records were either useless or misleading. The notion of subversion was being too widely drawn. This will be a continuing problem unless data protection and inspection over the activities of state officials have improved.

We have no Bill of Rights, another weakness, and little regard for the training of police and other government officials in human rights, in particular the European Convention on Human Rights. I propose to comment more fully on these weaknesses.

Community Policing

In my efforts to develop community policing and closer liaison between local government departments and the police, I came under fire from the political Left. Ever ready to see in the police a threat to freedom, they accused me of interfering with local government democracy, a charge which was later withdrawn.

Now a word about community policing. Community policing is based on the theory that undue reliance on criminal prosecutions is not the best way to control petty delinquency. Communities generate the problem and therefore have the means of controlling it through positive activity. The lynch-pin is the Community Policing Consultative Group. The Group is supported by all the social agencies including the police who work with the delegates. The police in making

7

themselves accountable to the community surrender some of their autonomy. They report on the state of crime in the neighbourhood and discuss positive ways of preventing it. Social causes of crime are highlighted by the social and welfare agencies and combined action is undertaken to ameliorate the conditions giving rise to crime. It is high visibility preventive activity. One of the difficulties facing any architect of community policing is the absence of democratic participation in community government—a device which is critical to a well ordered society. I will argue in this book for the establishment of a communitarian base for the improvement of the social order.

In my advocacy of a community based policing system I came under some criticism. In order to help refine and develop thinking on the subject of social order and the police, time to experiment was both in short supply and important. I reluctantly declined a proposed appointment to the Home Office Inspectorate of Constabulary in 1979 and later that year turned down the prospect of a senior appointment in Australia for the same reason. I certainly have no regrets on both scores—the search for a superior way of controlling social disorder is a compelling one. I campaigned vigorously over a number of years both within and without the police service for its introduction, at no small cost.

The culmination of my campaigning came when the Scarman Inquiry was set up following the Brixton disorders in 1981. Here was a legitimate and non-political platform for determined advocacy. My own evidence to the Scarman Inquiry is included in this book at Appendix 'A'. I later resigned from the police to campaign as a Liberal Party Candidate in the 1983 general election, believing that some of the issues concerning policing had become so politicised that this was the correct stance to take. I fully support the principle that police officers should not be allowed to participate in party political activities while they are serving.

I also came in for both derision and criticism within the police service, particularly in the 1970s when warning of the prospects of communal violence if changes in the policing policies were not implemented. At different times I urged these ideas upon the Home Secretary and the Commissioner of Police of the Metropolis, Mr. William Whitelaw and Sir David

McNee. For their own good reasons it was felt that, though they worked well enough in Devon and Cornwall, the theories were less applicable in inner-city areas. Experiments are now well under way in such areas and some success and progress is being reported. The Home Office are putting more pressure on police forces to speed up development. This is all to the good, I believe. The credit however has to go to Lord Scarman for the sagacity of his recommendations following his inquiry into the 1981 riots.

Repressive policing and lack of consultation with the public represent a threat to public tranquillity. This is particularly so when people live in squalor and relative deprivation. But when all is said and done, it is for governments to devise new ways of strengthening the social order, and I believe that the extension of democratic participation in policy making in all facets of government, particularly affecting communities, is an urgent requirement. Time is not on our side.

A Protest

It is unfortunate that, due to the lack of an adequate political forum at community level in which to discuss local issues, people are often brought into conflict with the law and the police. Some people suffer prosecution, humiliation and social ostracism as they feel obliged to protest. I refused to arrest peaceful anti-nuclear demonstrators at Luxulyan in Cornwall in 1981 because I believed they were not clearly to be seen breaking any law, although admittedly they were making a nuisance of themselves. But being a nuisance is not a crime. I will describe in the book what happened to me and to the demonstrators. Suffice to say that the conflict took six months to resolve, though not one arrest was made.

Law and Disorder

It is true that a nation will become more reliant on police power and the criminal sanction if democracy fails to provide adequate social justice, but there is a deep-seated idea of 'fairness' in the British psyche which is as capable of responding to well-intentioned effort.

Should future trends bring the courts and the police into a

9

dominant central political role, the social forces which thrive on liberty, equality and fraternity will wither, and within 20 years or so the face of British society will have become unattractive. Harmony and peace in neighbourhoods will give way to tensions and hostilities. A new role for the police, and even military forces in their support, will be defined. Civil strife and violence of spasmodic but unacceptable proportions may become a feature of life.

In anticipation of a continuing economic decline in real terms, it is to be doubted whether the juggernaut which is the state will be able to respond quickly enough to bring about changes which are essential. Existing bureaucracies are too inflexible for quick responses. While the machinery of government grinds on, things are happening. There are at least two credible reactions. One will manifest itself through increasing authoritarian, even ruthless political impulses. The state will seek ever more power to impose order. Freedom will suffer.

An alternative scenario, which I will seek to justify, lies in increased democratic activity and participation through the mass politicisation of society. It lies in a society in which every adult person (and, for some purposes, youth) is given a civic role. Because responsibility increases where political participation is generated, the social order can be within the active influence of all people.

Though the earliest socialising influences for social order are located within the family, the role of education will be critical. The production of a new generation with social, moral and political ideas capable of fashioning a new democracy to contain and ameliorate future social problems will be regarded as a touchstone. Those facets of government which touch upon, or fail to touch upon, the daily lives of people in their neighbourhoods will be tested, influenced and motivated by the activities of participatory democracy. Additionally the people will be encouraged to take neighbourhood initiatives. In this way, the social order will be affected by essential forces rising up from the bottom to balance essential governmental activity flowing down from the top. The control of crime and public disorder will be a shared political and social responsibility within neighbourhoods, since maintenance of the quality of life will no longer be seen to be entirely dependent on remote bureaucratic activity.

As society becomes increasingly aware of human rights, it will be more offended by their denial or by equivocation in their provision. The demand for a Bill of Rights as a constitutional guarantee will grow. The present position in Britain is unsatisfactory.

Magistrates' courts are at present often too remote geographically, as are magistrates in social backgrounds. There is a need to gear them more closely to neighbourhood environments. Justice delivered within the context of a local community, and aware of its advantages and disadvantages, will be seen to be 'better' justice, at least so far as juvenile offenders are concerned. Defendants with special problems of youth, old age, ethnicity, disability and poverty, for example, should have the advantage of assessors assisting magistrates, for in this way justice within the context of community courts will be facilitated. In turn, communities will expect to be active in preventing crime, assisting the police, and supervising and assisting offenders, and in the after-care of discharged prisoners.

Police—Friend or Foe

There has been a growing tendency in most Western democracies to place too great a reliance on the criminal sanction for social control and this in turn has required considerable increases in police power. The police in turn have more and more to be seen and to see themselves primarily as law enforcers. In the United States a disservice has been done to the idea of policing by labelling police 'law enforcement officers'. Police should be much more than law enforcers; to use an older term they should be 'peace officers'. The basis for the police role is to be found in the idea of 'peace' for they are 'keepers of the peace', and enforcement of laws is but one element in their function.

Neither have the police been well served by scholars and writers. Other professions—the Church, medicine, education, the law, politics, economics, and even the military—have been provided with philosophical and theoretical bases for their social function, but the police have lacked this vital foundation. It is small wonder that, when under pressure, the

11

criminal sanction is found to be their only refuge. As they play a growing and significant political as well as a legal and social role, it is important that the policing function should be seen to be grounded in adequate philosophical principles.

I have argued elsewhere the case for liberty, equality and fraternity to be essential foundations for the policing function.[1] Since the police are possessed of much power, that power needs more than its legal framework to qualify its application and use.

The police have to be seen and to see themselves as protectors of liberty within the law. Freedoms depend on the ability of the police (and the courts) to protect them equally, not unequally, and in doing so actively to generate fraternity not enmity. Unlike the soldier, the policeman should not think in terms of enemies, wayward, recalcitrant and anti-social though some people may be. Police are not cast to exact vengeance, for if society seeks vengeance at all this is the function of the courts.

In Britain at least, the political dimensions of policing are not yet sufficiently comprehended.

The police and policing were first drawn into the party political debate as a central issue in the general election of 1966. That was the year in which the Conservative Party made law and order a central plank in their election manifesto. The growth of permissiveness (or freedom, according to one's point of view) under the law reforms and influence of Roy Jenkins at the Home Office and the rise in the crime rate provided ready ammunition for reaction. It also found an echo and a response in police circles then and since. The Police Federation of England and Wales with their adviser, Mr. Eldon Griffiths, Conservative M.P. for Bury St. Edmunds, have mounted a number of political campaigns for the restoration of the death penalty, increased penal severity and police powers. Some senior police officers have openly criticised the policies of the political Left. Policing ideology, it seems, finds difficulty in accommodating progressive political thought.

In each ensuing general election until 1983 ascendancy in debates on law and order seemed almost to be a Conservative Party monopoly. The simple idea that more police, with greater powers and equipment, plus more courts and increased penal severity equals less crime is a seductive one. The other political parties seemed to be unable to provide alternative policies capable of catching the public imagination in the same way. It was to be the rises in reported crime and the serious riots in London and elsewhere during the first Thatcher administration which shook the confidence of the reactionary school of thought.

Even then the idea that equipping the police with death-dealing plastic bullets and noxious C.S. gas plus the re-introduction of capital punishment would somehow solve the problem of crime and disorder had many supporters. I campaigned hard against it. Meanwhile I had become convinced that there was an alternative to policing through escalating repression if only it could be clarified to commend itself to the police and the public and find its way into a coherent political philosophy.

Policing is a highly political function, if only because the laws which are enforced are a political creation and the discretion with which they are enforced often reveals the 'political' preferences of those who decide the policies of enforcement. In many ways the police are more comfortable with the politics of the Right. This should not come as a surprise, since the police are psychologically predisposed to maintenance of the status quo, the order of things. When a society embarks upon a period of the social upheaval which precedes change, it is difficult for the police to adapt. The confusion, even disorientation, of the police during the social upheaval marked by the permissive legislation of the 1960s and the advent of the plural multi-racial society was profound. For many, coming to terms with it all proved a somewhat painful business. Recent reactions, and the emphasis on the idea of order through law and penal severity, have restored some police self confidence. But overt attacks on the political Left have come from the Commissioner of Police of the Metropolis, chief constables and the Police Federation, who, for what they deemed no doubt their own good reasons, have demonstrated the willingness of the police to enter political controversy.

If Britain were to acquire a kind of police state it would not come about through a commitment to ideology but to drift. Should the social order become brittle due to difficulties arising out of economic deterioration, the drift would consist in the first place of a steady move towards bureaucratic centralism. Government departments would increase, are increasing, their own investigative branches both in numbers and in power. As more information on the populace would thereby be stored, it would be shared between those departments, the police and the security services. In the absence of adequate protection from a Bill of Rights, and data protection, the right of privacy would be eroded.

In such a scenario one of two things would happen to the police. A weakening of the bonds of attachments and loyalties to local communities would lead to the system becoming an institution in itself. This could be facilitated by police policies being decided by administrative rather than by democratic means. In a state of emergency, as happens now, the chief constables and senior civil servants would decide on the deployment of police from a central location. Decision making would cut out local police authorities. This happened during the urban riots of 1981 when the issue of plastic bullets and launching equipment was an executive decision—local police authorities were not consulted. Secondly, the Home Secretary by using his powers under the Police Act of 1964 could bring about a national police system in fact, if not in name.

The conflict between government secrecy and open government is at present a contentious matter. It tends to stimulate leaking of information, followed by investigation and trial. A kind of administrative resistance movement would build up. Protest movements would become even more vulnerable to the attention of the state. There are signs of a drift in this direction.

Police accountability has also raised its head as a political problem and I propose to discuss my reasons for recommending a Royal Commission to clear the air. The last time the problem was examined by such a Commission was in 1962 but Britain and her police system of 1984 have both been the subject of profound change since then. It is a matter for speculation whether the police would ever criticise a government for being too draconian with its measures for public order, though a doubt must remain. For these reasons alone it would not be prudent to grant the police in any society undue political influence.

14

A Communitarian Base

The theme of this book is the idea that the social order in any society depends on the healthy state of many and differing institutions. When those institutions weaken, the police and criminal justice are brought into play on a much higher level of social control. When this social condition prevails and is further compounded by seeming injustices, alienation and marked division, society ceases to be a cohesive one and crime and disorder, accompanied by heavier and more omnipotent policing responses, and demands for increases in penal severity, follow. Societies which develop these conditions become less attractive and less civilised. To avoid the drift towards such societies, a movement in the direction of communitarianism offers much to those prepared to understand and create it.

I believe that British society is entering a phase where community is becoming more important, meaningful and understood. My book concludes with a description of a communitarian society which is not only a good society in itself, but also one in which the police, the courts and the penal institutions have been relieved of some of the pressures being exerted upon them; and one in which the constant increase in powers and resources for policing have been slowed down and halted. In short, a society where tendencies towards law and disorder give way to tendencies towards order through justice and democratic participation.

Part One

THE SOCIAL ORDER

Chapter 1
Social Order and Disorder

I will comment on some aspects of the social structure in Britain today in order that the terms 'law and order' or 'law and disorder' may be seen in the cultural and political context. I have chosen to mention but a few of the more important political theories which in an eclectic work of this kind can receive but cursory attention.

It is a common error to consider the policing of a society in terms of laws, their enforcements, and the system of criminal justice as a whole. This particular error leads along false pathways since order in society depends upon a whole system of cultural and institutional networks. When those networks are strong and effective, the role of the police is placed on the social periphery. When social change is taking place at a fast, and, to some, disturbing pace, the role of the police may become central; the police might be strengthened and used to prevent social and political change taking place. When, however, it is realised that some change is inevitable if society is to become more tranquil, changes are forced upon society and the degree of police activity is thereby diminished.

Social Order

What is the importance of institutions such as family, school, neighbourhood and employment? How can we identify those forces which cause the condition of order to break down? It is only when answers to questions of this kind are discovered that the role of the police and laws can be seen more clearly. If we wish to understand the growth of crime and the outbreaks of public disorder and riots, we must first of all understand our social structure, its strengths and its weaknesses. Just as war is a failure of diplomatic activity so, too, is social disorder a failure of political, religious, or authoritative activity.

Most of us most of the time take the idea of social order for granted. Until some violent protest or a wave of disorder happens, we seldom question the adequacy of the existing order. We seldom ask ourselves why there is not *more* crime and disorder, though we regularly ask why is there so much. Neither social order nor social disorder, however, takes place in a vacuum. They are the product of forces, both good and evil, associated with society.

Evolution and reform seldom generate downwards from state to subject without there first being an upwards pressure. That upwards pressure often takes the form of disorder, as in the Civil Wars of 1642 and 1648 which toppled the Divine Right of Kings, or in the Reform movements of the nineteenth century, and the Suffragette campaign of the twentieth, which resulted in the achievement of universal franchise.

Man: A Social Animal

Man is a social animal. He needs society in order to survive and attain contentment. In turn, society makes demands on him.

Life without social order of some kind becomes intolerable. If social disorder persists some people may acquiesce in the imposition of order by strong and even ruthless government: the remainder will be coerced. People will give up their freedom for order. The history of the world is replete with examples.

The rise of Hitler and the Nazi régime in Germany in the 1930s grew out of the chaos of the Weimar Republic. The rise of Lenin and Stalin owed much to the chaos and degeneracy of Czarist Russia. The rise of Mao Tse Tung and the final victory of Totalitarianism in China established order out of the disintegrating, despotic and chaotic rule of the War Lords. In all these cases freedom was the sacrifice but order was the prize.

Henry VIII and Cromwell in England, Napoleon in France, Mussolini in Italy and Franco in Spain all owed their domination in some degree at least to the preceding social disorder. Societies are never totally immune from prospects of this kind. It would be imprudent to believe that Great Britain today has solved this dilemma for ever, though it has achieved more than many.

Society: Conflict or Harmony?

Man in a 'state of nature', and left to his own devices in pursuit of his own desires becomes dominated by his passions over his reason, said Thomas Hobbes (1588–1679). Every man becomes the enemy of every other man and in this way social order degenerates into chaos. There are indicators in contemporary problems of terrorism, serious disorder and serious crime, which serve to remind us that relapse into a 'state of nature' signals dangers for social society. People given to such extremes of behaviour are, as we know, quite capable of rationalising their actions as being in the pursuit of 'good'. The 'good' could be causing chaos as a prelude to a better order and the righting of wrongs, for example, or could be redistributing property in a society which encourages its acquisition.

The graffiti seen recently on a London wall, DON'T WORK—ROB THE RICH, is an expression of both passion and reason, if also dangerous and anti-social. Hobbes's comment, that 'if any two men desire the same thing which nevertheless they cannot both enjoy, they become enemies; and in the way to their end endeavour to destroy or subdue one another,' is certainly true of much of our understanding of today's serious crime and disorder. In the absence of some form of restraint, men will fall into behaviour which offers the most efficient means of achieving their own ends. These could be, for example, by force (small man with a gun dominates a big man unarmed) or fraud (a cunning man can dominate a stupid one).

Hobbes may well be right about the nature of man, but his solution of the problem is contentious to twentieth-century liberated thinkers. Hobbes's theory of the social contract requires that the individual surrender his natural liberty to a Sovereign authority (in his own day the Divine Right of the King). 'I give up my freedom for your guarantee of social order' may sum it up crudely. 'Relieve me of the fraud and force of my fellow man.'

This theory entails the centralisation of all power, since not all can be given equal power. The problem for today's liberated man, therefore, is to grapple with the centralised power of bureaucracies which include, of course, the police.

Other thinkers since Hobbes have stressed the constructive force of the rationality of man. They assume that man sees advantage in social order where life, health, liberty and possessions are the product of a natural order, only occasionally requiring intervention by government. John Locke (1632–1704), another celebrated English philosopher, propounded this view of the social order which is nearer to our more recent traditions than that of Hobbes. Where Hobbes sees the state as the *sine qua non* of civil society, Locke tends to regard it as an insurance, since man has his own vested interest in subscribing freely to the exercise of reason in a socially constructive way. This is a more positive view of man and provides the basis of many of our ideas of civil liberty and human rights. It is also borne out by our experience since, in spite of both opportunity and motive, most people most of the time neither commit crimes nor engage in public disorder. It is one of the reasons why we are not overwhelmed by crime and why we live in relative harmony with our neighbours.

Locke argued for two kinds of 'reasons' which operate among men—on the one hand, the pursuit of one's own selfish ends; on the other, the rationality of the need to cooperate with others, best summed up in the aphorism 'to live and let live'. Man therefore (according to Locke) has two conflicting forces operating in his motivations: a liberal democracy in pursuit of social order has to recognise them both.

The problem of order should not be disproportionately stressed against that of the liberating effects necessary for creative freedom to flower. The recent conflicts between the laws affecting private morality such as obscenity, homosexuality, abortion and censorship, and the upsurge of libertarianism in the 1960s illustrate this point. In a society where individualism challenges imposed conformity, those in authority—including of course the police—bear the brunt of the onslaught. The many protest movements of recent times provide ample evidence of this kind of social action. But individuals or groups each seeking fulfilment in a plural society (that is a society where diversities of culture, race and morals exist) at the same time need to acknowledge their 'identity of interests' with others.

It is argued, however, by some[1] that this identity of interests is not a natural order of things, nor will it maintain an acceptable social order under all circumstances. Take the conflict between capital and labour, for example, a matter which calls for consideration not only in economic theory but also in examination of the social order.

People begin to see that, in the harsh world of competition for the division of goods and wealth, the idea of identity of interests is questioned. (The growth in unemployment resulting from recession and technology in recent times is not only an economic problem but also one of social order.)

Ideas of inequality, injustice, oppression and coercion, if not in some way ironed out and balanced, begin to threaten the stability of order. Though competition may serve to regulate social affairs, producing its own form of balance, it might also lead to excessive exploitation and, once this kind of social consequence becomes subject to theoretical bases for positive action, the thin line of order through identity of interests is broken. When this happens, of course, the state has to rely further on its monopoly of coercive powers, which in turn can heighten social tensions and produce disorder.

The division of society into classes—on the one hand the employers and on the other the labourers—is the Marxist base of social dissension, that is, exploitation of the proletariat (the workers) by the bourgeoisie (the capitalists). Marx's view of industrial society cast its working class as a force destined to overthrow the existing social order. Neither Hobbes's theory of society as a permanent state of war nor Locke's idea of a natural non-coercive harmonious order was capable of dealing with this new challenge. Many of our industrial disputes are based on Marx's notions. The intervention of Marxism was to have profound effects on the ideas of social order which have marked most of the twentieth century. However, his prediction of a social revolution in which the workers would overthrow the capitalist system has failed to materialise in the West. The identity of interest within the social order was underestimated.

Marx's idea that the social order should be based on the dictum 'from each according to his labour and to each according to his needs' is still likely to inspire many to seek a more just social order. Yet the Marxist State as imposed by Lenin and Stalin in the Soviet Union has since been seen as a threat to the liberal traditions of the West—in fact, as its main enemy, alongside Fascism which no longer exists as a ruling force in Europe. As a consequence, those whose sympathies lie in this direction and who actively seek to promote Communism and Fascism are regarded as particularly subversive and are the subject of unfavourable police attention.

On the other hand, the liberal state believing, as it does, in free enterprise and the rights of the individual as against the corporate state, remains the main force against Marxist ideology. It does not, however, guarantee basic equality nor does it, as Professor Halsey has stressed, put a premium on that other essential ingredient of a healthy social order, fraternity. '...The market place promotes neither equality or fraternity.'[2]

The social destructiveness of the Industrial Revolution in early nineteenth-century Britain, and the disorder which followed, pressed hard on political philosophers and politicians alike. The Luddite riots in 1811 and 1812 were put down by military force. The identity of interest fundamental to good social order was fractured by a new technology. An economy or a social order based on the crude dictum 'every man for himself' is clearly inimical to both social justice and social order.

In 1831, riots and disorder connected with the pressure for the reform of Parliament and universal suffrage once again proved that the perpetuation of perceived injustices will sooner or later damage social order. The efforts of John Stuart Mill (1806–73) and others to refine political ideas began to effect changes in government policy. Meanwhile Robert Owen (1771–1858) developed socialist ideas different from those of Marx. Owen's thoughts on the social impact of technology have a peculiarly contemporary ring about them. 'Machinery,' he said, 'was displacing labour, and laisser-faire gave the working classes no adequate means of combating mechanical power.'[3] This change undoubtedly contained the seeds of disorder, and Owen's way of combating the evil gave impetus to the idea of socialism. Whereas Marx and Communism were to talk of revolution, democratic socialism was to be the product of evolution within a liberal democracy.

1984 and All That

As 1984 approached many began to wonder whether we were to witness a great division in society. Those who were doing well out of the new economic order, the product of Thatcherite monetarism and the slimmed down but more efficient industrial base, would provide one society; while the other would consist of those permanently or intermittently unemployed. Would the social order be held together only by a police system, strengthened numerically, trained to deal with public disorder on a scale not recently witnessed, and with increased legal powers? Would the great social divide first of all induce apathy, and then would the frozen anger which apathy represents break out into steadily escalating and spasmodic social violence? Would violent and organised crime increase to a scale already being witnessed in that part of John Bull's other island where the tribal divide resists both social and political solutions? What kind of police would such a society deserve?

The basis of order in society does not primarily depend on laws, police and judges, essential though they may be. A healthy, orderly society depends on such a multiplicity of interacting forces that there is no simple way of explaining how it may be attained. It is currently fashionable to emphasise more rigid enforcement of laws, increased severity of punishment, and other authoritarian measures as an end in themselves. This happens when problems of social disorder increase. It is to treat the symptom rather than the cause, which is more easily understood, and therefore more popular, than is the pursuit of knowledge and understanding of the complexities and intricacies of social development. But policemen and others concerned with maintaining social order have to pursue these things.

The Individual and The State

It is important to acknowledge the difference between the state and society. The state is the product of society not society of the state. The state is an artificial creation, capable of being changed either by social violence, where the institutions fail to give way to or adapt, or by pressure stemming from conflict of ideas about—for example—justice. Britain has experience of both these phenomena. A search for understanding of social order has therefore to begin not with a study of government and legislation but with man as an individual and man as a social being. It is precisely because of the preoccupation with laws and neglect of man in society that many of our problems arise. It is at least possible to argue that, if we understand how to bring about social order based on mutual respect and voluntary cooperation, then the dominant role of police and other bureaucracies of state could be diminished. The converse is to argue that man in our present society is so lacking in this spirit that laws and officials to enforce them have inevitably to increase.

The Making of an Individual

The first processes of socialisation are for the vast majority of people learned within the family unit. If we are born and mature within a family which is cohesive, loving, orderly and efficient, our chances of carrying such virtues forward into society are considerable. If, on the other hand, we are born and brought up in a family of thieves our chances of becoming thieves are very high. Every policeman knows this from experience; and countless sociologists, criminologists and behavioural scientists know it from their research.

Some children are of course exceptions to this rule. Well endowed psychologically and biologically, some will emerge unscathed from unpropitious circumstances, while others, even given all the advantages of the best family environments, will manifest delinquent tendencies. It is common knowledge, however, that the family is so important to the state of social order that, should it break down on a large scale, the consequences for widespread anti-social behaviour are considerably heightened.

The social disorder which exists in some of our crowded, poverty-stricken and disorganised neighbourhoods is often due to the concentration of large numbers of families which have broken down and have ceased to function as a socialising force for public order. Equally, where families continue to function well, the opposite applies.

West and Farrington[4] in their painstaking study of 400 male youths between the ages of eight and 18 commented, 'It seems that delinquent character formation begins early. An inherited temperamental disposition possibly contributes, but lack of attention, affection and consistent training from parents during formative years is a more obvious and probably more important factor.'

In discussing the important implications of their study they went on to say, 'It could be that one of the most opportune times to intervene in the delinquency cycle is before a child is born when young people are leaving their homes and beginning to produce families of their own.' This clearly indicates that not only is the family an important determinant of social behaviour but that some parents find familial duties to be a burden beyond their own capabilities. Happily the vast majority of families bring up their children without the disaster of ingrained delinquency. Nor is the family as a social institution, at least in Great Britain, in danger.

The Family

The Study Commission on the Family[5] reported in 1983 that, 'Surveys show more satisfaction about the family than with other aspects of life in Britain.' Cohabitation before marriage, while becoming more fashionable, does not appear to have affected the idea of the family. Certainly, the divorce rate rose from 31,000 in 1951 to 146,000 in 1979, but a high proportion of divorcees remarry, thus creating new families. One and a half million children are today brought up by one parent. In most of these families that one parent is also the bread winner. It is far better to be brought up in a happy loving household by one parent than in an unhappy one with two parents. Nevertheless, many children grow up without the advantages represented by the stable two-parent family, balanced in the psychological dimensions represented by mother and father. Children who are not genetically disposed towards delinquency can cope with many familial disadvantages but those who are so disposed are vastly more vulnerable.[6]

The impact of the emancipation of women, coupled with the economic realities of modern life, has resulted in some 52% of mothers being at work, full or part-time. Provided that such families are well organised, there is every indication that they can add to the quality of family life both in economic and cultural terms. Many women, however, are forced out to work to maintain children and home after desertion, separation or divorce. They need help. Their children are often among the vulnerable, though many of them cope admirably, particularly where they are supported by close family ties.

Family patterns and styles are changing. In addition, there are ethnic and religious differences. Roman Catholic families use divorce and separation less than others, though some would point to the evidence which supports the view that to be brought up in an unhappy family atmosphere is more damaging than being brought up in a broken but happy home.[7] Asian families also show fewer instances of one-parent families than the indigenous population, while the West Indian culture shows slightly more.

Considerable progress has been made by agencies such as the social services, the Marriage Guidance Council, churches and voluntary organisations. Problems, however, remain. Too many families are sacrificed to modern stresses and tensions and the children, who are themselves the victims, number among their ranks the future occupants of state institutions, from community homes to Her Majesty's Prisons. This is a blot on the record of a comparatively affluent society, which often hypocritically describes itself as a caring society.

Neighbourhood Pressures

Those who live in neat suburban homes, in tree-lined avenues, with all the many advantages of modern standards of living, are likely to have positive social attitudes instilled from an early age. Even in households where there is unhappiness and other psychological deprivation, such forces are not to be further compounded by neighbourhood defects. The patterns of behaviour set and demanded, however informal, are powerful social controls that only the most delinquent, the most rebellious and non-conformist—those of most independent mind—are likely to flout. The network of institutions, including youth movements and social gatherings, further strengthens conformity with what is regarded as a desirable way to live.

Experience indicates that the young who come from less 'desirable' neighbourhoods are particularly discouraged from entering this territory. Children may be forbidden to bring home friends with whom they play and work at school on amicable terms. Adults do not go to the same clubs nor join the same institutions. The golf club, the motoring club, and the many voluntary movements tend to reinforce the strong pressures for conventional behaviour.

These are the middle and lower-middle classes, or their aspirants, whose behavioural standards are generally regarded as those to be aimed for. They will seldom call for the police to deal with their family or neighbourhood disputes, preferring to keep such matters out of the public eye. Their delinquent failures come less to the notice of officials, though they do exist. If the police are called at all it is usually when people have been burgled or become the victim of other predatory crimes which, in most cases, have been committed by those who live elsewhere. Such neighbourhoods exert powerful influences for order.

Equally, well-kept working class housing estates, both private and council owned, are amongst the most orderly of environments. Here and there are likely to be problem families whose social behaviour is looked down upon and whose young seem to be out of control. Residents in such areas will be less inhibited about involving the police and other agencies when it comes to problem-solving. They tend to live closer to each other and have to come to terms with the invasion of their space and to put up with more noisy behaviour. There are, however, fairly well observed tolerance levels of what is and what is not acceptable as well as a cooperative attitude towards each other and each other's children. One exception to this state of affairs is often found in the conflict between young and old—the one seeking peace in their declining years, the other seeking outlets for their energy and exuberance.

In some of the more depressingly deprived neighbourhoods, things are different. Those who can get out, do so as part of the pattern of social mobility. Those left there are joined by other residents who have failed to make it in a fiercely competitive society. These areas manifest all the signs of decay and neglect. More rubbish in the streets, more graffiti on the walls.

More noise, more seeming disorder. More police intervention with arrests in the street, sometimes violent, and more juveniles appearing in court. More hopelessness with more families becoming the focus, not only of the social worker and the police, but of the housing manager, the school welfare officer (truancy is often high) and, for those found guilty of crime, the probation officer. It is in these areas that there develops the sub-culture which begins to work against the social order noticeable in other areas, and in which a loving and organised family is the main protection for many. But this is the archetypal area into which many broken families drift and in which many who cannot compete or cope are inevitably housed. It is fairly common for housing officers to concentrate problem families in such areas, thus compounding the problem. They become known as problem areas and all who live there become stigmatised by association, providing an additional handicap for those seeking self-improvement.

Not all neighbourhoods can, of course, be neatly packaged into a category. Neat well-ordered streets of well maintained houses will be found near depressed areas, though the inhabitants will have little or nothing to do with their 'less respectable' neighbours and will constantly use the police as their ultimate manifestation of non-acceptance. They are often victims of the misdemeanours and criminality of their less well-behaved neighbours.

Current social trends indicate that these demarcations of class, 'respectability' and affluence will multiply and harden, further impoverishing the social order in a reflection of Victorian England.

Schools—Socialising Institutions

School promises a disciplined environment (in one form or another); standards are set and non-conformity is discouraged. Additionally, and unlike the family and some neighbourhoods, school might represent a greater social mix. Pupils are able to compare themselves with others from diverse backgrounds and begin to learn to cooperate in achievement, at play and at study, which are important experiences to be carried forward into society. Such values as may be transmitted in schools will often be in harmony with those transmitted in the family and the neighbourhood and, when this happens, they represent powerful mutual reinforcement.

However, the impact of the socialising influence of school in relation to family and neighbourhood will vary. If the school is closely identified with a neighbourhood in its catchment area, it will almost inevitably take on some of those social characteristics. The social classes will be less mixed and those parents who cooperate with the staff will represent the social attitudes of the majority of the pupils. But where the school pupil catchment is over a wide and heterogeneous population, there will be a richer mix and a more complicated one. Not only will the school find it impossible to identify with one community only but it will also take on more of the characteristics of society at large. The head-teacher and staff, conditioned by their own experience, subject to their own prejudices (though, one hopes, able to submerge them most of the time), will face greater difficulty in coping with the social development of pupils living under widely differing cultures and classes outside school.

Schools are not alone in facing greater demands being placed upon them by society, but there can be no doubt that, as socialising institutions, they have a future as challenging as any. More and more are they being called upon not only to perform the essential tasks of education in subject matter, but also to help the young cope with the pressures of social survival.

'The range of necessary competence in the modern world includes not only the familiar basic skills, but also practical ability, the ability to get on with others, skill in solving real-life problems, and such necessary attributes for a full and effective life as judgement, responsibility, and reliability. It is in such areas that secondary education, seen as a whole, is falling short of what young people and the nation need.' Again, 'If we fail to build confidence through the educational process, we shall generate apathy, hostility and violence among the young.'[8]

Clearly much is expected of schools to reinforce positive social behaviour. They must encourage attributes which should, and often do, complement those transmitted in the family and in neighbourhood association. Like many things in

31

life, however, school is good for you if you are good at school. School is good if it helps to break down many of the social prejudices which disfigure the adult nation. The social order depends heavily on success in doing this. The words of Lord Scarman in his report on the Brixton Disorders in 1981[9] stress but one aspect. When referring to the under-achievement of West Indian youth in some of our schools, and its social implications, he comments; 'The problems which have to be solved if deprivation and alienation are to be overcome, have been identified—namely teaching in command of the English language, a broad education in the humanities designed to help the various ethnic groups (including the host community) to understand each other's background and culture . . .'[10] One would only add, 'to understand and respect' each other. If we are to seek fraternity in society at large the chances of success are greatly reduced if we fail at school.

An individual who experiences the care and guidance of a loving family atmosphere, who lives in a well-ordered neighbourhood, and attends a well-run and effective school, has the maximum chances of social advantage. At the other end of the scale, those who experience unhappy and violent family circumstances, who grow up in a deprived and depressed neighbourhood, and whose school experience is negative, set out in life with considerable social disadvantage. In both cases one advantage or disadvantage reinforces the other, as the two streams of young people move further and further apart in social experience.

It needs little imagination to conclude that the police, as enforcers of laws and quellers of disorder, will be more active in one area than in the other. The chances of becoming a juvenile offender are maximised in circumstances where example, influence, and control are defective and where police law enforcement activity is higher. This is not to suggest—on the contrary—that young people in disadvantaged areas are more innately criminal than those elsewhere, but that the way of life into which they have fallen, through little or no fault of their own, exposes them more to the criminal sanction. Naughty and even bad boys and girls in well organised families, neighbourhoods and schools have a much greater chance of avoiding the social stigma of an appearance at

Juvenile courts.

Work Discipline and Social Action

The most important socialising experience in adult life is
that of work in organised labour or management. This immediately raises the contemporary problem of widespread
unemployment, since those who are to be long-term
unemployed (and they are an increasing number) will be
deprived of the opportunity of work and of its socialising
effects.

The discipline of work is a powerful conditioner. To be
punctual, to use one's skills towards the collective good, to
maintain output of goods or services, to exert moral forces
which induce an obligation to others with similar interests, are
all socialising influence of considerable importance.

'The rules of occupational morality and justice ... force the
individual to act in view of ends which are not strictly his own,
to make concessions, to consent to compromises, to take into account interests higher than his own.'[11]

Members of the professions and of work forces are united by
mutual obligation which transcends the work place. They
develop an occupational solidarity which has wider social
implications.

The organisation of trade unions and professional
institutions leads to the establishment of social venues such as
working men's clubs, guilds, and institutes of numerous
varieties. Occupation has therefore two socialising
implications with important consequences for the social order.
On the one hand, the instilling of discipline and mutual
obligation at work; on the other, the social and political
organisations which stem from shared interests.

Where the interests of the occupational work force take on
political significance, workers and members of professions
form political movements (the classic case in Britain being the
creation of the Labour Party by the trade union movement) or
pressure groups with political undertones (such as the
Institute of Directors and the Confederation of British
Industry, with close affinities to the Conservative Party). In
this way lines are drawn and conflict ensues, sometimes with
disastrous consequences. The damage done to the British

33

economy in the pursuit of the sectional interests of power groups in conflict is a well accepted fact, while the withdrawal of services can and does cause hardship and creates a public climate in which disorder can flourish.

Individuals begin to submerge much of their individuality, they begin to understand and use collective power and influence, and to exert forces on the social order to bring about what they desire as necessary change. Where the social order is capable of adjustment without violence, the concept of change through conflict of ideas is realised; where it does not and 'iron enters the soul' of the masses, people talk of civil disobedience and revolution. All this, however, does not take place in a vacuum but within a moral and legal structure of immense complexity which holds society together even in conflict.

The Mass Media

No assessment of contemporary socialising forces would be complete without mention of the mass media of communication.

Children are the group which spends most time watching television—some 24 hours a week according to government statistics. That many of their beliefs and ideas are influenced by it is beyond question, as numerous studies have shown, but the position is less clear about its effect on behaviour. In their book, *Juvenile Delinquency*, Michael Rutter and Henri Giller comment: '... little is known on the extent to which films or television can have an enduring effect on attitudes and standards of behaviour. It seems unlikely that it could have much effect when it runs counter to other influences ...'

When family, school and social influences are positive there is less likelihood of television-viewing producing long-term aberrant behaviour. Conversely it is felt that the young with aggressive social tendencies may have them reinforced, particularly where their social experience is negative. So long as television-viewing over a long period of time gives the impression of the social acceptability of good forms of behaviour and unacceptability of the bad, its harmful effects are greatly minimised.

Though two in three adults read national morning newspapers regularly, according to the Royal Commission on the Press (1977), the young tend to rely more heavily on radio and television, particularly the latter. There can be little doubt that the modern generation is both better informed and more critical than its predecessors. For this reason alone its views have to be listened to, and where the urge for participation is kindled, ways should be found of accommodating it.

Morality and Law

Laws represent an interference with individual or collective freedom. A society without laws can hardly be contemplated. Even in the cloistered isolation of a Trappist monastery there are rules or laws with sanctions against the breaking of silence. But laws are a mere substitute for moral or cultural controls which, in a perfect society, would alone achieve social order. The ideal is that people would be so sensitive and conscious of rights and duties that laws would be unnecessary.

It would, on the other hand, be intolerable if *all* moral conduct were to be made the subject of laws. Laws follow morality to some degree, and in societies where mutual tolerance is high and there is wide consensus on what is moral and what is not, there should be less need for laws. In our society, with all its complexities, 'the flood of new laws continues, and shows no sign of abating.' In its Report on Criminal Procedure in 1981[12] the Royal Commission recorded: 'Some of the most fundamental social changes are reflected in the increased use made of criminal sanctions and the increased scope of the criminal law. No one measure is by itself a reliable measure of this change, but the trend is clear. In 1900 there were some 80,000 recorded indictable offences per annum; by 1950 the total was reaching the 500,000 mark; and in 1974 the figure was 2.4 million. In 1900 there were 36 high court judges whereas in 1979 there were 75 high court judges; the Lord Chancellor's department estimates that a further 69 full time judges are needed before the end of 1981. ... there were by 1975 over 7,000 criminal offences...'[13]

In 1978 five million people were dealt with for motoring offences alone. But if the chances of going through life without contravening the law are low, so are the chances of attracting moral censure of one kind or another. Socialising processes seek to render moral turpitude less likely, but moral values do

35

change more rapidly than laws.

In recent times we have witnessed the retreat of the criminal law from the field of private morality in a number of areas of human conduct. The repeal of the laws making criminal offences out of forms of betting and gaming, abortion, homosexual acts in private between consenting adult males, have taken place in the last 25 years and the laws concerning censorship and obscene literature modified by less stringent provisions. On the other hand new moral issues have become the subject of laws, including offences for damaging the environment, and those concerning unfair trading and discrimination on grounds of race or gender.

The gap between morality and law both narrows and widens as social change takes place. Sometimes pressure groups force changes through by persistent and well argued campaigns. The abolition of capital punishment was a good example of society's conscience being represented by a minority bringing about change at a time when perhaps the majority were against it. Certainly, if progress were to rely on majorities, little change in this and other fields would be brought about.

If the police continue to enforce unpopular and outmoded laws, they become the subject of controversy and sometimes hostility. The early nineteenth-century notion of 'suspected persons loitering with intent to commit a felony,'[14] the notorious 'sus' law, became the subject of a national scandal, due first of all to its abuse by some police officers against the young male residents of the poorer inner-city areas (particularly black citizens), and secondly because the idea was offensive to our more modern notions of justice. The law was repealed in 1982.

Social Morality

It is possible to assert, however, that most people most of the time do not require to know and understand the laws in order to know what is right and proper conduct. The idea of good and bad in some degree, however small, is one of the first notions of morality to be transmitted to the young. As people grow up and pass through various stages of contact and association they learn to understand what kind of conduct is approved. The idea that all people should be treated equally by the law and by public administrators is expected as part of social morality, and officials who fail to do this can expect to be challenged and criticised. The existence of such devices as the Ombudsman, Race and Sex Discrimination Boards, complaints procedures and consumer associations of many kinds, indicate the changes in the morality of equality which have led to progress.

The morality of fraternity is perhaps one of the highest and most difficult aspects of social morality, not only to develop but to enforce. It is possible for legislators to pass laws concerning liberty and equality and to enforce those laws until they become part of a social culture. It is impossible, however, to coerce people into loving others. In a modern liberal democracy which emphasises individualism and individual rights, the absence of fraternity gives rise to less socially desirable motivating forces, such as envy and greed. Unless a social morality balances the driving forces essential to material progress with adequate moral forces of fraternity in all aspects of its life, it will continue to be plagued by social disorder. It is in recognition of this that Christianity and other religious, philosophical and ideological movements have stressed the love of neighbour and the brotherhood of man. Without this element being developed to a high degree the social order, as we witness it today, will be impoverished.

Religion

As Max Weber[15] points out, religion not only helps people to cope with suffering through injustice, bad luck, sickness and so on, but it also helps those who experience good fortune, pleasure and largesse to believe that they deserve it. In short, that the social order is somehow pre-ordained.

If this is so, then there is little point in earthly struggle against fate or the gods; and submission to the social order is achieved. When Karl Marx said that religion was the opiate of the masses, he was making the same point, though here he viewed the impact of religion from only the perspective of community. He also pointed out that religion is 'the heart of a heartless world'. Further development is called for if the individual is to find an answer to his needs. In its more primitive form this is achieved through magicians, sorcerers, medicine men and the like. In its more developed form it takes on the emergence of prophets as the agents of gods through whom some form of salvation can be achieved. Whereas the more primitive forms tend to strengthen ethnic or community bonds, the individualised forms may free people from such ties. The religion transcends the tribe. The desire and need for social rules has to be met. 'Sins' require sanctions and good conduct requires formulation and reward if the social order is to benefit; the emergence of God-given laws or commandments fulfils this need. Those who obey the laws find salvation and a feeling of excitement, euphoria and satisfaction; those who do not obey feel guilt and remorse and only their confession to their God relieves them of their burden.

The rules espoused by religion, for example the Ten Commandments of Christianity, provide not only the early bases for moral codes and secular laws but challenges to the omnipotence of kings and rulers. Whilst the former contain the seeds of social order, the latter contain the seeds of conflict and disorder. Wars within and between nations and communities ensue. Religious movements, such as the Protestant Reformation, offering freedom of communication to God for the individual threaten not only the power of the priesthood but also the claims for the Divine Right of Kings. The social order is under attack, force is used to supplant the old with the new, society has marched another step forwards towards a secular democracy and order is reconstructed.

Secular Codes

The gradual transition from the social rules of religion to the secular codes is of the greatest importance in the evolution of modern ideas of social order, for it brings into conflict the freedom of the individual with the power of the state and with organised religion.

The American Declaration of Independence of 1780 speaks of 'self-evident' truths; 'That all men are born equal; that they are endowed by their creator with certain inalienable rights; that among these are life, liberty and the pursuit of happiness.' The idea that each individual has God-given rights may be contrasted with the French Declaration of the Rights of Man proclaimed in 1789.

The French Declaration offers a secular code and speaks of 'natural and imprescriptible rights of man'. These 'natural' rights include amongst other things 'freedom of religion' and 'freedom of expression'. This emphasis of rights no doubt reflects the age in which they were written, the Age of Enlightenment, when people were struggling to throw off a social order based on inequality and privilege. The new social order was somehow to be built on ideas of a social contract, in which rights and duties were to be so apportioned that people were to be freed from the rigidity of status defined by church and state. The theories of social contract continue to have a profound effect.

The Social Contract

If the social order is neither determined by Gods nor by Kings, people have to search for other theories and reasons. John Locke represents those who view civil Government as being based on a notion of contract between the state and its people. No doubt such ideas were influenced by the legal concept wherein parties to a contract enter into it freely, and so long as the obligations to the contract are carried out it remains in force. Both Governments and people could however be in breach of contract. Governments would therefore be changed by people and people coerced and punished by the state, if either party were in serious breach. The idea provides a secular reason for obeying Governments and is in the interest of social order. On their part the Government have to protect the people and punish those who offend on their behalf. People have to be both tenacious in defence of their freedoms and bold in facing up to social change, if John Locke's idea of the social contract in pursuit of the 'common good' (which he did not define) is to hold together.

The concept of the social contract was given further impetus by Jean-Jacques Rousseau, the French philosopher (1712–78). In his book, *Social Contract,* he addresses his mind to the problem which 'is to find a form of association which will defend and protect with the whole common force the person and the goods of each associate, and in which each, while uniting himself with all, may still obey himself alone, and remain as free as before. This is the fundamental problem of which the Social Contract provides the solution.' In this form the social contract provides that the people collectively have a 'general will' under which the individual places his personal power in a form of association. The social contract involves the individual being forced to comply with the general will of the association. 'This means nothing less than that he will be forced to be free' since the aim of the contract includes the giving back to the individual his birthright of natural freedom.

As Russell points out, this is a misuse of the word freedom since freedom to obey is no freedom at all, even if it accords with the general will of otherwise free people. The concept has been used to justify the right to obey the Police or the idea of the Police State, and contains the seeds of the Totalitarian State. But that it can produce a form of social order and control cannot be denied, though in doing so all individuals and groups who oppose the metaphysical 'general will' have to be forced to conform. There is a problem considering the social order in a multi-racial society which Great Britain, like other former imperial powers, has become. I will be considering the problems of disorder in such a society, but here it is sufficient to observe that, where the theory of submission to the will of the majority forms a narrow basis for Government of the social order, such a society cannot claim to be civilised. Nor can it expect to have an easy time in maintaining order. Where governments on the parliamentary model are elected by a minority, as in Great Britain, they tend to be unstable and there remains potential for social disorder unless the notion of the social contract implies equal concern for all its subjects. The race riots in the U.S.A. and, nearer home, the civil rights movement in Northern Ireland in the late 1960s, both owed something to a failure of government in this regard. Equally where the police and other parts of the apparatus of social control are drawn from the many differing communities which form the social mix, there is a better chance of their work succeeding.

The social order, therefore, depends for its relative tranquillity upon the healthy functioning of a wide variety of institutions but where those institutions fail to function adequately, reducing the capacity to cope in time with danger, the prospects of social disorder multiply.

Social Disorder

A society in which consensus is fairly well defined and understood, in which the laws and the manner of their enforcement appear just, in which the division of labour and goods is broadly acceptable as fair, even if by no means equal, has a very good chance of enjoying the benefits of a tranquil social order. This is a society in which the liberty of the individual, no matter what his religion, race or social standing, is protected and manifestly so protected by constitutional guarantees. Britain today is by no means so confidently poised that one might predict that it will be an orderly society in this sense, in either the short or the long term, unless some fundamental changes take place. What some of those changes may be will be the subject of the final chapters of this book, but here I am concerned with the signs which may indicate a more disordered society than we would wish.

Riots

The riots which took place in London, Manchester, Liverpool, and to a lesser extent in Birmingham and other places, in 1981 were predictable, and were predicted, yet nobody seemed to have the power or the imagination to stop them. Not only were the traditional social controls of family, school, religion and culture weakened in the affected areas, but the idea that the problem of social disorder could be cured by the police was a gross error.

'Where minorities have become described as a problem,' where they begin to suffer feelings of alienation, where tensions are compounded by the repressive use of police force and criminal sanctions, the resultant feelings of outrage will explode. In Britain we should know this well enough from our colonial experience and from events in Northern Ireland. The children of the repressed or oppressed have long memories, whether in the U.S.A., Ireland, Armenia, or the Basque country.

41

Both Protestants and Roman Catholics have described to me how they were brought up to hate each other and how this hatred was transmitted to each other's culture and institutions, particularly the police. The Royal Irish Constabulary, which was predominantly Roman Catholic before 1922, was regarded with scorn and mistrust by many Belfast Protestants, just as the Royal Ulster Constabulary of Northern Ireland, which is overwhelmingly Protestant, is regarded by many Roman Catholics today.

'I was brought up as a Roman Catholic in Northern Ireland never to trust the police. They were not our police but their police,' said a successful T.V. producer now with the B.B.C. This is quite a common experience of the children of minorities who sense prejudice and discrimination. All the more reason why the police often develop animosities towards minorities, unless they are carefully selected, highly trained and well led. This in turn can result in police and minorities developing a mutual disrespect leading to characteristics of warring factions. Social workers in Brixton before the riots noted, 'The lack of trust is highlighted in young males and adolescents, both black and white. When talking to these people one gets the impression of guerilla warfare. Reports of ill-tempered, aggressive attitudes among the police are rife. They may not always be true but it is what the youth believe that is important. This is compounded by the fact that the young people believe that they are winning the war. If the police believe that their attitude to the young is a deterrent then they have been sadly mistaken.'[16]

Similar comments have been made about policing the blacks in the United States. 'The United States today is a country in the grip of an internal cold war. Militant ghetto residents are pitted against militant members of metropolitan police forces. Each group watches the other with apprehension, and each plots counter-measures against expected aggression. On both sides are those who proclaim they will experience Armageddon in their day, in the shape of premeditated massacre by the opposing force.'[17]

Writing of the West Indian problems in Bristol before the riots of 1980, Ken Pryce commented that some 'had consciously chosen the criminal path of survival as an expression of contempt for the system which "puts them down", a stand which exposes them to continuous harassment by the State, represented by the police.'[18] He believed there were those 'whose revolutionary potential should not be underestimated'.

Norman Fowler, now Minister of Social Services in Mrs. Thatcher's Government, wrote a work called *After the Riots*[19] (sic) in 1979. It was a commentary on how European police forces were coping after a whole range of public disorders associated with students, activists and criminals during the late 1960s and 1970s. He concluded 'only a hopeless optimist would expect the next ten years to be any less eventful. New demands are likely to be made of the police and some policemen already see problem areas which they believe could easily develop into crisis areas.' I counted myself amongst Norman Fowler's 'some policemen', having warned throughout the 1970s the likelihood of widespread civil disturbance unless the policing of minorities and the social policies affecting the urban poor received more imaginative attention. I was less inclined than Mr. Fowler, however, to see the solution mainly coming from the police. In 1979 I wrote that 'The decaying inner-city areas are breeding grounds for crime and disaffection. To leave the problem to the vagaries of law enforcement would be unwise.'[20]

Some of us know that the excessive use of force in these tinder-dry situations holds dangers for both user and object, inviting as it does retaliation followed by reaction culminating in the escalation of violence. This has happened. Since the police went into the riots unprepared for the extreme levels of violence with which they were confronted, they are now of course better trained and equipped. The Home Secretary, at the time Mr. William (now Viscount) Whitelaw, speaking to the Police Superintendents' Association in September 1981, in the aftermath of the riots said that 'the police could no longer afford to be without riot equipment including water cannon, plastic bullets [known to be lethal] and C.S. gas [known to be capricious in a breeze].'[21] If, or when, social disorder breaks out again on any scale, the level of violence involved will begin on a higher threshold. What was once exceptional now becomes normal and acceptable. It is a policy of despair.

Will we ever take the lessons of Northern Ireland to heart? In the absence of social policies to reduce the prospect of

43

increasing communal violence, this despairing acceptance of disorder is the state's only answer. To embark on a social programme in which violence in all walks of life is to be *reduced* requires a massive change of heart. The police were once described as 'keepers of the peace'. Peace however does not come down like manna from heaven. It has to be worked for.

The Established Church

It is remarkable what little impact the church has had in securing a more peaceful social order in contemporary Britain. Individuals of course have done much. The Roman Catholic and Church of England Bishops in Liverpool did much to bring about peace in Toxteth in 1981, though they were sometimes criticised by the police for their interference.

It is difficult for the established church to oppose the existing social order, since it is an integral part of it and it is well known that some appointments which are within the gift of the Prime Minister are made as much for political sympathies as for theology. It would be of great benefit to the attainment of a more peaceful and just society if the established church were more vociferous about this. It must be said, however, that there are noble exceptions to such a wide generalisation. The movement known as 'Christian Action', for example, was well to the fore in the 1960s and early 1970s, but never seemed to generate the desirable momentum to make a dramatic impact for peace and justice.

With over one million Muslims now in Britain, the plurality of religion has increased. The occasional demand for separate education is heard and we have accommodated the Sikh religion by the remarkable exclusion of its members from one criminal offence, namely the compulsory wearing of crash helmets when motor cycling. In many ways it is remarkable how the various religions co-exist peacefully, though there are and will be tensions from time to time which threaten the social order.

Racialism in Britain

Anti-Semitic traditions are kept alive by organisations such as the National Front, and racism continues to rear its ugly head.

Many informed and open-minded people accept that racial prejudice and discrimination are more widespread than others are prepared to admit. I have encountered such attitudes amongst many police including some in the senior ranks. The whole ethos of the police has been built around a folk image of Englishness which does not easily accommodate multi-racial characteristics.

What was seen as a virtue in 1955 is now sometimes seen as a vice. Writing in 1955, before the increase in the immigration of black and coloured people, Geoffrey Gorer commented: 'but all the evidence available to me from my own research and observations and those of others strongly suggest that the amount and extent of the enthusiastic appreciation of the police is peculiarly English and a most important component of the contemporary English character. To a great extent the police represent an ideal model of behaviour and character.'[22] It is very doubtful whether the same sentiments would be expressed today. By 1975, Dr. William Belsen, in a searching study,[23] found that 66% of police officers questioned felt that 'immigrants should be obliged to adopt the British way of life.' Similar sentiments emerged consistently at the Police Staff College, during my time there as Commandant (1970–3) and as a visiting lecturer over the following nine years. Although Belsen found a generally favourable attitude between public and police, he was less sanguine about recent immigration and reported: 'It is highly desirable that a further survey be conducted, to check important indicators that coloured people's relations with the police were less favourable than in the general population.' As it turned out relations continued to deteriorate, finally breaking out in communal violence in 1981.

Racism is present in our prisons. In August 1983 the Home Office issued special guidance to prison governors to check its growth and to reduce abuses. Such abuses are, of course, wholly in contravention of the European Convention on Human Rights for prisoners and others.

Modern Britain, therefore, contains within the social structure the seeds of racial violence. A Home Office study published in 1981 reported: 'Our study clearly indicates that the incidence of racial attacks presents a significant problem.[24] It referred to a disturbing incidence of physical violence upon

45

people of ethnic minorities as a 'matter of fact and not of opinion'. The rate of attacks on people solely on the grounds of their racial origins was for Asians 50 times more than for whites, and for blacks 36 times more. This study revealed that whites bear a great deal more responsibility for racial violence than the combined coloured and black minorities put together. Racial violence, it is clearly revealed, is largely a white man's crime. The report further revealed that the police often underestimated the significance of racialist incidents for those attacked or threatened.

Once again, British society has to learn a lesson from Northern Ireland: when a minority feels itself threatened and inadequately protected by the police, it will not only cease to respect the police but will turn to its own protection through vigilantism. Once again, the prospects for social harmony are threatened.

Political Extremism

The extreme political Right represented by organisations like the National Front and its splinter groups are heirs to the Fascist traditions which caused such great havoc in Europe during the 1930s and 1940s. They espouse the cause of nationalism (sometimes wrapped up deceitfully as patriotism) and direct attention towards the racial minorities by intimidation and violence. During the 1930s (at the time of Mussolini and Hitler in Europe) Fascism raised its ugly head in Britain under the leadership of Sir Oswald Mosley. Its targets were both Jews and Communists. The excesses of violence and intimidation which ensued led to the passing of the Public Order Act in 1936, giving the police wide powers to deal with quasi-military organisations and the banning or routing of processions.

Following the horrors of Fascist bestiality and genocide during the Second World War and the defeat of the Fascist states by an alliance of Communist Russia and the Western and other allies, political extremism of the Right found little support in Britain. The public order was not threatened, in this particular way, until the increase of immigration of coloured and black people during the 1960s and 1970s. Since then, however, the Fascists have once more emerged from the crevices to generate prejudice and hostility against minorities. Now the Jews are joined by new social scapegoats for this small but increasingly aggressive political movement. Just as the extreme Left has its international links, there are signs that Fascism has managed to force at least some kind of international liaison.[25] The security services have been obliged to pay more attention to surveillance of the extreme Right than was the case some 15 or 20 years ago.

The movement to the Right in British politics following the last two general elections has encouraged some Right Wing extremists to seek to infiltrate the Conservative Party itself. The Federation of Conservative Students was reported to have been infiltrated in some branches by Fascist elements, and the National Young Conservative Vice-Chairman was reported to have presented a paper outlining 'continuing nazi infiltration' of young Conservative groups.[26]

The *Daily Telegraph* in May 1982 reported, 'Tales of forgery, vote buying, bogus conference delegates, infiltration by the British Movement, students in S.S. uniforms singing Nazi songs and suspicious bank accounts in false names have been enamating from the F.C.S. (Federation of Conservative Students) with increasing frequency since its swing to the right two years ago.'

There have been numerous reports of Fascist sympathisers standing as Conservative candidates in local elections, and in the 1983 general election it was revealed that Mr. Thomas Finnegan, Conservative Party candidate for Stockton South, had been a member of the National Front until recently and had twice contested a Birmingham constituency as a National Front candidate. Senior members of the Conservative Party quickly withdrew their electoral support. The newspaper *Searchlight* in its editorial of Tuesday 31 May 1983 opined: 'Refugees from the Nazi fringes are surfacing once again in the Tory Party as local council candidates and constituency activists, and the complexion of the Conservative Party parliamentary candidates is now much more overwhelmingly right wing. They have been attracted back by the ascendance of the far right within the party and Thatcher's own racism, her strident nationalism, and her apparent designs to do something about "law and order".' Mrs. Thatcher was reported in the *Guardian* newspaper on 1 June 1983 as saying

47

that 'she found the policies of the National Front utterly repugnant and the Tories did not want its support.' There are, however, indicators which suggest the possibility of the emergence of new Right Wing extremism to threaten the social order in Britain.

Right Wing extremism has often left its mark in conflict with the extreme Left. Though both extremes have similar characteristics (including authoritarian tendencies and a contempt for liberal democracy) they differ in the targets which they aim to attack. Where the Right attacks minorities and non-conformist groups in its assertion of nationalism, the Left attacks the establishment, particularly the police, and asserts its internationalism including its support of ethnic minorities.

Extremism in Action

Throughout the 1970s violent attacks on both police and National Front marches created public disorder of unacceptable proportions. The attack on the police in London's Red Lion Square in June 1974, the subsequent death of a young demonstrator, 46 policemen injured and unknown numbers of demonstrators hurt, caused particular alarm. The occasion was a National Front rally. Lord Scarman's inquiry, which followed, found that the main blame for the violence which took place lay with the International Marxist Group. The police, however, came out of the inquiry with some criticism for faulty tactics. Other clashes occurred during National Front marches in Lewisham in August 1977. Considerable damage was done to property, two police officers received stab wounds, 134 people required hospital treatment including 56 police officers. After the incident an organiser of the Left Wing violence was reported as saying, 'We want to make it absolutely clear to the police that we are not going to allow the Nazis to walk the streets of this country.[27] They threatened to crush the National Front in subsequent confrontations. During the 1979 general election the violence which broke out in Southall during a National Front meeting in the Town Hall was particularly vicious. One man was killed and many hundreds injured.

The degree of violence threatened whenever the National

Front declared its intention to march caused Chief Police Officers throughout the country to seek a ban on such marches under the provisions of the Public Order Act 1936. The banning of extreme Right Wing marches became commonplace during the early 1980s.

Clearly the clashes between political extremes remain a prospect of social disorder whenever conditions and circumstances present an opportunity. Richard Clutterbuck in his book on the subject[28] provides a masterly account of almost a decade (1970–7) of political violence in which the extreme Left created numerous and serious industrial disputes leading to violent confrontations on the picket lines. There can be no doubt that, should political polarisation in Britain become more pronounced with greater numbers aligning themselves with the extremes, there are considerable dangers of communal violence, exceeding that in the 1970s which caused Clutterbuck to label the period, 'Britain in Agony'.

Division of Labour and Goods

The greatest revolutions in modern history have been concerned with the just distribution of work and goods, and it can safely be predicted that the issue will continue to dominate British politics. It can also be predicted that from time to time violence will break out, as sections of society seek to obtain more for themselves while often demanding that others take less.

Among those characteristics of social behaviour which lie at the root of much social disorder are, of course, covetousness, jealousy, envy, greed and fear. Secular laws are impotent in suppressing such feelings, although they punish many of their manifestations. But any society which wishes to be peaceful has to develop ways of containing such attitudes within constructive and socially harmless bounds.

It had been said[29] that the Christian religion was (or is) the most successful in this. God, whose children we are, will judge us, not by success in the material sense, but in terms of courage in accepting our earthly destiny. We shall be rewarded in heaven. In this way irregularities are explained away to the satisfaction of the disadvantaged, while relieving the advantaged of their guilt. The same writer argues that

49

Western society has moved from a hierarchical society relatively free of envy, anxiety and guilt to an egalitarian society riddled with envy, anxiety and guilt. Be that as it may, the Western world has to secure novel ways of coping with inequality and reducing the prospects of disorder which covetousness and its companions make probable. They have to start thinking about social justice in the here and now, and not in some unknown and doubtful after-life. The distribution of labour and goods heads the list. We have seen industrial dispute heaped upon industrial dispute reflecting a genuine search for social justice on the one hand and a less endearing mixture of envy and greed on the other.

In Britain—one of the minority of countries calling itself a liberal democracy—the solution offered by Communism has never found favour with the people. Conspicuous by their failure to succeed at the ballot box, the proponents of this authoritarian egalitarianism have resorted to industrial warfare. The enemy is Britain's capitalist system, based as they see it on exploitation and representing social injustice. The conflict between the two has been mitigated in Britain by democratic socialism, the mixed economy and the Welfare State.

The brand of Conservatism evolving in the 1980s, now determined to rid Britain of socialism, poses new possibilities of social instability. The police could inevitably be drawn into a major political role of the kind envisaged by the late Arnold Toynbee writing in the *Observer* in April 1974.

Commenting on the inevitability of economic recession resulting in a scramble for a share of dwindling resources, he forecast that society would have to be severely regimented by a rule 'imposed by ruthless authoritarian government'. In this of course he was echoing Thomas Hobbes (see page 21). To envisage the police in Britain forming the spearhead instrument of ruthless authoritarian government should be enough to concentrate the mind wonderfully. If a liberal democracy is to avoid the poison and disaffection that a drift into illiberalism would engender as it faces up to the new world of mass unemployment and financial limitations and inability to pay for the social welfare of its most needy, regard for the development of its traditions of social justice is an urgent necessity.

Justice in the liberal society has taken on new meanings since Jeremy Bentham and the Utilitarian school of philosophy propounded the idea that society should seek the greatest good for the greatest number. A modern and celebrated philosopher, John Rawls,[30] describes justice as 'fairness' and 'for this reason justice denies that the loss of freedom for some is made right by a greater good shared by others. It does not allow that the sacrifices imposed upon a few are outweighed by the larger sum of advantages enjoyed by many.' Equality, however, does not always mean justice either, since to level all down is to deny those capable of achievement; and to level people up is to reward incompetence and sloth. In order to make any social order work within bounds tolerable to fair-minded people, fraternity needs encouragement and opportunity to manifest itself.

Crime

A great deal of the crime in Britain, both reported and unreported, has little to do with social injustice.

Crime is not confined, as we know, to any particular class of society or any particular group within it. Anybody who has spent much time in our criminal courts will, of course, notice that the poor represent a high proportion of accused people. It should not come as a surprise that those courts which deal with poor areas will manifest high levels of the prosecuted poor, for they represent the majority of potential defendants, and the police are more active here. Nor should it come as a surprise that the unemployed and casual manual workers find their way into the courts and the prisons, since they are more likely to be reported, prosecuted and imprisoned than those able to settle for compensating their victims informally or whose punishment lies in dismissal rather than prosecution. Additionally, the unemployed and unskilled and semi-skilled workers represent a large percentage of the population—some 30%. On the other hand, there is a growing awareness that higher levels of criminal behaviour exist among professional and skilled workers than was hitherto thought to be the case. Fraud, corruption, theft, falsification of accounts, dealing in stolen property, are among the classes of crime most frequently committed by 'white-' and 'blue-collar' workers—

51

people who generally have little excuse, certainly less than the poor, for increasing their possessions in this way. Greed is more often the motivation than necessity.

Although much crime has no direct connection with social injustice, where social injustice happens to be marked it produces unnecessary and disproportionate poverty and squalor, and allows this to exist cheek-by-jowl with affluence. A social order which is dominated by such characteristics, as for example many of the unstable countries of Central and South America, and to a lesser extent parts of Italy, can hardly expect crime and spasmodic public disorder to go away.

Alienation

People who feel alienated, and whose alienation is compounded by whatever cause, begin to opt out of social responsibility, including the responsibility for keeping the peace. They also lose respect for the wider society and its values. Disrespect for the social order, once internalised, may result in vandalism, burglary, theft, and other property crimes. Those who do not share in the delights of a property-owning democracy, and have little prospect of doing so, may develop anti-social attitudes towards the property of others, unless other socialising influences have strengthened their feelings towards respect for that ideal.

Some Crime is Inevitable

Crime as a social phenomenon, however, does not always indicate that a society is unhealthy. On the contrary, for crime is, as Durkheim put it, 'an integral part of all healthy societies'.[31] What Durkheim was getting at, when he wrote that comment, was that the very nature of a healthy society not only provides greater opportunity for the commission of crime but that behaviour is always changing, new rules are being brought into play and old rules are being discarded. This must be so, since social morality itself is always changing. It is possible, however, when crime reaches such morbid proportions that either the social order is defective or it goes unprotected. When these characteristics intervene, a society becomes a more unpleasant one in which to live. Fear increases and freedom may be curtailed in order to deal with the problem.

Crime will Increase

It can be predicted with some confidence that crimes reported to the police in Britain will continue to increase. This is not the same as saying that the volume of crime will increase, although it may. The dimension of actual levels of crime has long defied rational measurement. Traditionally crime has been measured by statistical information based on crimes reported to the police; this represents a known quantity. But it may also be a reflection of opportunity or of inclination to report by the victim. There are many victims who lack both. Just as opportunity makes the thief, so does opportunity make the recording of theft. Criminologists have long speculated on what they call 'the dark figure' of crime, but until recently have not known how to measure it. The British Crime Survey carried out in 1982 broke new ground. It is a most welcome trend towards a less irrational examination of crime.

The first report indicated, for example, that around four times more property loss and damage existed than official figures recorded. Around five times more cases of personal violence were committed than were reported to the police. Cases of shop-lifting were notoriously under-reported. On the other hand, serious crimes rate a higher level of recording than do the more trivial. Contrary to popular belief, the people safest from personal violence are the elderly (as some would hope in a civilised society) and the most likely victims are young males. The survey also found that victims of crime were less punitive in their attitudes towards offenders than might have been imagined from the results of public opinion polls. This kind of survey provides a valuable step forward in a proper understanding of the phenomenon of crime, revealing, as it does, that many people who are its victims have a much more sanguine view about it than some politicians and police would have us believe.

The Law's Overkill

Trends since the beginning of this century, however, indicate that the number of criminal offences recorded will go on increasing by the very nature of social change. There are now more offences to commit, more opportunities to commit them, more opportunities to record and process them. But the so-called rise in crime does not necessarily mean that people are innately less respectful and decent than in times past. What it does mean is that society has developed higher expectations of behavioural standards in new areas and is prepared to legislate for better control. There are now more than 7,000 criminal offences though as recently as 1940 these were less than 2,000. This increase in criminal legislation reflects not so much lowering standards of behaviour as the social complexity of a modern society. It also has had a dramatic effect on the resources required to maintain enforcement, and there is every sign that this demand will continue to increase.

In 1978 there were 2,400,000 recorded indictable offences.[32] Crimes in 1982 reached 3,250,000. Crime reported to the police over the next five years is likely to increase by at least one third again, according to Home Office forecasts.

Increase in crime cannot be attributed to a reduction in the resources provided by successive governments to combat it. The strength of the police forces has steadily increased from around 50,000 in 1947 to about 130,000 in 1983. Civilian staff in support of the police has increased even more dramatically.

Responses to Crime

Not only have the police vastly increased in manpower but they have taken advantage of developments in equipment and technology. A largely foot police has become a largely mechanised police. Manual systems of recording information and intelligence have been replaced by computers. A whole battery of equipment, including firearms and riot gear, has become standard issue and in many respects police training and deployment of resources has become a highly specialised function. It cannot be said that the rise in crime is due to the insufficiency of police resources.

It follows that, as more crimes are recorded, investigated and prosecuted, there arises a need for more courts and judges.[33] The body of magistrates, those who try over 90% of all criminal cases, has similarly grown. From 14,100 in 1951, they now number some 26,000.

Our prisons held some 16,000 prisoners in 1945, and this has increased to a prison population of some 45,000 in 1982. The necessary increase in prison staff has followed the same trends, although successive governments have failed to construct adequate penal accommodation. Our prisons are now full to overflowing and are in a dangerous and explosive condition. Prisons built to hold some 36,000 prisoners now have a population of around 45,000. The need for places will undoubtedly increase. Recent plans by the Home Office to improve and extend the prison accommodation are belated and still inadequate.

The idea—which is put with much force by both politicians, mainly of the Right Wing persuasion, and the popular press— that the imposition of more severe penal sanctions will somehow reduce the amount of crime is almost completely without foundation. In my own experience I have met very few ex-prisoners who have been reformed by the custodial sentence, necessary though it may be in some cases. Some 70% of discharged prisoners are reconvicted within a matter of two or three years. The cost of all this in purely financial terms is considerable. Expenditure on prisons alone grew from £88,450 millions in 1972–3 to £242.535 millions in 1977–8 and continues to grow.

It is now generally accepted that there are many people in prison who should not be there. The petty thief, the alcoholic, the fine defaulter can be dealt with by less costly but effective social sanctions. Care and supervision within communites, and curtailment of freedom through community service orders and attendance centres, are among alternative means. Paradoxically, the qualities which we admire in law-abiding people are often to be found in those who commit crime as a calculated course of action. Initiative, daring, determination, skill, imagination, persuasive powers, the energy to go after 'the good things of life', are some of the driving forces which are to be found in successful businessmen, politicians, policemen, tradesmen and skilled workers. They are also among the characteristics of those who commit company fraud, burglary, bank robbery, planned shop-lifting, and theft generally.

Violence

Violence poses particular problems, notably when large numbers are involved. The violence which some individuals use in their daily lives is more manageable—though extreme cases certainly excite public indignation, an indication of healthy social order. The British are more ready to condemn violence than dishonesty, no matter how grave the latter may be. The Great Train Robbers, whose haul exceeded over two million pounds, were condemned by the public (though not the courts) more for violence to the engine-driver than for their theft. Of course, the constant reportage, and sometimes unduly sensational reportage, of crimes of violence may lead us to feel that the problem is greater than it is.

A sense of proportion was cultivated in the British Crime Survey of 1983: 'In contrast to other offences covered by the survey, the chances of being assaulted were no higher in the inner-city than they were in the country. Age, sex, and lifestyle were the determining factors.' The survey concluded that the odds of being assaulted were much higher for those who were male, under 30 years of age, single, widowed or divorced, spent several nights a week out, drank heavily and themselves assaulted others.[34]

The vast bulk of criminal violence takes place within families and groups of people prone to violence, both as victim and offender. Violence upon strangers is comparatively rare. Violence as an ideological or political weapon, though happily extremely rare, is of another dimension altogether.

Terrorism

Terrorist violence in some ways resembles war, though it is not. The terrorist may regard himself at war, but, at least overtly, there is no declaration of war between identifiable states. The police and security forces, therefore, cannot act as if opposing enemies in war where laws hardly apply, but have to act within laws enacted for times of peace.

Healthy and stable liberal democracies are vulnerable to superficial damage from terrorist violence but have infinite capacity to contain it. An unstable, shaky, social order can fall like a ripe cherry to a small handful of determined ideological warriors, however, as countless modern examples testify.

In attempting to goad a liberal democracy into excessive and inhuman reaction and into abandoning the rule of law, the terrorist seeks to bring about such a state's self-destruction or self-damage. The amount of counter-violence which such a state can deploy is limited by its very nature. Liberal democracies are, therefore, in a sense trapped. While wishing to reduce and eliminate violence, they are of necessity forced into using it. But in order to retain their own humanity and the rule of law, some suffering and sacrifice have to be endured. It is a dilemma. And yet liberal democracies possess the means to see terrorism defeated wherever the social order is robust and stable.

Chapter 2

Justice and the Police

'Justice is fairness,' writes John Rawls and then he explains himself in 600 pages.[1] Justice as an abstract principle is one thing and generally not within the police officer's purview. When a police officer walks or drives out of the police station yard he does not say to himself, 'I am going to do justice today.' He may say, 'I am going to enforce the laws today,' but that is a different thing.

Selective Justice

Laws do not guarantee justice or order, though the aim of the law-maker may lie in that direction. For laws to be just they have to be founded in a notion of justice, that is, in liberal democracies they accord with the rule of law. They are intended to apply to all persons equally, yet all persons are never equal. It can be argued that it is as unjust to treat equals unequally as it is to treat unequals equally. If a police officer sees two cars equally exceeding the speed limit and he stops and prosecutes only one of the drivers, the laws have not been equally, i.e. justly, enforced. The prosecuted driver may say that his prosecution was not fair. But he cannot complain that the law itself is unjust. The police therefore do not and cannot ensure justice in the wider meaning of the term, i.e. equal enforcement, though they may do so in particular cases.

Since the police cannot enforce all the laws all of the time, they have to be selective; and it is here that they are most likely to be judged. They will be judged by the people against the people's notion of fairness; and in many cases that will differ from culture to culture, from neighbourhood to neighbourhood. To prosecute an offence under the Litter Act for dropping a piece of litter in a street full of other people's litter would be judged unfair. Whereas to prosecute the same offence in a tidy neighbourhood would not be so judged. To condone minor breaches of motoring offences for a long period and then to prosecute those lulled into the belief that the police are permissive in that regard would be judged to be unfair police practice, though it is patently lawful.

There are many reasons, therefore, why laws cannot be enforced justly if by justly we mean that they should be enforced universally. Not all crimes are reported to the police, therefore the offender cannot be prosecuted. Not all crimes reported to the police are cleared up, thus further reducing the universal application of the law. The police are (and have to be) selective in their enforcement activity, which implies a use of police discretion. Here, the police decide the who, when, why and where of prosecutions. All this must be tested against a standard of fairness, though, as has been pointed out, that standard itself will have different meanings.

One of the standards against which police enforcement will be judged is that of unfair discrimination. Discrimination in enforcement of laws on grounds of class, religion, race, sex, nationality and so on is contrary to Article 14 of the European Convention of Human Rights, but it is also morally repugnant. Therefore, although it is understood that it is fair to exercise discretion in enforcement, it is both unfair and unjust to discriminate on the grounds mentioned.

Though justice and equality do not always coincide, equality, even in chance prosecutions, is 'fair' as long as no particular discrimination has been made. Persons never stand equally before the law in the sense that they start from equal conditions, but they should stand equally once the law is activated. The first activation is carried out by the police; in a sense, the police are the gate-keepers of criminal justice.

Invisible Justice

Take the police role as just one entry point in the panorama of justice. The police officer operates in those areas of society where notions of legal and social justice and injustice are seen in the raw. Far removed from the debating chambers of Parliament and the forensic clinical atmosphere of the courts, he walks and observes the public in its kaleidoscopic form. He carries with him on behalf of his fellow citizens the most awesome battery of powers, greater than any other public official in the realm. The activation of his powers, though prescribed by law, and ultimately to be considered by the courts, is within his personal discretion. He has the power and often the means to kill, to use violence, to take away liberty, to detain, to search, to invade privacy and to summon, all within the law. How and when he uses these powers will depend not only on the law but on his own judgment in particular cases. He may be as young as nineteen years of age and have had some three months training.

At least one element of justice lies therefore within police discretion. Police discretion is an intangible thing, but at least it contains both legal and moral elements.

In the first place the police presence should be seen to personify legality as officers of the law, and that law should be democratically enacted and should not offend the notion of fairness. Legality, however, is more easily defined than fairness. It is more exact and is in writing and can be understood. Fairness, on the other hand, is a qualitative moral issue. If a law is deemed unfair and sufficient people regard it as such, then the legislature should address its mind to repeal. When police have to enforce laws which they themselves regard as unfair, they are placed in a moral dilemma: on the one hand they have a duty to enforce such laws since they are extant, on the other they face a moral pressure in such enforcement. They can draw attention to the dilemma or they can let the law lie unenforced, in which case they may face further criticism.

Laws, on the other hand, may appear fair but be unfairly enforced. Into this category fell the laws under the Vagrancy Act of 1824 concerning suspected persons loitering with intent to commit crime, the infamous 'Sus' law repealed in 1982. The enforcement of this law fell very much within police discretion, since only suspicion was needed to bring about the arrest. Every police officer was aware that this law was abused by local police, particularly in London, to maintain pressure on street loiterers and on members of the criminal fringe, particularly young males and, in recent times, young black males. It required considerable pressure from ordinary people to bring about change. Although politicians are active in

60

passing new legislation they are often dilitary in repealing the old.

It is an interesting cultural phenomenon that ever since 1824 the 'Sus' law had been enforced on a fairly pliant white community and that it only reached a high and controversial level in the 1970s when the ethnic minorities, together with the National Council for Civil Liberites and others, campaigned against it.

The pursuit of a more just society cannot and, of course, should not rely on justice filtering down from the top; there have to be pressures from the bottom also. As a result of pressures for the repeal of the 'Sus' laws, the Home Affairs Select Committee in 1980 unanimously recommended its repeal describing it as unacceptable in a democratic society.[2]

The uses and abuses of police discretion, therefore, lie at the heart of justice at that point where the criminal law is first activated and, unless it is affected and guided by ethical considerations, its power is potentially damaging to both police and public.However, if the police were to be prevented from exercising proper discretion, our system of law enforcement would work less well than it does. This is the problem which faces the police in the Federal Republic of West Germany where what is known as 'the principle of legality' operates. In effect, this means whenever the commission of an offence comes to the notice of a police officer he has to report it; the decision to prosecute rests with legal officials. Exactly the opposite operates in Great Britain: the police themselves decide not only whether to report or not to report a particular offence but (in over 90% of criminal cases) whether or not to prosecute. This means that, throughout the entire enforcement and prosecution process, no independent viewpoint or opinion is brought to bear, save in those few serious cases where the Director of Public Prosecutions takes responsibility. A product of history, perhaps, but nevertheless now being regarded as unacceptable.

Discrimination or Discretion?

When the Road Traffic Bill 1968 was being guided through Parliament by the then Minister of Transport, Mrs. Barbara Castle, and the breathalyser was to be used to detect driving

61

under the influence of drink, there was considerable consternation about police discretion. Pressure groups, such as the motoring organisations and civil libertarians, stressed the need for adequate limitations. Some Members of Parliament were alarmed at the prospect of being breathalysed at the whims and fancies of police discretion. A compromise was reached: police discretion was not to extend to random checks. It was to include only those incidents where police attention was drawn to the manner of driving or some defect of a mechanical nature.

Now, this may be contrasted with the Misuse of Drugs Act 1971 under which police have power to stop and search any person or vehicle suspected of carrying or being in possession of listed drugs. This includes cannabis resin. There is no limitation on police discretion. Only reasonable suspicion is required, and this can be interpreted very loosely. 'Police officers have to be prejudiced and discriminatory if they are to do their work properly,' a senior police oficer told a seminar in Oxford. A Detective Superintendent of the West Yorkshire Police, he said that checking long haired youths in bedraggled clothing would result in a seizure of drugs, and checking West Indians 'wearing short jeans, T-shirts and multi-coloured tea-cosy type hats who hover around pedestrian precincts, walkways and subways in city centres will detect outstanding handbag snatchers and what has become commonly known as street mugging.' The Superintendent said, 'That is the sort of discrimination and prejudice we want from police officers.'

These two examples provide interesting insights into the exercise of police discrimination. On the one hand, the entire range of social class and economic standing is represented in the motoring public, the vast majority of whom would strenuously object to the police stopping and testing them every time they leave their clubs and pubs at closing time. Yet the police know full well that many of them will drive off with an illegal alcohol content in their blood, sometimes with lethal and horrifying consequences for themselves and other road users. The random use of police powers in these circumstances is regarded as socially unacceptable. On the other hand, scruffy youths and colourful West Indians in leisure clothing of their choice are to be stopped and searched on the grounds solely of their appearance. The motoring lobby is able to gather its forces to resist random breath tests for alcohol; long-haired boys and West Indians who are innocent of any crime have no such lobby, save perhaps violence at the end of the day, and by resisting a search render themselves liable to further criminalisation for obstructing the police in the exercise of their discretion.

These examples also indicate that, wittingly or not, the police do not enforce laws in a politically neutral manner or, as George Orwell would have put it, that 'All men are equal but some are more equal than others.' Clearly, it behoves the police to improve their intelligence gathering and observations on suspected offenders before embarking on wholesale random stop and search exercises.

Deadly Force

But the exercise of police discretion is brought to its highest and most dramatic level when the use of deadly force is contemplated.

Authority to use force (which is given to the police on behalf of the people) has both legal and moral dimensions. It is a power on loan, so to speak. I have known police officers in some countries—outside the United Kingdom, I hasten to add—who have developed an attitude best summed up by the phrase 'shoot first and ask questions afterwards'. At times this may be within the laws, for example where it is permissible for the police to 'shoot at fleeing felons' or in cases where the police officer genuinely believes that he or someone else may be shot at unless he shoots first.

There are three important reasons why the use of deadly force should only be used as a last resort, and they all fall within the exercise of police discretion. In the first place, the killing of a person by a police officer is within the law only if it is done to avert the apprehended killing of another person. Colloquially known as the doctrine of minimum force, the force used should be commensurate with the object it is used to achieve. Secondly, the killing of a person by a police officer is a judicial act since the officer is the agent of the law. If he does it within the law it becomes excusable homicide, but if he does it outside the law it is either murder of manslaughter and he may be charged accordingly. Thirdly, the act is irrevocable.

63

Nothing can restore the status quo.

Since the right to life is a fundamental human right (see Chapter 3), life should never be taken by a police officer even if he has a legal excuse, if he can resolve the problem without doing so. There have been numerous examples in my own experience where officers who were armed could have killed and invoked the law to excuse their acts, but they have refrained from doing so even at some risk to themselves. When this happens, it is a triumph for morality over legality.

This problem is seen at its height in the U.S.A. 'The national debate over the State's right to take life has been sidetracked, in a sense, on the issue of "capital punishment", or more precisely, execution after trial. Far more deadly in its impact is the body of law permitting execution without trial through justified homicide by police officers. In 1976 for example, no one was executed and 233 persons were sentenced to death after trial, yet an estimated 590 persons were killed by police officers justifiably without trial. Even in the 1950s when an average of 72 persons were executed after trial each year, according to official statistics, 480 a year were killed by police officers according to one unofficial estimate. Since record keeping in 1949, police actions have been by far the most frequent method by which our government has intentionally taken the lives of its own citizens.'[3]

It is also important to take into account the statistics of the killing of police officers in this same culture. Over the years 1961 to 1980 the average number of police officers murdered in the U.S.A. was 89 compared with an average of one per year over the same period in England and Wales. Even allowing for bigger population there are considerable differences as the table on p. 65 shows.

As the incidence of firearms used in the commission of crimes began to increase in Britain and the threat of assassination of public figures by terrorists became more wide-spread, more officers required the issue of firearms to carry out their duties.

The first decision to be made was that only selected officers would be trained. They had to be stable in personality, accurate shots, and of sound judgment. Only one in five were selected. A senior officer's permission was required to unlock the safe where the firearms were kept. After each issue the

MURDER OF POLICE

Country	Total	Years (to 1980)	Average	Rate per 1,000,000 population*
England & Wales	20	20	1.00	.020
Japan	26	8	3.25	.029
Sweden	3	8	0.38	.045
Denmark	2	8	0.25	.049
West Germany	13	3	4.33	.071
Finland	3	8	0.38	.079
Australia	9	8	1.13	.079
New Zealand	2	8	0.25	.080
Belgium	8	8	1.00	.102
France	59	28	7.38	.138
Canada	73	20	3.65	.155
India	1,361	8	170.13	.266
Italy	132	8	16.50	.291
United States	1,780	20	89.00	.408

*Statistics: Canada: June 1982

The unarmed British police officer heads the list as among the least likely to be the victim of homicidal attack.

officer concerned had to record details of the incident, whether weapons were fired, and why. The underlying principle was defence of life, and no other use was permitted. In effect, this meant that an officer who discharged a firearm for any other purpose was in breach of discipline. He was also liable to criminal prosecution if a person were injured or killed in cases where he posed no immediate danger or threat to the life of another.

Over the years this system has worked well. But there is no guarantee that this position will not deteriorate, if the trend towards the use of firearms for criminal purpose increases and the police discretion in the use of deadly force to match its escalation is not adequately controlled. Imprudent use of firearms by the police would undoubtedly arouse public indignation; it would lead to alienation, thus diminishing police effectiveness.

The Waldorf Case

On the evening of Friday 14 January 1983, Mr. Stephen Waldorf was shot and battered in Kensington, London, by officers of the Metropolitan Police. Mistakenly believing that they had identified David Martin, a man, charged with attempted murder of a police officer by shooting and later escaping from custody, the officers had opened fire, seriously wounding and later knocking about the head an unarmed and innocent person.

Speaking in the House of Commons three days later, the Home Secretary said, 'I am sure that the House will agree with me that this was a most serious, grave and disturbing incident. Nothing like it must happen again.'

The Home Secretary and indeed the entire House of Commons may hope that 'nothing like it must happen again', but the subsequent acquittal of two officers on charges of attempted murder and one of grievous bodily harm indicates that there may be times when it will happen again. Whether it recurs will, to a great extent, depend on the ability of individual police officers, who are armed, to control their fire and of their senior officers to exert the required discipline.

During the same debate, the Home Secretary revealed the degree of the use of firearms by police in London over the preceding three years.

> 1980   firearms issued on 5,968 occasions
> 1981   4,983
> 1982   (first nine months) 4,346

In spite of this widespread issuing of firearms only in six incidents were shots fired, numbering twenty eight, and only three persons wounded.

These figures are a testimony to the self-control of the police and the high standards of their training.

Police discretion in the use of deadly force should continue to receive attention of this sort if the police in Britain are to retain public confidence. It is equally important, if almost a paradox, that police officers should keep their reputation for going generally about their duties unarmed. In those countries where the police have a reputation for hasty shooting they seem more likely to become victims of murder themselves, at least so far as available evidence is concerned.

The Bounds of Discretion

In addition to our laws and internal regulations, both the United Nations and the European Parliament have endeavoured to lay down standards. But it is not in the more dramatic forms that the exercise of police discretion will impinge on the lives of those citizens with whom the police, in their law enforcement role, will come into contact.

It is youth—and male youth in particular and motorists in general—who will have noticed that the police officer on the spot can issue warnings or cautions instead of resorting to methods of prosecution in a variety of minor cases. These methods are generally approved by chief constables in their orders and instructions. When it comes to that category known as 'indictable offences', however, the officer on the spot is left with no room for manoeuvre, since he must report them no matter how minor they may be. A warning or caution may later be approved by a senior officer within his discretion, again delegated by the chief constable. The more serious offences— of murder, manslaughter, rape—must go to the Director of Public Prosecutions, and it is only at this stage that the law in the form of the Prosecution of Offences Regulations removes discretion in prosecution from the police.

Justice and ethical fairness are very much within the discretion of the police at the point of contact between police and offender, true offender and suspected innocent alike.

This discretion is backed up by powers of considerable force. It has to be so, if the enforcement of the law is to be carried out effectively. In the vast majority of cases police officers acquire a skill, a reasonable attitude and a feel for the operation. This still leaves room for the abuse of discretion— including interference with liberty as a summary punishment, use of force for similar reasons, use of the prosecution system (in weak cases expected to fail) as a punishment, use of power

67

to intimidate, unnecessary invasion of privacy, and so on. Some control of police discretion is undoubtedly in the interests of police. That is not to say that the police in the main do not act with considerable impartiality, though they are possessed of power of considerable proportions in the exercise of discretion in relation to less powerful members of the public. Nor is it to deny that the proper ethical exercise of police discretion is essential if our system of criminal justice is to function properly.

It is now some 25 years since Lord Devlin wrote of the role of the police in our system, 'Since the police force cannot be excluded altogether from the field of inquiry—and since the worst thing of all is to have an irresponsible police force, and the next worst is to have one that is responsible only to the executive and in no way answerable to the courts—is it not better, it may be argued, to leave the police in sole charge of the inquiry but to see to it that they act under a sense of responsibility to the courts for what they do?' Lord Devlin was seeking to justify the English judicial system and the role of the police within it. He saw the courts and the High Courts at that as the main check against police excesses. But much of the use of police discretion never reaches the courts at all since it includes the discretion not to prosecute or to arrest, but to discharge with no charges preferred. Nor does all but a tiny fraction of criminal prosecutions ever reach the High Courts— around 8% only. The vast bulk of criminal prosecutions are dealt with by magistrates, some of whom also serve on police authorities.

Whichever way one looks at it, the police in England and Wales exercise their own discretion, unsupervised, in the enforcement or non-enforcement of the law, the method of investigation and, in the vast bulk of cases, the discretion whether or not to prosecute. It was announced in March 1984 that the Home Secretary was to introduce a Bill in Parliament to set up a prosecution system independent of the police. True, there exist ex-post facto means of challenge both in the trial itself and through remedies such as action for malicious prosecution or false imprisonment. Habeas corpus as a discipline and control has virtually fallen into disuse.

It remains to be stressed that much of the exercise of police authority and power is carried out unobserved by independent persons or police supervisors. In spite of laws, policies and procedures, individual police officers have it within their several powers to modify policy and fashion it on the streets and in other places where their duties take them. Police discretion is too much of a power to be placed in the hands of persons other than those of the highest personal probity, training and behaviour.

Since Lord Devlin's book[4] was published in 1960, increasing interest has developed in bringing about changes in our system of criminal justice. The Scottish system, which embodies elements of the procurator fiscal more common in continental Europe, has been urged by its supporters; and most significantly of all the Royal Commission on Criminal Procedure in its report published in 1981 recommended the setting up of a system of Crown Prosecutors (a modified version of the Scottish system and one based on Canadian experience in Ontario and British Columbia) to separate the policing function from that of the prosecutor. It was encumbent upon the Commission to do so since it recognised, among other reasons, that its recommendations for increased powers of the police would be too dangerous to be linked to the existing discretion in prosecutions. One of the mistakes made by the government in 1983 was to introduce the controversial Police and Criminal Evidence Bill without at the same time introducing a prosecution system independent of the police. This was tantamount to ignoring the strong case for a new balance which the Royal Commission had recommended.

I had held, and hold still, strong reservations about linking up the system of criminal prosecutions with the political system. At least, as long as the police are held responsible for the exercise of their discretion to prosecute, the prospects of narrow political interference or manipulation are minimised. All our great legal officers of state, the law officers of the Crown, the Lord Chancellor, the Attorney General and the Solicitor general are political appointees. They are, in the words of one former Attorney General, 'political animals'. The police are not political animals. The Director of Public Prosecutions is accountable to the Attorney General who is almost invariably a cabinet minister.

Now, as long as such people are capable, as they are, of

maintaining political neutrality when exercising their legal function, it may be held that this is acceptable. But it cannot always be guaranteed for the future. The complete political control of the system of criminal prosecutions would certainly offer hostages to fortune. For these reasons, I always opposed the idea of a system politically linked to such an extent. The proposals of the Royal Commission, however, make it possible to have a system of prosecutors in much the same constitutional position as the police themselves. That is, they would be accountable for the proper discharge of their function to elected police authorites but not directable in the manner of this function. This seems to me to be an admirable middle road and in keeping with our best traditions. The first step, therefore, towards the better control of police discretion is to remove the decision to prosecute from the police altogether, and to hand over this function to Crown Prosecutors.

Police Orders

The second source of control of the discretion of individual police officers lies in the instructions given by chief constables in police orders of one kind or another. For example, I was able within three years of issuing an order for the better exercise of discretion in minor motoring offences to reduce prosecutions in Devon and Cornwall by ten thousand; while at the same time preserving safety of travel on the highway which is the main object of Road Traffic Laws. The wider use of advice and cautions brought this about, but not without some disagreement from senior police officers who were of the opinion that the proof of a police officer's industry could only be measured by the number of prosecutions. A chief constable can, therefore, influence the use of police discretion by his administrative orders and his system of management. He can be questioned on his policies by the police authority, but cannot be directed by them. Also, active police authorities can be successful in imparting feelings of the public and in this way endeavour to bring about reasonable modifications. It is, however, a very sensitive area in which the parties involved have to tread with care.

The third element in the control of the exercise of police

discretion lies within the embodiment of an ethical dimension in the attitudes of the police as individuals. As Lord Devlin put it, 'There is the expectation by the public that the police will act fairly, coupled with a general desire among the police force as a whole to satisfy this expectation.'

But this feeling on the part of the police requires reinforcement in their training, through awareness of human rights (particularly the need to act without discrimination on grounds of social standing, race, religion, etc.), and through the precept of their leaders. The codes of police practice of both the United Nations and the European Parliament point the way.

A further element in the control of police use of discretion is to be found in the Police Discipline Regulations which provide sanctions against abuse of authority.

The best chances of providing reasonable and responsible control of police discretion lie in the combination of these four measures. First, the prosecution of offences should be separated from the policing function; secondly, the orders of a chief constable should provide a framework of directions; thirdly, the training of the police should embody ethical principles of fairness and objectivity; and finally the sanctions of police discipline should deter abuse of authority.

Policing the Poor and the Homeless

When a society manifests comparative affluence on the one hand with comparative poverty on the other, it is likely that the affluent will develop anxieties concerning the potential of the poor for disorder and crime. In such societies, as in early nineteenth century England, the legislature will look to its laws and to their enforcers, the police, to protect society and to maintain social control of the poor.

Though crime in Britain is not confined to any particular class or social group, it is the crimes of the poor which appear to threaten the social order. The 'white collar' criminal may practise fraud, falsification of accounts, tax evasion and illegal use of his clients' or investors' money, but he fails to attract fear and apprehension, though the economic damage of his actions may be large. On the other hand, the petty thief who commits his crime in the streets and who in due time may band

71

together to riot and to loot, is seen to induce fear and an apprehension of the breakdown of the social order. Yet, almost paradoxically, it is not the battalions of the poor and demoralised who cause revolt; rather it is the disaffected of the middle classes. The thousands of unemployed graduates are much more likely to contain within their ranks the leaders of organised revolt. From Lenin to Chairman Mao, they are the people with ideology, powers of organisation and leadership.

The number of police engaged in the investigation of fraud is tiny though the economic value of such crime makes street crime pale into insignificance by comparison. If society were to view the problem of crime purely in economic terms there would undoubtedly be a demand for many more hundreds of police to be assigned to tax evasion. As it is, the policing of the poor becomes a priority. It is no accident that the term 'the criminal classes' was often used to describe the poor.

The Vagrancy Act of 1824 and its later amending statutes indicate the intention of Parliament to control the lower social orders through prosecution and imprisonment. The preamble to the Vagrancy Act of 1824 says that 'it is expedient to make further provision for the Suppression of Vagrancy and the Punishment of idle and disorderly Persons, Rogues and Vagabonds, and incorrigible Rogues in England.'

The poor law had harsh consequences for those who were chargeable to the parish or township. (If a person were deemed able wholly or in part to maintain himself or his dependents by work or other means and he refused or neglected to do so, or if he were chargeable on the parish and went from one parish to another without a certificate, he committed a criminal offence and as an 'idle and disorderly person' could be punished with a month's hard labour in a penal institution.) The mobility of the poor was heavily restricted, due partly to the official policy of preventing people unsettled by rural poverty from drifting to the towns. Nobody wanted 'scroungers'.

Hawkers and pedlars wandering abroad and trading without a licence and Persons wandering abroad or placing themselves in any public place to beg, or causing or encouraging children to do so are among those labelled 'idle and disorderly persons'. Other offences include *Persons wandering abroad and lodging in any barn or otherwise unoccupied building or* (believe it or not) *in the open air ... and not giving a good account of themselves* or *wandering abroad and endeavouring by the exposure of wounds* (returning soldiers) *or deformities to obtain alms.* The Act of 1824 not only gave the power to arrest such persons to any citizen who was thereby required to take them before a justice of the peace, or a constable, but it provided a punishment for any police constable who failed to 'use his best endeavours in such cases'.

Throughout the nineteenth century the police were pre-occupied with harassing and moving on vagrants and controlling the petty infractions of the poor, while the magistrates, mainly drawn from the landed squirearchy as Justices of the Peace, passed judgment on the lower orders. It is a further irony that the police should be drawn from those who did not have 'the rank, habits or station of gentlemen', namely from those same lower orders, according to the policy of recruiting the police in 1829 laid down by Sir Robert Peel in his instructions to the early Commissioners.

I well remember that, even in the mid-1940s, before the provisions of National Insurance and the Welfare State, the police had a duty to arrest vagrants and take them before the magistrates if they had no visible means of support and refused to go to a work-house. A tramp or a drifter always attracted the attention of the patrolling police constable. After the new provisions for social security in 1948, the sight of the wandering destitute person became rare. It is all the more distressing to find that—as recession deepens and unemployment grows—homelessness and poverty are once again on the increase in the 1980s to the point where the policing of the poor takes on some new dimensions. In 1982 the police in Oxford found themselves cast in much the same role as their nineteenth century predecessors in relation to questions of the homeless poor, though parish poor law administration is by now well established with the Department of Health and Social Security. Equally, the homeless poor of 1982 are as likely as their 1824 predecessors to drift into petty crime.

Homelessness is a condition of social disorder, at least in a so-called advanced society. The report *Single and Homeless*, published in 1981 under the sponsorship of the Department of the Environment, highlighted this. It found that 'The incidence of unemployment amongst the homeless is disproportionately high, as is the incidence of certain medical and social problems. Half our respondents had been in prison, borstal, mental hospitals or had been in children's homes.'

As a society becomes more affluent and caring, provision should be made in one form or another for housing the homeless. The provision of public housing for rent has been the main social policy in this direction. But there is a shortage of such housing and in Oxford alone in 1982 over 7,000 families were on the waiting list. Furthermore, there was a shortage of accommodation for single people, due partly to social policy which makes private renting of property difficult and bureaucratic (for good social reasons, to avoid exploitation) and partly to local demand from university students. Voluntary and statutory agencies working together had been unable to meet the demand.

To alleviate the problem, statutory provision under the Housing (Homeless Persons) Act 1977 places a duty on local councils to provide accommodation, but single homeless persons are not regarded as 'priority' cases and have to seek other means. The 'other means' for those homeless and of no fixed abode and those who have no other source of income includes application for supplementary benefits from the local office of the Department of Health and Social Security. Claimants seeking to improve their minimal claims by exaggerating their costs (akin to false expense claims in business) because some landlords were willing to encourage such claims and to profit thereby, combined with the bureaucratic problems of the Ministry to reduce Oxford in 1982 to a mess. The police had acquired information about the large number of petty frauds, and a decision was made between the Ministry and the police to act. Thus the social problem of homelessness and single and itinerant unemployed was not to be solved by improved procedures and better provision of accommodation—but by the criminal system.

A Major Operation

The combined police and Ministry operation, called 'Operation Major' was launched on 2 September 1982 and on the first day 283 people—some guilty of petty fraud, including some hundred who were innocent—were arrested and

74

detained, all of them in one way or another representing social problems, including poverty.

This strategy is of interest, since it was quite close to the police being associated with soliciting or inciting offences which, interestingly, does not appear to have been raised in subsequent proceedings. To solicit or incite another to commit an arrestable offence is itself an offence at common law. The possible incitement in this case lay in the manner of the operation. Persons suspected of having made false claims in the past or suspected of being about to make them were invited to present their claims in special decoy premises in Oxford. They received the following notice: 'In order to ease overcrowding of unemployment benefit offices, a temporary benefit office has been opened at South Oxford Middle School, Cromwell Street (see map below) for the issue of giro-cheques to personal issue claimants.' To put it bluntly the D.H.S.S. set a trap.

The claimants were invited along on Thursdays when it was fairly obviously believed by the Department of Health and Social Security officials and the police that offences in the nature of fraudulent claims would be committed. Steps were not taken to prevent such offences but to condone them before activating the criminal law. Although such offences need to be stopped, it is at the very least a questionable practice for public officials to conspire to allow the commission of offences in order to detect offenders. When such offences arise out of social problems it becomes ethically dubious, to say the least.

Over a hundred of those arrested were not charged with any offence, and since those who were charged were homeless they were mainly detained in prison. The cost of the operation was estimated at £180,546 and frauds by some 175 persons, which were discovered, at £800,000. The offences committed were small amounts over a period of time, probably over some seven years. One may rightly pose the question that if such minor frauds were known to have been going on for seven years, why was not adequate crime prevention within the system adopted? It equally follows that, since the guilty were poor, there were no alternatives to custodial sentences, since most of them could not have paid any fine. For some of those sentenced it was their first offence.

The operation caused considerable controversy. The

Campaign for Single Homeless People, Child Poverty Action Group, Claimants Defence Committee, National Association of Probation Officers and the National Council for Civil Liberties produced a report.[5] Allowing for special pleading and some inaccuracies, the report provides the gist of the problem. Nobody concerned with the operation seems to have come out of it well. The Chief Constable of the Thames Valley Police, Peter Imbert,[6] felt it was another example of the police being 'left to pick up the tab—as usual', and that he was 'glad that other people have now heard about homeless itinerants'. Some members of the Police Authority felt 'an operation like this must never happen again', and that the cost to the taxpayer of the frauds and the operation, 'would have been better spent on new housing'.

There should have been a major *preventive* effort in the first place, say the simple warning by a uniformed police officer to each claimant for benefit who approached the office of the Ministry. Ministers have a duty to make their systems proof against the petty miscreants who, in order to supplement their meagre income, are tempted to 'gild the lily' of their claims, a course of conduct not pursued only by those who live on the margins of society. The losses to the Inland Revenue through tax evasion alone are estimated in billions of pounds.

Morally, the issue is quite uncomplicated. If it is felt that the police should be placed at the disposal of departments of government in order to diminish illegal practices which cause a drain on government funds, some form of fiscal police branch to include the fraud squads should be set up to do so. But if that is to be done it should begin its operations at the *top* of the social order rather than at the bottom. Of course, this would be more difficult than policing the poor. To start with, there would be an articulate outrage concerning the abuse of police powers; the best lawyers would be in great demand; very few if any suspects would be remanded in custody in our rotting prisons; and the police would find themselves in protracted business and fought every inch of the way.

There is more than a whiff of hypocrisy about the type of operation inspired by our social security services in Oxford in 1982.

Police Power

Throughout history, police in one form or another have been given power over their fellow citizens to maintain order, including the enforcement of laws. They are the long arm of the law which reaches out to activate the criminal processes which should result in justice being done. In democracies, the important question of 'who guards the guardians' has become a constant theme, and sometimes a problem. Police can be used to *deny* true justice, that is fairness and equality under the law, and a whole range of human rights. In modern times, the two most notorious examples have been the K.G.B. and its predecessors in the U.S.S.R. and the Gestapo of Nazi Germany—one the product of the totalitarian Communist state; the other the product, at least in the beginning, of a distorted and hijacked democracy.

In the preface to his well documented book, *The Soviet Police System*,[7] Robert Conquest records; 'It has so far been the rule that the power and activity of the police have increased enormously during periods of crises in the Soviet Union, whether spontaneous or created by official policy (like the collectivisation terror). The first wave, starting in 1918 and culminating in the terror against the Kronstadt rebels.' This, he records, was followed by a period of reduction in police obtrusiveness but during the period 1930 to 1933 the collectivisation campaign, the victory of Party and Police cost the lives of millions of the peasantry. Torture by the police was explicitly sanctioned during the Stalinist regime. A circular quoted in a Khrushchev confidential report in 1956 explained: 'The question arises as to why the socialist intelligence service should be more humanitarian (than all bourgeoisie services) against the mad agents of the bourgeoisie, against the deadly enemies of the working class and of the collective farm workers. The Party Central Committee considers that physical pressure should still be used obligatorily, as an exception applicable to known and obstinate enemies of the people, as a method both justifiable and appropriate.'

In his famous 'secret' speech, Khrushchev (Conquest records) 'confined himself to uncovering some—but not all—of the horrors of the period between 1934 and 1952'. The political and repressive role of the Soviet police system is carefully documented, however, and Conquest comments, 'The requisites of the Party have often conflicted in the past with the requisites of justice. They may do so again. Leadership conflicts may still precipitate the use of police action the scope of which is per se, not readily kept within the bounds set for it'[8].

Meanwhile in neighbouring Nazi Germany the use of the police as a political battering ram and a tyranny was reaching new and appalling dimensions. As for the Gestapo. 'Thousands upon thousands of unseen eyes seemed to watch every step taken by every German. The tentacles of the police octopus wrapped themselves round the community; any trace of anti-Nazi sentiment was duly noted by 45,000 officials of the Gestapo distributed over 20 Leitstellan (Regional Offices) and 39 Stellan (Sub-Regional Offices) fed by so called 'antennae' in a further 300 Leitstellan and 850 Frontier Police 'Commissariats'. The security of the State was guarded by 65,000 men in the Sicherheitspolizei and 2,800,000 men in the Ordnungspolizei (Regular Police) headed by 30 HSSPF (Senior S.S. and Police Commanders). 40,000 guards terrorized hundreds of thousands of actual or supposed enemies of the regime in 20 concentration camps and 160 afiliated labour camps. A shadowy army of 100,000 S.S. (Security Service) informers kept a continuous check on the population's thinking.'[9]

The guardians of the guardians were the guardians themselves. A catastrophic political recipe.

In the United Kingdom the many checks and balances in the system of criminal justice and our democratic Parliamentary organisations have prevented such grotesque distortion. But it hasn't stopped a recrudescence of the debate on police accountability.

Ordinary mortals perpetuate excesses and, in all systems known to us, individuals or small groups are capable of degrees of tyranny. No man should ever be given power over another man in any degree whatsoever unless that power is, first, essential in the wider interests of the people and of justice and, secondly, that in the use of that power its functioning is accountable to the people. There can be no justification whatsoever for giving power to one man over another for mere convenience or expediency, or in the interests of one political party or group. The power is given so that order be maintained and that in maintaining it justice may be done. Justice is a tender plant, though a fine one, and demands constant protection, not only in the grand manner in parliaments and courts but in our neighbourhoods and at the individual level.

It is possible to live in a society where the theory of justice and some of its practices appear on the surface to be healthy, well controlled and at the service of all, irrespective of race, creed, religion or social standing. But every day, in our society, justice is denied or distorted or remote from individuals who are unable to seek it—unable, that is, through their own incompetence, social condition, or because of discrimination and prejudices against them. This condition will continue and may get worse as long as justice is dispensed through large, remote, bureaucracies. It is easier for people of influence, higher social standing and affluence to get justice than for those less well endowed. In a society that really cares about justice for all, some rearrangements are necessary. That is not to say that our present institutions are not well intentioned or better than many.

Chapter 3

Police and Human Rights

The development of the human rights movement in national and in international law has taken place as a response to the inhumanities perpetrated upon people by powerful governments and their bureaucracies. One of those bureaucracies is the police. Police systems, being an arm of government, reflect the regard of that government for basic principles of human rights.

The struggle between a government's discharge of its duty to maintain law and uphold order and the assertion of the rights of the individual or group is a permanent one. The appalling atrocities committed by the Nazis in Germany before and during the Second World War, and by the Stalinist regime in the U.S.S.R. and its satellite countries, contributed to the birth of the United Nations and the Universal Declaration of Human Rights in 1948.

The European Convention

The Council of Europe, of which the United Kingdom was a founder member, drew up the European Convention on Human Rights which was signed on 4 November 1950 and came into force in 1953. It is the only bill of rights to which a British subject can turn in the final defence of his rights as an individual.

It is remarkable how, in the intervening years since 1953, so little of this great charter of human rights has percolated into the training and management of our police forces. (The same is true in most if not all member countries.) It was for this reason that the Committee of Ministers of the Council of Europe adopted Resolution ((78) 41) in 1978 which, among other things, recommended the governments of member states to take whatever measures are appropriate to teach the subject of human rights at all levels of education. Member states are required 'to promote the teaching of the safeguard of human rights and the relevant protection machinery in an appropriate manner as part of the training for members of the civil and military services'. Although this recommendation is not legally binding on governments, it places a heavy moral duty upon them to promote training of police officials in this subject. In the United Kingdom that burden falls primarily on the Home Office and the Scottish and Northern Ireland Offices, together with their professional and academic advisers.

Demeanour of Police

Free people expect much of their police. In such societies, the police stand at the point of balance—on the one hand securing human rights, and on the other exercising their lawful powers (given to them by governments in the name of the people) to protect the people and their institutions.

Societies which are not free acquire omnipotent police, who serve only those in power. Laws are promulgated to give police wide powers to deny human rights, in some cases even the most basic civil liberties. Police in such corrupt systems are themselves corrupted and, through degeneration, are permitted to indulge in arbitrary conduct, including torture and inhuman or degrading treatment.

Of course police authority is abused even in democracies. It can become more the master and less the servant. It can snuff out more freedom than it protects. The main problem lies in control. This is particularly so in the growth and practice of secret police. Abuses can flourish not only because of official negligence or acquiescence but because, rightly or wrongly, broad sections of the people identify with such practices and consider that, in spite of their excesses, the police are carrying out a necessary and unpleasant task if both state and society are to be preserved and protected. Considerable moral burdens are placed on decent police officials whose actions to check drifts of this kind are of paramount importance to the preservation of human rights.

In an ideal world there would be no need for police. Society would achieve order through agreement, mutual tolerance and through the leadership of true authority. There would be no call for physical coercion and its threat. But human experience indicates that noble sentiments alone are too weak to control those whose ambitions, greed, aggression and anger give way to threatening and damaging activity on either a small or on a grand scale. From rebellion to simple theft, there are requirements for laws and for some form of enforcement of those laws. The great instruments of enforcement in most states are the police and the judicial processes.

In creating such instruments, free societies have to take great care on two counts. First, they have to ensure that the system created to protect them does not become the instrument of their bondage. In containing crime and disorder, the system must never take away those basic freedoms enshrined in the best of domestic laws, in the United Nations declaration, and in the European Convention and its extensions. The police have to be seen to be carrying out their function within the law to which they themselves are subject.

Secondly, nations have to ensure that those who are chosen to exercise power and authority are carefully selected for their human qualities, properly trained to perform their difficult duties in an ethically correct manner, and, very importantly, are led and directed by persons with high qualities of human excellence. Nothing less than this will help to secure the balancing of human rights with adequate control of excessive human misbehaviour.

Even in the best of regulated democratic police systems, aberrations will emerge from time to time in which groups and individuals will fail to maintain the high criteria which are sought. In such cases measures have to be available to maintain correct standards by the imposition of disciplinary regulations (having regard to the human rights of the malefactors) to be followed by such internal reforms as are necessary to reduce repetition.

It has been said that 'Power corrupts and absolute power corrupts absolutely.' Police officials have to be on guard to avoid the potential and insidious corrupting influence of power, if it is to be neutralised in them as individuals and in the groups to which they belong. Power for the police is not to be seen as an end in itself but as a means towards a free social order.

In ideal circumstances, all the many parties would so respect and trust the police that they would offer maximum assistance to them in their functions of law enforcement, investigation of crimes, maintenance of public tranquillity and prosecution of offenders. Where the police are seen to be at the service of human rights, in particular, and humanitarian acts, in general, such public support is more likely to follow.

Individuals or groups, who are exposed to inequality, victimization and denial of human rights and civil liberties may well resort to anti-social or criminal behaviour. If the police have a highly developed social awareness, they will often be presented with opportunities for the prevention of crimes and the maintenance of social order, through bringing their influences to bear. In this way, police will enhance their own stature and function and, in so doing, will improve their position as law enforcement officials. Police officials should see their relationships with the many differing sections of the public as *positive*.

As a society becomes more civilised, free, educated and informed at all levels, its expectations of police along with other public servants are raised. Among other things, it requires not only that the police carry out their primary functions but that they do so with greater sensitivity and understanding. As peoples become more aware of the dignity of the individual and of human rights, they are likely to criticise and complain about police behaviour which in another age might not have been regarded as wrong. I think that the impression that our police have deteriorated is often false; sometimes it is simply that higher demands are being made upon them.

The general demeanour required of the police is not necessarily constant. A society which is homogeneous, monocultured and classless would require less adaptability from police officials than our real world in which there are ethnic, religious, cultural and other differences. Police at the service of human rights must develop an instinct for human dignity. Because they often see human beings in degrading and degraded situations, police are exposed to the influence of cynicism. They have to avoid becoming indifferent, however difficult that may be.

The foundations of good police practice are, therefore, an understanding and acceptance of ethical principles of duty to the enforcement of laws, not as an end in themselves but as a means of securing fairness and justice to all manner of persons irrespective of their race, creed, religion or social standing. The provisions of human rights legislation seeks no lower standard of police behaviour. The police in the United Kingdom at the time of writing receive little or no training in ethics and human rights. This is a serious omission which it is hoped will soon be put right.

Discrimination Forbidden

The police from time to time act in breach of the fundamental provision of the European Convention forbidding discrimination in the performance of their duties. 'The enjoyment of the rights and freedoms set forth in this Convention should be secured without discrimination on any grounds such as sex, race, colour, language, religion, political or other opinion, national or social origin, association with a national minority, property, birth or status.' When Lord Scarman in his report on the Brixton and other disorders in 1981 recommended that racial discrimination should be an offence under the Police Discipline Code, his recommendation was opposed from within the police service and the Home Office failed to press it. A serious omission. What he had to say is fully supported in the European Convention. The European Convention affects many aspects of the day-to-day performance of the policing function, but unless police officers are well trained and educated in the subject they are likely to commit breaches of it. They are less likely to perform within the spirit of the Convention as well as within its letter. This is particularly so when police activity is subjected to severe strain, as for example in Northern Ireland.

Interrogation Abused

In 1978 in Northern Ireland the police and security forces in 'that tragic and lasting crisis', the 'longest and most violent terrorist campaign witnessed', in the words of the European Court, were found to have been operating in contravention of that part of the Convention[1] which forbids 'torture and inhuman and degrading treatment' of prisoners under any circumstances.

I am well aware that in military training, interrogation techniques for use in time of war have been developed beyond anything contemplated by civil police even when facing a terrorist campaign. The end can never justify the means. Once the police begin to believe that tacit government approval is given to their excesses, they embark on that slippery slope which in a number of countries has led to summary executions by the police as well as torture[2] and other inhuman practices.

The techniques found to have been used by the police in Northern Ireland included wall standing (spreadeagled in a 'stress position'), hooding, subjection to noise, deprivation of sleep and of food and drink for long periods of time. These techniques, while not committed to written instructions, were approved at a 'high level'. The government of the United Kingdom was taken to the European Court of Human Rights in Strasbourg by the government of the Republic of Ireland and there judgment was delivered against the United Kingdom.[3] In the interim period the controversial police practices had been forbidden. Where police and military work together in peace time operations, it is of the utmost importance that the police provide the standards of law enforcement demanded of them.

It is not only in times of emotional and sensational stress that police denial of human rights can take place, but in the everyday business of arresting, interrogating, invasion of privacy, surveillance and so on. Sometimes this is done deliberately and sometimes by omission, ignorance or mistake. Such treatment as unnecessarily long detention, stripping and searching, neglect of prisoners' rights, gratuitous assaults, overbearing and intimidating conduct, racial prejudice, all accrue to the deprivation of human rights, and all chip away at the reputation and standing of the police. Practices such as these are rarely condoned at a 'high level' and are in any case forbidden by the provision in the Police Discipline Regulations against 'abuse of authority'. Nevertheless they continue to occur.

Greater attention at all levels of police activity to the overriding principles of the European Convention on Human

Rights would go a long way towards establishing a standard of professional conduct which is demanded in a liberal democracy.

Training of Police in Human Rights

Early in their training, junior police officials are faced with the considerable task of assimilating a great deal of domestic law and procedure. It is important that they are also made aware of fundamental human rights as set out in the European Convention.

The short handbook, published by the Directorate of Press and Information, Strasbourg and entitled, *The European Convention on Human Rights* sets out the basic text. The trainee might first be introduced to the Convention in general terms (stressing in particular Article 14—which forbids discrimination at all times) and, as his education progresses, he should be made aware of the particular Article of the Convention which touches upon the subject being dealt with. Thus, when a trainee is being taught domestic laws and procedures of arrest, Article 5 should be drawn to his attention. The aim is to ensure that at the end of their basic training all junior police officials should not only be aware of the existence of human rights provisions but of their relevance to the daily police function. The Declaration on the Police of the Parliamentary Assembly of the Council of Europe should therefore be studied in detail, as should the United Nations Code of Conduct for Law Enforcement Officials.

Where trainees are being prepared for promotion and leadership, the importance of their own example and the supervision of their subordinates should be highlighted. There are useful texts published by the Secretariat of the European Commission on Human Rights, such as *Stock-taking on the European Convention on Human Rights*.

Training among the higher echelons of police should focus on responsibilities of governments and the entire range of the function of the Council of Europe. The senior police official not only requires the knowledge and ability to ensure that his organisation is functioning in accordance with the intention of the Council of Europe and his own government, but he should be in a position to advise those higher officials whose work takes them into the Committee of Ministers, Parliamentary Assembly, Court of Human Rights and the Commission of Human Rights.

A Bill of Rights

I wish we had a Bill of Rights. The absence of such a document impedes education as well as justice at all levels. To understand the ramifications of the existing principles and remedies for denial requires the knowledge of a first class international lawyer. To secure justice under the European Convention requires not only that an aggrieved person should exhaust all domestic legal procedures before a complaint will be considered by the European Commission, but that even then another two or three years may elapse before the decision is promulgated. That 'justice delayed is justice denied', has long been a cliché in English law, and under the existing conditions it is clear that justice is denied.

As long ago as July 1969 Emlyn Hooson M.P. sought unsuccessfully to introduce a Bill of Rights in the House of Commons. In 1979 Lord Wade's private Members' Bill in the House of Lords suffered the same fate, though attracting much support. The voices of Lords Hailsham, Denning and Scarman, among others, have been raised in support of the incorporation of the European Convention on Human Rights into the constitution of the United Kingdom. I am of the opinion that had the time and enthusiasm given by the House of Commons to the issue of restoration of the death penalty been accorded to the much greater issue of a Bill of Rights, its achievement might well have been brought about. The Prime Minister, Mrs. Thatcher,[4] has expressed doubts about such a measure ever becoming part of the domestic law of the United Kingdom. We have therefore to await the ascendency to political power of those who are willing and prepared to take an historic step in the evolution of the liberty of the subject.

The interplay between rights and duties is of considerable importance. Those without rights (for example, slaves) have no moral obligation to perform civic duties.

Barely a day passes without some important personage speaking from Olympian heights to those whose lives are comparatively humdrum, enjoining them to be responsible, to perform their civic obligations and so on. People who are aware of their civic rights and freedoms and of the state's determination to protect them, are much more likely to respond to such calls than those who believe, rightly or wrongly, that power threatens.

The modern state is the biggest threat of all to human rights. This is true not only of totalitarian states but of democracies as well. Anyone who doubts that the United Kingdom falls short in this respect only needs to study the list of applications for justice to the European Commission of Human Rights at Strasbourg—of all member states, citizens of the United Kingdom form the single largest number. There are of course member states of the Council of Europe who do not permit petitions, but these are very few.

A Bill of Rights, therefore, is designed to discipline the power of the state. Its effect is to make life more difficult for officials. It encourages people to make a nuisance of themselves. It is of vital importance to the continuing aspirations of all people for justice. It will only come about if enough people of influence, knowledge and authority combine to bring it to fruition. Political parties have to be challenged to act.

Part Two

POLICE AND THE SOCIAL ORDER

(Police and Politics 1959–84)

Chapter 4

Royal Commission 1962

'I decline to submit a report of my investigations into an allegation of corruption implicating members of the City of Nottingham Corporation.' With these sentiments Captain Athelstan Popkess, Chief Constable of Nottingham, fired the first shots in the battle over reform of the police system of England and Wales—which has continued, to a greater or lesser extent, to the present time. It was May 1959.

Popkess, one of the last of the 'amateur' chief constables and formerly an officer in the British Army, had received information alleging corrupt practice by members of the City Council. He decided to call in outside detectives from New Scotland Yard. This action infuriated some members of the City Corporation as well as the Town Clerk who wrote to the chief constable demanding a full report. Popkess refused, relying on the constitutional principle that he was not, in the legal sense, a servant of the Corporation. The Town Clerk insisted that he would carry out the inquiry and would only involve the chief constable if and when he had made up his own mind to do so. Popkess remained intransigent. On the 3 June 1959 the Police Watch Committee passed a resolution that the Town Clerk and the chief constable be instructed to submit reports concerning the activities of the officers from New Scotland Yard. Once again Popkess refused on the grounds that law enforcement was a police matter, and not one for the Watch Committee.

These exchanges, though quite formal in content, were in fact peeling off layers of encrustation which for a hundred years had attached to the office of chief constable. The system had in the past worked in a fashion, but had now become head-on conflict. The Watch Committee made the next move by suspending the chief constable from duty as from 9 July 1959.

The Association of Chief Police Officers rallied to his defence and sought legal advice. Deputations called upon the Home Office to intervene. The Home Secretary, then R. A. Butler, was informed and on 22 July the Watch Committee were advised to reinstate Popkess. They refused, and countered by advertising for a new chief constable. After considerable pressure from the Home Office, buttressed by the best legal opinions, the Watch Committee finally capitulated and Captain Athelstan Popkess was reinstated to the office of chief constable. But things were never to be the same.

Following the dismissal of the Chief Constable of Cardiganshire due to incompetence, the Chief Constable of Brighton for alleged corruption (he was later acquitted), and the Chief Constable of Worcester for fraud, the Home Secretary was already under considerable parliamentary pressure. In November 1959 he faced a censure motion for his action in making £300 of public funds available to settle an action brought against a constable in the Metropolitan Police on grounds of alleged assault.

Allegations were made that the police were not subject to adequate accountability (still a familiar sound in 1984); that their constitutional position in the state was ill-defined; and that the method of dealing with complaints against them was ineffective and not always fair to the complainant (yet again all too familiar in 1984). On 25 January 1960 Butler appointed a Royal Commission on the Police. The debate had begun in earnest.

In the light of the recent clamour concerning the accountability of the Metropolitan Police to locally elected representatives advocated by the Greater London Council and some of the London Boroughs, it should be noted that the Report of the Royal Commission on the Police, 1962, gave scant attention to that particular issue. It does not seem to have engaged the debate at the time. It was no doubt felt that the Home Secretary's answerability to Parliament for the policing of London was an adequate guarantee of accountability and that it was the provincial arrangements which needed revision. After all, the Commissioner of Police of the Metropolis clearly came under the authority of the Home Secretary who required any orders governing the general conduct of the Metropolitan Police to be submitted for his approval. The general policy of the force in discharge of its function could be questioned in Parliament and the Commissioner was accountable to the Home Secretary. In the provinces it was a different matter.

Under the heading *Arrangements for the Control of The Police*, the Royal Commission observed: 'The problem of controlling the police can therefore be re-stated as the problem of controlling chief constables.' The problem to be overcome, however, was how to establish control without giving Watch Committees and Police Communities the power to interfere with and direct law enforcement policies in general, and prosecutions in particular. There were strong arguments put to the Commission urging an end to all this nonsense of local police forces and demanding total nationalisation. One can only speculate what the position of the police would have been in 1983 had we had a national force controlled by a Minister: it might well have become extremely unpopular and consequently less effective. There were, however, those who maintained that all that was needed was a reform of the localised police system and traditions and in the end their views prevailed.

Control of chief constables, it was recommended, should be achieved through supervision by the Home Office Inspectorate of Constabulary, and through the power of police authorities to call for reports, to dismiss the incompetent and to discipline the wayward. At the same time, as Tom Critchley (Secretary to the Royal Commission) pointed out, 'No one should have power to give him [the chief constable] orders even on broad matters of policy. The chief constable should be free within the limits of his duties, to act as he saw fit both in enforcing the law in individual cases, and also on questions of policy.' It is the latter part of that statement, namely, 'questions of policy' which caused subsequent conflict between some chief constables and their police authorities.

The Commission believed that local police authority committees should have the following functions: to provide, pay, equip, and accommodate the force; to give advice and guidance to chief constables about local problems; to foster good police public relations; and (subject to approval of the Home Secretary) to appoint, discipline and dismiss senior officers.

The Home Secretary, it was felt, should be responsible in the provinces for general police efficiency and should have powers to achieve it. This function would include the power forcibly to amalgamate many of the 126 separate police forces. The Association of Chief Police Officers viewed the prospect of amalgamations with alarm—after all, their own evidence to the Royal Commission indicated that, in their view, there was little wrong with the police service as it then existed, and they were certainly, probably naturally, opposed to the decimation of their ranks. An exception to this point of view was that of the Chief Constable of Lancashire, T. E. St. Johnston, who submitted evidence recommending sweeping amalgamations. Needless to say, this alienated him from most of his colleagues. (An experience I shared when giving evidence to Lord Scarman's Inquiry after the riots of 1981.)

A new Police Act

In November 1963, the government introduced a Police Bill which was to find its way into the Statute Books as the Police Act of 1964. The Bill followed closely the recommendations of the Royal Commission and set out, for the first time in police history, to define the respective functions of the Home Secretary, policy authorities and chief constables. The Home Secretary was given powers to promote police efficiency including compulsory amalgamations of police forces. The police authorities were to be responsible for maintaining adequate and efficient police forces. Chief constables were to be responsible for directing and controlling those forces. The Bill was a detailed one reforming almost every facet of the police system. It caused few problems during parliamentary debates and was felt to have created a satisfactory clarification of constitutional and administrative principles. It could hardly have been foreseen that within less than ten years the controversy over police accountability would once more swirl about council chambers throughout the country and within the debating chambers of Parliament itself.

R. A. Butler, a splendid and respected Home Secretary, had done much to bring the issue into the open and, by setting up the Royal Commission in the first place, had not only found his own refuge from parliamentary attacks but had made possible a welcome shift in police affairs towards essential evolution. In 1964, however, a Labour government took up office and it fell to Roy Jenkins as the new Home Secretary to implement many of the changes made possible by the Police Act.

Amalgamations

Roy Jenkins set about amalgamation with gusto. By the time he had finished, the 126 police forces were reduced to 49. Many chief constables were demoted to lower ranks of deputy and assistant. Some left the service.

Even Robert Mark, the excellent Chief Constable of Leicester, felt the Jenkins' axe. As he was to write in his memoirs, 'When the amalgamation was proposed the bottom fell out of my world.'[1] If the bottom was to fall out of his world in Leicester, his new world at Scotland Yard was to be another story. He was to become one of the boldest Commissioners of the Metropolis and will be remembered chiefly for the courage, determination and success with which he pursued his campaign against corruption in the force—a campaign that was waged in the glare of maximum publicity. He can be said to have set an example, as a more aggressive publicist for his views than any senior officer in the annals of police history. Towards the end of his period of office even the Home Office became nervous and no doubt breathed a sigh of relief when Mark resigned. For better for worse his new style—combining publicity, openness and the forthright expression of (often controversial) views—was inevitably adopted by other senior police officers. It was a difficult act for his immediate successor to follow.

Following the provisions of the Police Act of 1964 new police authorities were created in the provinces. Further amalgamations followed when the Local Government Act of 1974 reduced separate forces from 49 to 41. The intention of the Royal Commission and of Parliament to lay the bogy of police accountability was not entirely successful. The issue was to re-emerge with intermittent intensity throughout the 1970s and early 1980s. It is still on the political agenda.

Chapter 5

Democratic Accountability and the Police

As every democrat knows, power should be distributed not only wisely but in miserly fashion. Power given to individuals over other individuals can and does have a corrupting influence. On the other hand authority and the power that goes with it are essential to get things done, to govern and to maintain order. It would offend common sense to envisage a society in which officials charged with responsibility are denied the authority with which to discharge it.

The only acceptable way for a democratic government to manage the distribution of power and its control is through some form of accountability. On the whole this is fairly clearly defined. Civil servants are accountable to their ministers, who are in turn accountable to Parliament and thereby (in theory, if not always in practice) to the electorate, the people. In local government, officials are accountable to their committees who are again accountable to the electorate. Both civil servants and local government officials are servants in the eyes of the law and can be ordered to implement agreed policies. The position of the police is in some ways quite different and this anomaly continues to give rise to misunderstanding as well as to controversy.

It has long been accepted that a 'constable' (and all police officers are constables) does not in law have a servant-master relationship with his superiors or politicians, as do civil servants and ministers for example. For legal purposes he is an independent officer. Not even his senior officer can forbid him to enforce the law. This independence has been transmitted to the legal duties of the chief constable; in the words of Lord Denning, 'I have no hesitation in holding that like every constable in the land, he (the Commissioner) should be and is independent of the executive. I hold it to be the duty of the

Commissioner, as it is of every chief constable to enforce the law of the land.' He went on to say, 'No Minister of the Crown can tell him he must or must not keep observation on this place or that, he must or must not prosecute this man or that. Nor can any police authority tell him so. The responsibility lies on him. He is answerable to the law and the law alone.'[1] These principles were further reinforced by the Court of Appeal in a more recent case (see chapter 11).

No one can tell a chief constable how to enforce the law or prosecute individuals. However, it is a mistake (and a common one) to interpret this to mean that the Home Secretary in London and police authorities in the provinces should have no say in the administration of a police force or in its overall policing style and strategy or in the provision of resources. On the contrary, in London all police orders concerning the administrative function of the Commissioner have (at least in theory) to be approved by the Home Secretary.

The relationship between the chief constable and the police authority is further clouded by the vagueness of the Police Act of 1964. The Act places a duty on the chief constable to 'direct and control' the force under his command but this is not defined and therefore buttresses the position of the chief constable. The combined effect of the cases declaring the autonomy of chief (and other) constables when enforcing laws and the wording of the Police Act is to create a situation which some believe is unsatisfactory while others, particularly chief constables, believe is essential if undue political meddling is to be avoided. After all, it is argued, the chief constable is accountable to the law and to the police authority for the efficient discharge of the task.

At this point, it becomes apparent that there is a potential source of conflict, which is more than semantic, since the police authority is itself charged with the duty, under the same Police Act, of maintaining an 'adequate and efficient' police force (again not defined). How can this authority maintain an 'efficient' police force if it lacks the power to control, or at least strongly to influence, policing policies? This uncertainty is the nub of the problem. How far can a police authority go in bringing about the kind of policing it wants without clashing with its chief constable? I came near to a conflict in 1981 by insisting that I would not purchase plastic bullets nor train the force in their use, and at the same time advocating the constitutional establishment of local Community Policing Consultative Groups. Fortunately, it never came to a show-down since the police authority accepted my advice, but a number of councillors were clearly agitated by my strong views.

Apart from controlling the supply of money in the annual budget, and ensuring that item by item this control of expenditure restricts the chief constable's administrative and operational options, the only power over a chief constable held by a police authority is the power to dismiss him. But this only applies if the chief constable is inefficient (or guilty of misconduct)—an extremely rare occurrence.

Professor Goodhart in his dissenting memorandum in the 1962 Royal Commission report put his finger on the problem with unerring accuracy. He commented: 'The emphasis placed in the report on the power to enforce dismissal is, I believe, evidence of the weakness of the present system, because no private organisation could function efficiently if the only method of control lay in a threat of dismissal.' He went on to say, 'This virtually uncontrolled position of the chief constable is unique,' and 'I find it difficult to accept the view that to give such unfettered power to chief constables is in accord with a democratic form of government on which so much emphasis has been placed.' Professor Goodhart clearly foresaw many of the present day problems and dissatisfactions.

A Fiction

In 1929 the Royal Commission on Police Powers and Procedures commented: 'The police in this country have never been recognised, either in law or by tradition, as a force distinct from the general body of citizens. Despite the imposition of many extraneous duties on the police by legislation or administrative action, the principle remains that a policeman, in the view of the common law, is only a person paid to perform, as a matter of duty, acts which if he were so minded he might have done voluntarily.' The Commissioners went on to say, 'Indeed a policeman possesses few powers not employed by the ordinary citizen and public opinion expressed in Parliament and elsewhere has shown great jealousy of any attempts to give increased authority to the police. This attitude is one we believe not to any distrust of the police as a body, but to an instinctive feeling that, as a matter of principle, they should have as few powers as possible which are not possessed by the ordinary citizen, and that their authority should rest on the broad basis of consent and active cooperation of all law-abiding people.'[2]

I have quoted these passages at some length since they give rise to a fictional theory about the police which has long been overtaken by a new reality. The truth today is that 'To say that a constable is a citizen in uniform is no more accurate than to say that all citizens are constables in plain clothes.'[3] Not only have the police much more power than the citizen but they have become much more professional than their predecessors.

The police derive their power not only from the law, but from their organisation and their equipment, from the enormous amount of information in their possession and from the discretion with which this is used. A chief constable today controls and directs a vast and increasing number of sophisticated systems. Furthermore the range of human activity subject to the sanctions of the criminal law has grown from 1,000 separate offences in 1929 to over 7,000 in 1983.

Not only do the police now enforce thousands of laws affecting the daily lives of an increasing number of people, but they do so from a position far removed from the idea of the police officer as a citizen 'performing for pay that which he might do voluntarily if he were so minded.' The widening of the scope of the criminal sanction is but one step with far reaching consequences for police and public alike. Where laws and police are fewer, the police role is less obtrusive, for the police operate more on the margins of society. Where laws and enforcement are all-pervasive, the police operate at the heart of society; and this is one of the reasons for the controversy surrounding the issue of democratic accountability of the police at the present time.

Choices of Policy

Since the police cannot enforce all of the laws all of the time, they have to be selective and establish priorities. Of course, serious crimes demand and always receive priority and there is little or no argument about this. But the bulk of laws and their enforcement are not concerned with serious crime but with social control and regulation. The laws about morality, public order, freedom of speech, conduct of businesses, drug usage, consumption of alcohol and motoring are among the many which police enforce from time to time, depending on the resources available and the directions given by the chief constable. According to his own standards, he may concentrate on one or more of these regulatory offences. Some chief constables, with declared moral attitudes, may spend more of their resources on prosecuting pornographic literature; others have purges on motorists. The chief constable's own preferred standards of law enforcement are not always those of the wider public, though of course there are always pressures from one source or another. The chief constable may react to local pressure groups and media opinion, or may respond to members of the police authority. But he may do none of these things. As has been said, he is under no obligation to enforce particular laws in particular ways.

The Office of Chief Constable

Chief constables are appointed by the local police authority, subject to approval by the Secretary of State at the Home Office. Applications for the post are advertised from within the police profession only. The local police authority then prepares a short list of applicants which is submitted to the Secretary of State who, with the advice of his Inspector of Constabulary, approves the list. He may delete names of those considered unfitted for the post but he has no power to add or substitute names. Subtle pressures to do this have been tried from time to time, but local police authorities almost always guard their prerogative jealously.

Having been appointed, the chief constable can be dismissed only on two counts, that he is found guilty of a serious breach of discipline or he is deemed unfitted to carry out his duties. In both cases he is entitled to a proper inquiry and has a right of appeal against any decision.

On appointment the chief constable becomes solely responsible for the 'direction and control' of the force. Internal policies, including enforcement and prosecution policies, the deployment of resources, the priorities of his organisation, are all matters within his control and direction. He may receive guidance from time to time from the Home Office but he is not obliged to implement it, though persistent refusal to do so may conceivably render him liable to be regarded as unfitted for his duty; however, this course has never been implemented in recent years.

So far as resources of manpower, equipment and buildings are concerned he has to persuade his police authority and the Home Office of his needs. This, together with the demands of the law, are the only controls to which he is subject. His is an influential and powerful position.

The position of the Commissioner of Police of the Metropolis is different from the provinces. The appointment is in the gift of the Secretary of State as police authority for the Metropolitan Police District. The post is not open to applicants nor does it carry the security of tenure associated with the office of chief constable. The office of Commissioner of Police of the Metropolis is held 'for the duration of Her Majesty's pleasure'. This means in effect that the Secretary of State can relieve him of his post should any conflict leading to a crisis of confidence occur. Following the scandal surrounding the entry of Michael Fagan into the bedroom of Her Majesty the Queen in July 1982, Sir David McNee, the Commissioner of Police at the time records (in his memoirs) that he was pressed by his Under Secretary of State to resign.

'The Commissioner controls the force by virtue of the Metropolitan Police Act 1829, as amended, and not being a police officer enjoys no security of tenure, unlike provincial chief constables who enjoy a measure of protection from arbitrary dismissal under the Police Act 1964. Dismissal for any reason would, however, be likely to attract the attention of Parliament, but if the Home Secreatry felt that he was on strong enough ground there is no doubt at all of his right to dismiss the Commissioner if he thinks fit.'[4]

Furthermore, orders for the administration of the Metropolitan Police are subject to the approval of the Home Secretary. Operationally the Commissioner functions with the freedom of a chief constable though he should be and is alert to the political pressures exerted on the Home Secretary in Parliament.

Parliament has therefore made the Commissioner of Police in London more accountable than his provincial counterparts. Successive Home Secretaries have at least assured that, as police authority for London, they have few accountability problems.

It has become established practice in recent times for Commissioners to serve for about five years, whereas in the provinces it is not unknown for chief constables to hold their office for twenty years or more.

Chief constables (and the Commissioners) are collectively organised as the Association of Chief Police Officers of England, Wales and Northern Ireland, (known as A.C.P.O.) which also includes deputies and assistants. A.C.P.O. is not legally accountable collectively to either the Home Office or police authorities though by convention it advises the Home Office. Its main objectives are to promote the welfare and efficiency of the police service, to provide opportunities for discussion and to give advice on matters affecting the police service. It also acts to protect the interests of its members.

Although A.C.P.O. has no constitutional standing nor any authority over its members, it is a powerful organisation: with the Home Office, the A.C.P.O. steers the police service in this, that, or the other direction. The A.C.P.O. is organised into a number of committees for such matters as crime, traffic, communications, training, anti-terrorism, computers and other techology. Its expertise and advice is given not only to its members but to the Home Office through joint conferences with senior civil servants. In what is known as the Central Conference, senior officials of A.C.P.O. and senior civil servants thrash out general policies and formulate guidelines on the pressing issues of the day. The findings of this conference are usually confidential, which often means that elected members of police authorities are not privy to the results of these deliberations. As far as training policies at national level are concerned, there exists a form of accountability to which local Police Authorities are party. There is, however, no equivalent arrangement for the discussion of other police policies at national level, particularly in the field of police operations. Each year a conference is held between the members of the Association of Chief Police Officers and representatives of local police authorities where an exchange of views takes place, but this is also a social event and as a rule little in the way of accountability or policy making emerges.

A Shifting Balance

Since 1962, when the Royal Commission believed it had solved the problem of police accountability (as did Parliament also), much has happened to throw the delicate arrangements out of balance. The police are in effect less democratically accountable now than they were before the passing of the Police Act in 1964. There are a number of reasons for this.

The police are more professional, particularly at the level of chief constable. The legacy of the amateur police chief, associated with the pre-Second World War policy of appointing retired army officers, particularly in counties, has disappeared. At the same time, the training and preparation of officers for the top posts has given them a unique body of knowledge and a near monopoly of inside information. They have learned to use rhetorical skills to defend themselves and their organisation against attack by appealing over the heads of politicians to the general public, to control the power of officials continuing to demand some constitutional adjustment.

Conflict

Take the example of Mr. James Anderton, the Chief Constable of the Greater Manchester police. A long running argument between Mr. Anderton and some members of his police authority coincided with action by a local M.P., Mr. Jack Straw, to table a draft Police Bill in November 1979. The main thrust of the Bill was to improve the accountability of chief constables. This was a sensible attempt to achieve greater control of the general policing policies of Chief Constables by police authorities, while at the same time ensuring their independence in day-to-day operations and prosecuting functions.

When introducing this Bill in Parliament in November 1979, Mr. Straw said, 'Some of the chief constables have not confined themselves to policing policies but have been willing to engage in political controversy. The best publicised example of this new breed, although by no means the only one, is the chief constable of Greater Manchester, Mr. James Anderton.'

Mr. Anderton 'threw down the gauntlet' shortly afterwards in an article in the magazine *Police*, the monthly organ of the Police Federation. He commented, 'Mr. Straw when moving his Bill in Parliament saw fit to select me as his major target of criticism.' Describing Mr. Straw's assertion as 'entirely unfounded and unsupportable', Mr. Anderton produced his own flow of rhetoric designed to appeal to 'the people'. 'Political control of police forces must be avoided at any cost,' he declared. Referring in his article to the problem of accountability Mr. Anderton commented, '... does it mean that chiefs of police should be legally required to take orders from elected representatives, not all of whom are well advised and properly motivated, and who have no justifiable reason for taking command?' In fact Mr. Straw's Bill made no mention of elected representatives (or anyone else) 'taking command' but aimed at the strengthening of accountability and the determining of general policies of the force. This is the kind of action that the Home Secretary, a politician, might take in London. For example, Roy Jenkins, while Home Secretary in 1966, directed the Metropolitan Commissioner to introduce a system of unit beat policing (a system based on motorised and foot patrols) which he did reluctantly.

Mr. Anderton's retort however was a classic example of the claim by a professional police chief to autonomy over elected representatives 'not all of whom' to use his own words 'are well advised and properly motivated'.

Mr. Straw (The *Guardian*—14 January 1981) retorted, 'If the Chief Constable of Greater Manchester doesn't like the heat, he had better get out of the kitchen.' Strong stuff. He went on, 'My Bill specifically safeguards, through appeal to the Home Secretary, the necessary day-to-day independence of the Chief Contable. But the Bill does greatly increase the accountability of chief constables to their police authorities and enables the authorities to decide on the "general policing policies" for their areas. For that I make no apology.

'It is high time that the community, through its elected representatives, was able to decide on the basic policing philisophy for its area. Whether an area is policed by a "community policing" approach or the reactive "fire brigade" approach is too important to be left to chief constables.'

Mr. Anderton later refuted some of Mr. Straw's comments and again the nub of the controversy was about styles of policing and the police authorities' right to influence them; it also mirrors the internal police debate and controversy which for some years before 1981 had caused much argument. Later that year Lord Scarman's recommendations on policing strategy were to move it towards the 'community' style.

The Professional Chief

The modern police chief has a great deal of power at his personal disposal in the promotion, discipline and placement of his officers. He has the power to decide, ultimately on his own judgment, policing strategies and tactics and prosecution policies. In these circumstances it is not surprising that the importance of professionalism is becoming increasingly recognised. Neither is it surprising that those who are concerned with the principles and applications of democracy are continuing to demand some constitutional adjustment to control the power of public officials generally.

The power of the media, while sometimes turned against a chief constable, can also be mobilised in his support through his own direction of public relations departments. Sir Robert Mark, when Commissioner of Police in London, was the past-master at this and some (including myself) learned much from his example. It was quite a sight to watch his manner when debating with the hardened editors of Fleet Street in television interviews. Referring in his autobiography to his invitation to deliver the prestigious *Dimbleby Lecture* on B.B.C. Television, he wrote that the occasion 'allowed me to explain to the British public for the first time what policing London is all about. The event was to cause shock waves which have not yet subsided.' He clearly relished any opportunity to wage a professional policeman's rhetorical battle, and laid about politicians and lawyers in particular with gusto. But he was skilful and accomplished. Others who have tried it have failed. Nevertheless, the modern police chief is in a position to develop and use this style. Writing on this subject recently, Stuart Morris of the University of Manchester commented about Sir Robert Mark[5], 'The abandonment of reticence which Sir Robert Mark dubbed "a tradition of questionable value", is bound to owe something to vanity and ambition,' but he went on to point out that a chief constable is constrained to show solidarity with his own profession irrespective of rank. 'There is an expectation of public leadership on the part of subordinates particularly those who have come to regard themselves as a "misunderstood minority,"' he concluded. Mark argued that a chief constable 'has a right, indeed a duty, to speak out on behalf of his men even though what he has to say may not be entirely to the liking of those to whom he is accountable.' That may be so; but there is another side to this coin and one which I personally regard as of equal importance and that is the chief constable's right—and duty—to speak out against the professional sub-culture and the police establishment itself when the occasion demands it. To be the 'hero chief' is one thing, and brings some internal popularity, but to use the platform of the office of chief constable for the wider purpose of serving the public or common good is much less comfortable.

Stuart Morris is right when he says, 'The enhanced authority of chief constables has increased their public prominence'. This 'visibility' has in turn strengthened their position in relation to police authorities, and 'chief constables have enough autonomy to outrank other local executives in official status, and they have the potential "public strength" to overshadow local politicians in notability.'

This may be so in some cases, but generally speaking the conflicts and disagreements between chief constables and their police authorities are resolved in committee from which the press are excluded. When it comes to the full meeting of the police authority, usually quarterly, with the press and public present, neither side is anxious to create an appearance of disharmony. From time to time differences of opinion become marked even in open meetings, and the conflict becomes public.

In London, however, there is no public meeting between the police authority (the Home Secretary) and the Commissioner to be reported. Certainly the Home Secretary can be questioned in Parliament but what goes on between himself and the Commissioner is kept behind the scenes.

It is also noticeable that those police authorities where disputes have been marked tend to be from a Labour controlled authority or from the Labour minority. Conservative controlled police authorities are less inclined to open up the differences in public, at least as a general rule. It may be that the Conservative Party regard the police as part of their own establishment. On the other hand, the Labour Party is perhaps more wary of the police role in industrial disputes and policing of the underclass and ethnic minorities. At all events, the disputes between the chief constables and the police authorities in Manchester, Merseyside and Sheffield in recent times seemed to reflect this hypothesis. Commenting on his first three years (1976–79) as Chief Constable of Greater Manchester, Mr. James Anderton remarked that, 'I have had no difficulties with the police committee in almost three years. That's no small achievement in the north-west, where politics are played hard.' This was a period when the Conservatives had a majority in the police authority. A different picture emerged when Labour achieved a majority in the 1979 local government elections.

There were conflicts between the chief constable and the Labour majority over operational matters and over his public pronouncements denigrating some Labour and Left wing politicians. When discussing the chief constable's report on the operations involved in the July 1981 riots in Manchester, Labour members were critical while Conservatives and magistrates supported him.[6] Again, when reporting to the police authority on the police operations in an industrial dispute, a Labour member proposed a critical resolution which the Conservatives sought to amend by expressing full confidence in him. Put to the vote, this amendment was lost by sixteen-to-twelve.[7] At the same meeting he was called upon by the chairman to clarify earlier comments which he had made 'including very derogatory references to members of police committees and wide ranging allegations'.

In an interview reported in *The Times* on 18 March 1982 Mr.

Anderton was alleged to have said, 'There are serious attempts now being made to undermine the independence, the impartiality and the authority of the British police service. I honestly believe we are now witnessing the domination of the police service as the necessary prerequisite of the creation in this country of a society based on Marxist/Communist principles.' At least one chief constable was finding the debate on police accountability a subversive threat to society as a whole. In the same interview he roundly criticised 'political factions' whose interest lay not in better policing but in the first step towards a 'totalitarian one party State'. It was rather strong stuff and reflected little confidence in the robustness of British democratic institutions. Eleven months later it was reported in *The Times*[8] that Mr. Anderton had 'conceded defeat' by withdrawing 'remarks about people being unfit to serve on police committees'. He made it clear that he had not been referring to members of his own police committee, who had taken serious exception to his comments and were prepared to take legal action unless he withdrew them. The dispute had of course centred around the entry into the political arena of a chief constable while still a serving member of the police.

In Britain today the policing function has in places become very much part of the party political debate, and it is easy for senior police officers in particular to fall into the trap of appearing to be partial. But since it is the duty of the police to serve all people irrespective of their politics (provided they are within the law) it is clearly unacceptable for them to take sides. If they wish to do this they should resign.

Take the example of the dispute between the Merseyside Police Authority and the Chief Constable, Mr. Kenneth Oxford. A Labour member of the police authority complained that the police authorities were being treated as 'rubber stamps' and deplored the position which gave chief constables too much autonomy in the running of the force. This went to the heart of accountability. Lady Simey of the Merseyside Police Authority, and its chairman, said of the British policing system[9], 'In effect, we have a system of workers control of the police service far beyond anything that even the most revolutionary amongst us would dare to dream of.' She deplored the fact that police authorities in the past had failed to use their powers, small as they are, to make the police more accountable. She had also put her finger on the effect of growing police professionalism as one of the pillars of autonomy of chief constables.

The matter came to a head after the riots in Toxteth in the summer of 1981—the chief constable had spent some £50,000 on protective equipment without approval of the police authority.[10] 'All this makes a mockery of the traditional precept that control of the budget is the ultimate sanction in a democratic society,' wrote Lady Simey.[11] To add a fresh dimension to the controversy, the Merseyside Police Federation warned the police authority that it would take legal action if the ban on acquisition of protective equipment led to police officers being injured in any fresh outbreak of rioting.

The same indefatigable Lady Simey had been frustrated by being unable to extract information concerning the death in police custody of a James Kelly when the chief constable blocked any reporting of the issue on the grounds that the matter was sub-judice. She wrote, 'The strain put on the relationship between the police and the public by dissatisfaction with the complaints system as a means of obtaining the redress of grievances, and by the recent outbreaks of public disorder has brought the question of "who polices the police" sharply into focus.'[12]

This provoked a counter-blast: what was being sought in the name of accountability would result in political interference, if not actual control over the operation of the force. The fury with which this argument has been pursued has distracted attention from the question of the accountability of the police authority itself, a matter wrapped in some obscurity. Lady Simey rightly defined a solution to the issue as one of political will to pursue the use of such powers as a police authority has to call for reports, to debate policies and to make chief constables account more for their stewardship. She felt the problem not to be a failing in the police but in neglect of democratic activity. A telling point.

Mr. Eldon Griffiths, M.P. for Bury St. Edmunds and adviser to the Police Federation, entered the argument about chief constables by declaring in February 1982, 'that the Home Secretary needed to give his own Whitehall police department a short, sharp, shock'.

He went on to say that there were many able chief constables but 'there are also second-raters—men who cannot stand criticism; who surround themselves with toadies; who do not read enough; whose temperament and training no longer fit them to carry the heavy duties or to handle the social complexities of late twentieth century Britain.' The report in *The Times* of 6 February 1982 also commented: 'It is known in Westminster that Mr. Whitelaw has expressed doubts about the ability of some chief constables to cope with crisis.'

The President of A.C.P.O., Mr. Barry Pain, Chief Constable of Kent, described Mr. Griffiths's attack as 'unwarranted and unfounded' as well as being 'extremely offensive'. He called upon Mr. Griffiths to substantiate his allegations.

In an open letter to the President, Mr. Griffiths offered either a public debate or a private discussion on the issues raised. He concluded his reply by the retort, 'that the time has gone when chief constables individually or collectively, could live in ivory towers. Your members wield too much power, spend too much public money and carry too many heavy responsibilities any longer to expect that their individual qualities, as well as their professional competence (not to speak of their ability to handle huge budgets) will not come under closer scrutiny.'

In the event, the A.C.P.O. decided to let the matter rest. It could have pointed out that the training of chief constables at the Police Staff College and the Home Office and police authority selection procedures have never been so good. If there is fault to be found it is to be explained in part by the isolation of chief constables in their larger bureaucracies, resulting in more tenuous links with both the people and their officers—a problem of scale as well as accountability. Mr. Griffiths was right to imply, however, that the matter of the direction and control of a modern police force often places too much responsibility upon the shoulders of one man.

Problems of Scale

The Police Act of 1964 swept away the powers of the former City Watch Committees who hitherto, together with the chief constable, had been responsible for promotions and discipline.

110

There had been questionable practices of nepotism, for example in Liverpool where it was said that local politicians had considerable influence in police promotions favouring their friends. It was even suggested, not always without cause, that membership of organisations such as the Freemasons helped here. In Wigan it was often alleged that being a Roman Catholic was an advantage.

The smaller county borough forces disappeared under the 1964 Act. The Royal Commission had not recommended such a sweeping programme of amalgamations as Mr. Roy Jenkins eventually brought into effect. They considered that the optimum size of a police force should be about 500 officers. In fact, forces of 2,000 and upwards became the norm, and by the time the Metropolitan counties were created under local government reform in the early 1970s forces such as Greater Manchester, West Midlands and Merseyside were around the 5,000 mark. They became large and remote bureaucracies. My own force of Devon and Cornwall, the largest in geographical terms in England, covered an area of 1,027,348 hectares with a population of 1,360,800. It is approximately 140 miles in length and some 100 miles at its widest point. By no stretch of imagination could the force be considered 'local'. The idea that police authority members would generally have a wide understanding of local problems could no longer be supported. Individuals would know their own patch and that was about the extent of it. The effect was that the chief constable held most of the cards and only the budget control prevented his power becoming autonomous. (At least in my own experience. The budget was the only issue upon which I was seriously challenged.)

Police in the United Kingdom are neither local nor central, but regional. The net effect of this has been to make more tenuous the reality of accountability. The police organisations occupy a kind of 'no-man's land', and this in turn strengthens the position of the chief constables vis-à-vis their relationships with elected representatives and local officials alike.

Community Accountability

I first became aware of the damaging effects which these new developments were having on police relations soon after taking

111

over as Chief Constable of Devon and Cornwall in 1973. Complaints that the police had abandoned their prevention and caring role were numerous. Parish councils were particularly vociferous in making known their dissatisfaction. People in the cities and towns felt that their streets were not being adequately patrolled, as they had been in 'the old days'.

I never ceased to wonder at the ease with which so many facets of local government, particularly the police, had been wiped from the British scene. I urged, therefore, that the police should not wait for further such legislation but should take steps to strengthen informal accountability at the local level. In the cities, towns and parishes the establishment of Community Policing Consultative Groups became the policy of the force, fully supported by the police authority. I lectured, I wrote, I publicised the need for greater informal accountability, through arrangements which were to foreshadow some of Lord Scarman's recommendations in his report on the 1981 riots.

The idea of an 'ethic of responsibility' and informal accountability aroused scorn in some professional circles, but in others there was growing support, ironically in the inner-city and racially tense areas. My book *Policing Freedom* was an attempt to develop this theme. Observations by academics and politicians varied. One academic commented, 'It can be construed as a kind of prefectoral ethic ... This emphasis on what John Alderson ... calls in *Policing Freedom* "an ethic of responsibility" serves as a surrogate form of accountability to a more independent professionalism.' Surrogate or not, it at the time encouraged in the police an awareness of accountability, which the recent trends in reorganisation of police forces had, at least in my view, seriously undermined.

If accountability to local representatives had been weakened in the provinces, in the metropolis it had not existed since Sir Robert Peel's Metropolitan Act of 1829. The City of London retains its autonomy and with it police accountability, but elsewhere the police of London are accountable to the Home Secretary. The Home Secretary is, of course, subject to interrogation and criticism in the House of Commons; additionally, as has already been pointed out, the Commissioner is clearly accountable to the Home Secretary.

The controversy at present engaging attention in London is

112

not so much about the quality of accountability as about its political nature. The pressure for change comes largely from the present Greater London Council (under sentence of death by the Conservative government) and some London boroughs, notably those controlled by the Labour Party. Policing is now firmly established as an issue of party politics.

The argument of the Greater London Council (which incidentally does not raise taxation for the policing of London) is set out in their pamphlet *Policing London*, 1982.

The Council refers to 'a crisis of policing in London' and criticises the then Commissioner (Sir David McNee) for 'skating' over the distrust, scepticism and even hostility which is widespread throughout London, particularly among the young and black communities, referring of course to the Metropolitan Police. Some of the Council's grumbles about the nature of policing are likely to be satisfied by the implementation of the essential recommendations of Lord Scarman's report and the actions of the Home Office. However, the main thrust of their opposition is (as in the past) that 'the Metropolitan Police is still the only Force in the country which is not answerable to a locally elected police authority.' The G.L.C. are fighting against 150 years of history.

The pamphlet goes on, 'There are several historical reasons for Londoners being treated differently from the rest of the country. Not only was the Metropolitan Police the first "modern" police force to be established, but Parliament and the people shared a long standing fear that police could be used against them by the monarch or the government. In 1829 there was no local government for the London area to challenge parliamentary control [they overlook the power of the City of London!] and as a result the Met was made answerable to Parliament through the Home Secretary. Another reason which is still used to justify the exceptional London arrangements is that the Met has a national as well as a London role and as such, requires special treatment. In its comments on Lord Scarman's Report, the G.L.C. has argued that the separation of these national and local roles would be welcome and would be a step in the direction of a more accountable and responsive police force. At present, Londoners have no say in the expenditure of the third of a billion pounds which they contribute to police costs in the Metropolis.'

The nub of the question then is taxation without representation!

I had always been aware of the latent dissatisfaction with the issue of accountability of the Metropolitan Police to the London ratepayers, while at the same time being aware of the national services provided by New Scotland Yard. For these reasons, I recommended to Lord Scarman at his inquiry a compromise in the form of a Metropolitan Police Board, for the metropolis as a whole, to which the Home Secretary and the Commissioner would recognise a degree of accountability, not for the national functions of the Metropolitan Police, but for the ordinary day-to-day policing of London, its crime, its public order and so on (see Appendix A).

The Home Secretary has agreed to meet the Members of Parliament from the London constituencies from time to time in an informal manner but, good as this may turn out to be (or not), it still leaves local government out of the picture. On the other hand, the recent formation of Community Policing Consultative Groups based on the London Boroughs as developed in Devon and Cornwall in the 1970s and recommended to other areas, including London, by Lord Scarman, recognises the acknowledged need for improved accountability at local level.

The Greater London Council has made out a strong case for a London Police Authority. In their Police Committee report of 22 December 1982 (*A New Police Authority of London*, a consultation paper on democratic control of the police in London) they recommend a police authority resting on a partnership between the G.L.C. and the London Boroughs. In their scheme, the Home Secretary would continue to be accountable for the national services of the Metropolitan Police. Each London borough would have its own police committee, and together with the G.L.C. police committee, would form the police authority for London. In a 65-page report, the case is argued cogently, though its chances of ever reaching fruition are at present remote.

A former Home Secretary has however come out in support of the idea.

114

On 17 March 1982 it was reported[13] that 'Mr. Callaghan, former Labour Prime Minister, last night weighed into the argument over who should control the police by saying that he no longer believed the Metropolitan Police should be solely accountable to the Home Secretary.'

Mr. Callaghan, who was Home Secretary from 1967 to 1970, said he would prefer a new police authority to be established, with representatives from local councils and the Home Office. This suggestion comes close to my own recommendations to Lord Scarman and to the recommendations in his report on the Brixton riots. It is now official Labour Party policy to introduce a London Police Authority along the lines of those existing in the provinces.

If the police in Great Britain, and certainly in England and Wales, are to continue to be regarded as a locally based system with a national coordination, then some adjustments are essential.

In the first place, it is my view that chief constables should be appointed on principles akin to those of the Commissioner in London with allowance made for the different constitutional arrangements. For example, the Commissioner is appointed by the 'sign manual', in other words by the Monarch. There is no need for this procedure in the provinces. Instead, chief constables might be on a contract of service. The parties to the contract would be the chief constable himself, the local police authority and the Home Secretary. The contract would provide the usual and necessary safeguards. It would state the period, say seven to ten years. Few chairmen of nationalised industries, managing directors of large organisations, or senior officers in the armed forces, occupy demanding and responsible positions for longer than this period. A chief constable takes a year or thereabouts to get to know the force; three, four, or five years to implement his ideas; and a year to have them consolidated. He has given all that he can. There are other talented people following up behind him. He would be able to apply for posts of chief constable in other forces and thereby to spread his experience.

The contract would provide for the security of tenure of the chief constable so long as he performed his duties to the satisfaction of at least one of the other two parties. Thus if he were at odds with his police authority but not with the Home

Secretary, he would be secure. If on the other hand he were seriously at odds with both, his contract would be terminated, with financial compensation (unless of course it were terminated through misconduct). Such a contract could be terminated by any of the parties on its expiry or it could be renewed for a shorter period—say two or three years. This would allow for the implementation of recent policies or the preparation of a successor, but ten years in office would generally be regarded as the maximum. I suggested all this a few years ago and received short shrift from the chief constables, although some deputy chief constables thought it a good idea!

When it comes to the vexed question of policing policies the position is more complex. Police authorities already have adequate control over the budgetary process, and the Home Office keeps a watchful eye and has a right to intervene, albeit cautiously, in practice. It is also clear, and rightly so, that criminal prosecutions should remain outside the province of a politically constituted body. The first step, however, is to remove the responsibility of criminal prosecutions from the police altogether, as recommended by the Royal Commission on the Criminal Procedure, 1981. To remove that particular issue from the area of contention between chief constables and police authorities would be a major step forward. (The Home Secretary, Mr Leon Brittan, has announced the government's intention to introduce a Bill in Parliament to do this.)

We are then left with two areas of potential friction: the administration and operation of the force. The Home Secretary does not have to face this problem in London since, under the Metropolitan Police Act as amended, he has the right to approve orders affecting the administration of the force. Provincial police authorities should have the right to discuss administrative orders of a major kind—for example, alteration in force structures such as divisional and sub-divisional boundaries. In cases of disagreement the Home Secretary's word would be final, although it is unlikely that many cases would reach this situation. This is not the point. The point is effective accountability as of right.

So far as the day-to-day policing of the area is concerned, criminal investigations, control of public order and so on should be the sole responsibility of the chief constable. The police authority has the ex post facto right to call for and discuss reports and should use this power, for example, in cases where things go wrong. Cases where excessive police violence is reported, deaths in police custody, matters involving compensation for wrongful action, and disputes of one kind or another should be monitored as a matter of routine.

At present the police authorities have the duty to examine the records concerning complaints against the police. There remains however a grey area, which is the general nature and grand strategy of the policing function. This has caused much of the present controversy. Mr Jack Straw's Bill (see page 103) and his comments were written just before the urban anti-police riots of 1981. Since then, many people, both in the police and outside, have had cause to reflect. The Home Office, as police authority for London and with general responsibility for the efficiency of the police throughout the country, has been quick to act to generate a new attitude to local accountability. It has also, somewhat reluctantly, included a clause in the Police Bill at present before Parliament to render local consultation a statutory responsibility. Riots have their positive side too!

The prospects for the extension of this 'surrogate' form of police accountability cannot at present be estimated. It can be forecast that some police authorities and chief constables will make a success of it.

Success in making the police more accountable at the community level depends on many factors. The concept has to be promoted and encouraged from the highest official echelons down to the operating level. There must be powerful political will to bring about change (politicians, both national and local, are very wary of trusting the public with genuine participation).

Police authorities and chief constables alike must recognise that this new approach brings with it new problems. Both sides must act with sensitivity and imagination in order to avoid conflict between them. There will be a need for a different administrative structure to facilitate local account-ability and, within their own organisations, chief constables will have to introduce this new, largely untried and contro-versial policy in the face of some inevitable opposition. There

117

will be much public support. Nevertheless, when something goes wrong (as it occasionally will) all parties will need to appreciate the value of healthy criticism.

A combination of all these proposals for securing greater democratic accountability of the police will go far towards holding the delicate balance between two possible extremes—on the one hand the growing power of the police with defective democratic accountability, on the other excessive party political manipulation of that power.

It is however my view that the time has come for a powerful Royal Commission to be appointed. The terms of reference for the Commission and its membership should be drawn up by an All Party Parliamentary Select Committee. By this means political bias could be avoided, and the Commission could embark on its work in the knowledge that it had the backing not only of the government but of Parliament as a whole. The last Royal Commission on the Police which reported in 1962 was unable to foresee the considerable social, economic and political changes which affect society in 1984. Such changes have to be accommodated by all institutions of government, and the policing systems are no exception.

Chapter 6

Change: Cause and Effect

In the 1960s changes in policing style were introduced which, within ten years, could be seen to have a harmful influence on the effectiveness of the police and their relations with ordinary people. These changes involved motorisation on a universal scale which, together with the advent of personal radio, gradually but inexorably established a gulf between police and public.

After experiments in Lancashire, the Home Secretary Mr. Roy Jenkins, in 1966, pressed upon all police forces (including the Metropolitan Police) a style of policing known as the Unit Beat system. It entailed greater motorisation for improved response to incidents and ideally was intended to be super-imposed upon a system of traditional foot patrols. Gradually but inevitably the foot patrols were absorbed into the motorised section, and within a few years patrolling police had all but disappeared from the streets. Initial resistance to the whole concept was voiced by traditionalists at New Scotland Yard and in the provinces but was overcome by Home Office insistence. In many parts of the country, too, the public were incensed at the disappearance of the 'bobby on the beat'. But the new system was put across as a substitute for an increase in costly manpower and a necessary response to rising crime rates.

Now that the police were motorised and hundreds of officers were moved into central locations, doubts were raised even about the need for the local police stations. Police officers gradually lost the art of talking to people, of taking an interest in the young on the streets, of providing a reassuring presence. Despite the new professionalism of the technological cop and the advent of police computers, the preservation of public tranquillity became harder to maintain and the control of crime remained an illusion. Police were like fire brigades, swooping into neighbourhoods where they were unknown and where that element of cooperation so essential to effective policing was eroding. The creation of special groups of motorised police took away more officers from preventive duties and, as crimes reported to the police continued to increase, officers were more and more frequently transferred from prevention to detection. Bewildered and often disorientated by growing anti-police sentiments, policemen tended to harden in their attitudes as they rarely experienced ordinary contact with the public except in terms of conflict. Assaults on the police increased. Chief constables became concerned and sought increases in their establishments which, when granted, were often absorbed by the growing specialisations and failed to appear on the streets.

The front line of police activity as represented by preventive patrols in contact with the public was weak or even non-existent. The second echelon as represented by motorised response patrols was stronger, however, and inevitably its contact with the public only took place when something had gone wrong. For many, policing seemed to be changing fundamentally.

In 1967, after a re-shuffle of Mr. Wilson's Cabinet, Roy Jenkins became Chancellor of the Exchequer and James Callaghan took his place at the Home Office. Jenkins had carved himself a reputation not only as a member of that rare breed, a reforming Home Secretary, but as one who had shaken up the Home Office Police Department while at the same time providing enough money to fuel the new police technology of mobility and communication. In addition, with Robert Mark's considerable support, he was responsible for introducing majority verdicts in the courts of England and Wales. Some of his more liberal ideas grated with the high command at New Scotland Yard where the Commissioner, Sir Joseph Simpson, came under particular pressure. The so-called permissive society with its cults of drugs, civil disobedience and growing anti-police sentiments, had disorientated traditional police thinking. Complaints against the police had multiplied and pressure to change the system built up almost before the Royal Commission's proposals had

120

had a chance to prove themselves. Any change in procedure, however, would have to wait until Roy Jenkins returned to the Home Office in 1974. Meanwhile the issue smouldered on, causing damage to the reputation of the police and dissatisfaction to many police forces themselves.

In the mid-sixties the police were facing a crisis in manpower, due to full employment in both public and private sectors combined with heavy wastage rates among trained and experienced officers who found it easy to get more congenial and lucrative jobs elsewhere. London was particularly hard hit, as wastage exceeded recruitment at a time when its resources were fully stretched trying to cope with increasing crime and public disorder. To compound these problems, the new Home Secretary, James Callaghan, imposed a freeze on police recruitment as part of the Labour government's economic policies.

In 1968, as a result of anti-Vietnam war sentiments, massive demonstrations in London caused such a strain on police manpower that suburban preventive policing virtually ceased to exist, as more and more officers were required to control protests numbering many thousands of participants. In the main, the police succeeded admirably.

Throughout the country the university campuses were restive and the police found themselves confronting a generation of militant undergraduates in Cambridge, Oxford, Warwick, Essex, the London School of Economics and elsewhere.

Change Overtakes Policing

The 1960s saw the emergence of the multi-racial society. The widespread immigration of Commonwealth citizens to man our buses, to work in our mills and factories, to staff many of our hospitals and other public institutions, began to test the capacity of the police to adapt. Having become used to being accepted as objects of respect and admiration, more and more police officers met people from other lands where this was far from the case. Newcomers who had had experience of police as an oppressive arm of the state or of their colonial masters had little respect for the police, who were often slow to realise this. Equally important were the new patterns of behaviour and

121

customs which at times resulted in breaches of commonly accepted minor regulatory laws. The parties where alcohol was sold without a justice's licence, the use of marijuana, the noisy street scenes, often regarded in lands from which the immigrants had come as tolerable behaviour, brought the police as enforcers of the law into frequent conflict. Ignorance of personal susceptibilities and use of thoroughly disagreeable words—'nigger', 'wog', 'coon' and so on—by the police often gave grave offence. All this and more contained the seeds of a deterioration in police relationships with monorities.

Racial discrimination and prejudice were also rife in housing and employment. Children of school age began to grow up to regard the police, not as their friends, but as a threat to their families and neighbours. Young males in particular grew sullen towards the police, and violence, on both sides, became more common. Black people felt threatened by a seemingly hostile society and in particular by the uniformed police and their plain clothes colleagues who represented that society.

The growth of racialist movements such as the National Front, and speeches of an inflammatory nature, notably by Mr. Enoch Powell, M.P. began to sour the relationship between the host nation, Great Britain, and immigrants arriving hopefully in a better and civilised land.

Police Training

In 1968 a report[1] on British Race Relations—*Colour and Citizenship*—arrived on my desk at New Scotland Yard. At the time I was Deputy Assistant Commissioner with responsibility for the training department. The report made startling reading: it is remarkable how it anticipated some of the findings of Lord Scarman's inquiry some 13 years later, and the findings of the report on the Metropolitan Police by the Policy Studies Institute published in 1983. It said, for example, that 'The problems that concern the police and coloured immigrants in their mutual relations are frequently the problems of the area in which they meet.'

It was considered that the police are themselves a minority group and by the nature of their organisation tend to be isolated from the communities they serve. This isolation was marked in the areas where the majority of coloured immigrants were living. Current training programmes had failed to do justice to the complexity and importance of the role of the police in urban areas with the result that they were isolated from sources of opinion, information and knowledge, which could have helped them to adapt themselves to the changing situation in which they had to function.

Police training, it was felt, should focus on controversial or problematical aspects of policing, as they relate to the social role of the police and to relations between police and the community—including complaints against police; the police use of force; discretionary decisions by individual police officers and police forces; civil rights; public attitudes to policing; and the accountability of the police to local and national political structures.

The Report concluded: 'To help the police to operate in multi-racial communities and to understand the needs of coloured communities in our cities, we recommend the inclusion in police training of lectures on race relations, on the cultures and customs of minorities, on the nature of prejudice, and on the legal and social background to recent race relations and immigration laws. The present arrangement of including occasional lectures in a term cannot be considered in any way adequate.' 13 years later it was clear that we, the police, had not succeeded in achieving the high ideals contained in this prophetic document.

Although the problems were complex and demanded a national response by the Home Office, the Commissioner, Sir John Waldron, was soon convinced that the Metropolitan Police should move to deal with the growing problem. I convened a working party and was soon able to report to the Commissioner as follows.

The Changing Role of Police in Society

'In considering the training of newly appointed members of the Service we became increasingly aware of the importance and relevance of the first item of our terms of reference, viz., "The adoption of new methods of policing and the changing role of police in society."

123

'It is axiomatic that we live in an age of intellectual turbulence when the social conscience is restless and uncertain. Technological advances in the last 20 years have radically altered the way of life of a majority of our people and have raised standards of living dramatically. They have conferred upon large sections of the community a sense of financial security which earlier generations never knew and an independence of thought and action which, even as recently as the 1930s, would have been regarded by many as almost revolutionary. This new-found freedom from the fears of unemployment (sic) and want has released the mass of the British people from a necessity to conform to the wishes of the privileged and has freed them also from their earlier bondage to those who represent established authority. The influence of the upper and middle classes has at the same time been eroded away, largely by political action, and we have seen a significant degree of merging of the social classes. This trend has been accelerated by the accessibility of vastly improved educational services to greater numbers of children and adults from all sections of the community.

'In addition, the community is now rich enough to support in far greater numbers those who find their vocation in cultural and political activities. These are the artists, authors, designers, radio and television producers, university students and lecturers, journalists and, to some extent, commercial and industrial advertisers, whose occupations tend to make them critics and analysts of the society in which they live. Many of them have seized the opportunity to feed and encourage the doubts and uncertainties created by a widespread rejection of accepted beliefs and moral standards.

'In these changed conditions the fundamental police duty of keeping the peace is perhaps unalterable, but the ways in which that duty is discharged have been subjected in recent years to exceptionally close public scrutiny. For police to fulfil their role as servants and guardians of the general public, it is essential today, as it has always been, for them to retain the approval and co-operation of the great majority, so that the life of the community may continue on a stable and civilised course, despite the social upheaval of our times.

'To do this, we feel that all members of the police service must be able to show by their actions and their attitudes that they are aware of the major sociological forces which influence our way of life; that they are alert to the changing patterns of community living, the merging of the social classes, and the broad effects of immigration, particularly by coloured peoples. The impacts of the Welfare State on members of the community, whether as beneficiaries or as contributors, need to be understood, and the relaxed attitudes of established authority, illustrated by the so-called permissive legislation of recent years, must be so woven into the pattern of police training that all members of the Service are equipped to perform their essential functions in an enlightened and acceptable way.

'There is abundant evidence in contemporary reports that the medical, legal and teaching professions are reforming their training programmes to emphasise the need for an understanding of human and social affairs outside the hitherto accepted limits of professional technical expertise. The junior police officer, who soon finds himself at the eye of the storm, has an equally pressing need for training of this kind.'

The writing was clearly on the wall during the second half of the decade of the sixties, as subsequent events have proved, and in spite of changes in both the content and emphasis of training it was too little and too late. Policing in London, and elsewhere for that matter, was moving closer to the North American pattern.

The benign incorruptible P.C. George Dixon of *Dock Green* began to lose credibility and the dramatists turned their attention to the reality of 'Z' Cars, the new type of motorised policing, then to *Softly, Softly* with the Regional Crime Squad and their irascible senior officers and tougher dialogue. The police were being portrayed in a new light. During the later 1970s some of the more brutal portrayals evoked criticism from the police. The *Law and Order* series of the B.B.C. depicted corrupt detectives, while *The Sweeney* covered the drama of life in London's Flying Squad with regular shoot-outs between police and organised and violent criminals. If the police had become tougher, then their toughness was both a response to more violence and a warning that our police may begin to take on a role not envisaged when Ted Willis created his heroic P.C.

Training in the Metropolitan police was later reviewed

during the period when Sir David McNee was Commissioner (1977–82) and the new programmes being introduced drew praise from Lord Scarman in his report on the Brixton disorders in 1981. Time alone will tell whether the hopes of the sixties will fructify in the eighties.

Reaction in the 1970s

The decade of the seventies opened with the police restive and crime rates rising. Relations with ethnic minorities were deteriorating fast. Reginald Maudling, now Home Secretary, faced not only public dissatisfaction but a lower police morale. The Police Federation, as well as the chief constables, were pressing for improvements which were slow in coming. By now the debate about policing was constant and universal and the police, accustomed to widespread questioning and criticism, understandably reacted by making their own views known publicly as spokesmen became familiar figures on television and radio.

Sir Robert Mark, by now Commissioner of Police of the Metropolis (1972–77), led the debate on the police side with verve, criticising the criminal justice system for its failure to ensure conviction of a sizeable proportion of offenders. Mark demanded a number of changes including abolition of the accused's unfettered right to silence in criminal trials, which brought him into conflict with both Parliament and the legal profession. However, he gained the support of the Criminal Law Revision Committee whose Eleventh Report advocated many of Mark's suggested reforms. But the system failed to budge.

It was just before this time that I began to have my own doubts about the way police affairs were drifting. Having been Commandant of the Police Staff College from 1970 until my appointment as Assistant Commissioner of New Scotland Yard by Robert Carr at the close of 1972, I had had time for reflection. On 16 August 1971 I had invited Robert Mark, then Deputy Commissioner at New Scotland Yard, to deliver a lecture setting out some of his ideas, and I agreed to press coverage of the occasion which raised a few eyebrows at the Home Office. I had perceived that Mark himself was not only locked into internal controversy at the Yard, particularly his conflict over police discipline and allegations of corruption within the C.I.D., but also that he was on the threshold of initiating an even more dynamic confrontation with old fashioned thinking about the role of the police in society.

The occasion was followed by publication in *The Times* of the text of his lecture which was later contrasted with an interview with senior C.I.D. officers at New Scotland Yard. Whereas Mark had displayed his customary intellectual grasp of some police essentials, his adversaries had resorted to sweeping condemnation of the law, the Home Office and Parliament. The arguments about the police generally and the Metropolitan Police in particular had been opened up to public gaze for the first time in recent history, and Fleet Street was not slow to grasp the implications of the new situation. Internal debates about the police were no longer to be confined to the quarterly meetings of the Association of Chief Constables.

I agreed with Mark that the issues were too important to be confined purely to establishment circles, and I supported his initiative whenever possible. Mark himself did not have much time for A.C.P.O., an organisation which had failed to back him in his campaign for majority verdicts in criminal trials. He declined the office of President, rightly believing that it would only impede his campaigns for reform. He was determined to go his own way, and in doing so he inspired many who believed in his ideas.

My own efforts to carry on the debate on police issues in public were equally frowned upon by A.C.P.O. and successive Presidents tried hard to discourage me. Meanwhile the Police Federation, anxious about the deteriorating situation, embarked upon a publicity campaign in 1975 under the title of *Dear Fellow Citizen* in which they appealed directly to the public, over the heads of police leaders and the Home Office. It was the first sign that the Police Federation, counselled by their parliamentary adviser Eldon Griffiths, M.P. for Bury, St. Edmunds, were becoming politically aware and active. In this they had stolen a march on the chief constables who, by reason of their independence, always found it difficult (and still do) to express the combined views of their own Association.

The Police Federation campaign was not calculated to please a Labour Home Secretary, at this time Roy Jenkins, who in 1974 had returned to the Home Office. In many ways the campaign was critical of his more liberal views. But its tone fitted into the politics of the Conservative Opposition. The Police Federation publicity spoke of police officers' frustrations, many of which stemmed from failure to grasp the impact of social change of the times. They were critical of new and well intentioned legislation, particularly that which was contained in the Children and Young Persons Act of 1969. This placed heavy emphasis on keeping young people out of penal institutions. It had taken its place in the Statute Books during the previous Labour government and had been strenuously opposed by many Conservatives. The thrust of the campaign was directed against the policies of the Labour government of the time. The Federation also backed Sir Robert Mark's proposals for increasing the likelihood of criminal conviction of the guilty and cited him as an example of the outspoken policeman: 'In recent years, Sir Robert Mark has spelt out the increasing frustration of the police service in very forceful and forthright terms. What he has been saying in public, police officers have been feeling in their hearts for many years.' They raised their voices loudly in support of Mark's criticism of some members of the legal profession in his 1973 *Dimbleby Lecture*. For their pains, the Police Federation were criticised by Labour and other Members of Parliament as well as by the National Council for Civil Liberties, the Howard League for Penal Reform, and the National Association for the Care and Resettlement of Offenders. Many others felt that it was not acceptable for the police to be proposing greater penal severity and expressing opposition to reforms. In the event their campaign marked an increase of Police Federation activity in political comment and generally reflected what would be called Conservative and reactionary views.

An Important Seminar

As part of this campaign the Police Federation convened a seminar at Emmanuel College, Cambridge, which took place in April 1976. Among the distinguished speakers were Enoch Powell and Justice Melford Stevenson.

Although the Association of Chief Police Officers had been

invited to nominate a speaker they not only declined but advised their members not to speak. I was personally invited to deliver a paper and decided to do so, much to the annoyance of the President of A.C.P.O. I thought it too important an occasion for police leaders to boycott as speakers, since it was bound to become a matter of public interest, and the debate was likely to dominate police affairs for some time to come.

Mr. Justice Melford Stevenson spoke of the need for more condign punishment and of the dangers of an alliance 'between the crook and the high minded', and no doubt his words fell just where the Police Federation hoped that they would. But it was Mr. Powell's speech which captured the headlines as he waded in with unabashed relish. 'Let me start with the case you mention first,' he said, 'the growth of mugging. Although there are aspects of mugging which are continuous, permanent, old fashioned, the new word is describing a typically new thing. That new thing, as is recently admitted, is connected with the change in the composition of the population of certain of our great cities. To use a crude but efficient word for it, it is racial. Its prevalence is due to the fact that an implant in our society has changed a community that was previously homogenous into a community which is no longer homogeneous and self-identifying. I am fascinated to notice that your profession has at last started not merely to say that, but to criticise those who refuse to allow so manifest a fact to be stated in order that it may be examined. I was delighted with the terminology of the Metropolitan Police Report to the Select Committee on Race Relations and Immigration, a fortnight ago. No politician could have bettered it. "Experience has taught us the fallibility of the assertion that crime rates amongst those of West Indian origin are no higher than those of the population at large." Splendidly expressed! Beautifully expressed,' he enthused.

There were two main points here, with which to take issue. First, mugging (street theft from the person) is no new phenomenon, and existed *long* before the advent of Mr. Powell's 'alien wedges'. The urban alienated poor—whether black or white—have always shown a propensity for street crime. They know their own area with its escape routes and safe dens. Secondly, Mr. Powell's comments were intended to generate feelings of hostility towards a whole section of the multi-racial society. Failure to understand the changes taking place over 20 or so years had already led to poor relations between the police and the growing ethnic minorities, and this in turn had deterred the better educated young blacks from joining the police. (The die was being cast for the street riots of 1981.)

I decided to make the thrust of my own paper towards the prevention of crime, a cause which I determined to promote over the ensuing years in order to counteract the growing (and in my view erroneous) belief that mere reaction to crime and severity of punishment following conviction were in themselves likely to succeed in controlling the bulk of petty street crime, burglary and vandalism, the main concerns then as now.

I argued that we were losing the art of preventive policing and that much of the crime then plaguing society was preventable but only if we were to develop new strategies. The concept which I argued for then and since was the establishment of community policing. I had already set my sights on such a concept in Devon and Cornwall from which I hoped it would spread, and be adapted and used in our major cities, and London in particular.

I argued along the following lines in my paper, entitled *The Fulcrum*:

'I suggest that contemporary problems of crime demand greater resources for its combating than our present economy can afford. To combat crime the police and the citizen have to get down to the business together. Thus the police instead of feeling they are alone should take steps to convert the ample sympathy for their cause into active support. Equally the citizen can no longer say: "I have paid for a police force to do this job, it is therefore no longer my responsibility."

'Let me illustrate what I mean by a somewhat hypothetical example. Suppose that an area is beset with sporadic outbreaks of public disorder or potential public disorder, of terrorism and other violence, of a frequency which demands that police resources earmarked for the routine of crime prevention patrol and preventive duties generally are constantly diverted to deal with these major problems. A force obliged to turn itself from a proactive into a reactive body. This in turn results in vulnerability of neighbourhoods to the

130

main scourges of street and off-street crime such as robbery and theft and of burglary. The inhabitants of this neighbourhood seek further protection which the police cannot give nor can the community afford the necessary resources. What then are the options?' A question which still continues to fuel argument.

I argued that in such events the police have a legal as well as a moral duty to take the initiative by allocating such resources as they can spare to organise community self-help. The alternative would be to leave the community to its own devices, in which case the quality of life in its neighbourhoods would fall below civilised standards or it would sprout its own leadership and organise itself, neither of which is desirable. The apathy of the first course was as unpraiseworthy as the inherent dangers of the latter. The choice of anarchy or rule by vigilante or gang was unacceptable.

Given the lead, the vast majority of the people would, I knew, respond. It was only for the police to have planned and organised and to have given that lead for that response to have been harnessed.

There was sufficient evidence to suggest that much of the crime which plagued society was preventable. But it was only preventable where the police and the public cooperated in a community plan. The plan had to be in depth and to start in that stratum of society which proportionately produced most of all recorded crime—the under-sixteens. The young people themselves could be influenced through their parents, through schools and through their social groups. This part of the plan could be designed to protect youth from criminality. It would be wider than the juvenile liaison schemes and would involve an organising committee to inform parents through every medium possible and to offer a consultative facility. Police and parent associations might be viable in some neighbourhoods. Inadequate parents, as all police officers know, require greater help and support.

Police contact with the young at school could be based on the best of the schools liaison projects and in a progressive commitment to appropriate education up to sixth form.

I argued for a community crime prevention plan to grapple with the problem of safety on the streets and security in the houses within each neighbourhood itself. At the first socially

131

possible level, the good neighbourhood plan would need to be encouraged. Any concern for other people's safety would need stimulation and emphasis in areas where street crime and burglary exceed the tolerance level.

Muggings, auto theft and housebreaking could, I knew, all be greatly reduced by a patrolling presence. The will to protect one's own community or neighbourhood carried into effect through police leadership of a selected and trained voluntary or special constabulary had to be, I knew, the superior answer. Under a professional police team leader, ideally the neighbourhood constable, active men and women who were prepared to give a little time to preventive patrol in uniform, with professional resources on call, could go a long way towards reducing the incidence of street crime. Such patrols would need close supervision as well as being strictly limited in function. People should be encouraged to regard this service as a civic responsibility, which traditionally it is.

All police officers know that the street patrol on foot with good communications and adequate mobile responses is the classic champion over the scourge of street crime and will always triumph. To fail to consider its creation in mixed police and volunteer form was to eschew a socially constructive measure. I did not, however, believe that in any one area a dynamic integrated neighbourhood crime prevention plan, backed up by adequately trained professional resources, had yet been fully tested.

The first step was to acquire the will to act, which required objectivity and the frankness to accept that the drift away from preventive policing had produced a dangerous or potentially dangerous vacuum.

The second step was to create a motivating instrument in the nature of a Crime Prevention Task Force—a specialist police team. Composed of eight or ten selected senior police officers, it would need to be trained and tasked to provide stimulus for the latent goodwill and enterprise of the community. With involvement from primary school through place of work to preventive patrol, the scheme offered a multi-level opportunity to stem the incidence of violent street and property crime and, of equal importance, fear of crime.

The Crime Prevention Task Force, having served one neighbourhood or community, would hand over to neighbourhood police and move on to the next, and so on until the whole police area had been covered save for those few earmarked as not sufficiently receptive for this consensual policing style. In such areas, though cooperation with the police be inadequate to sustain joint action, there may be some opportunity for the development of non-conflict contact leading to better mutual understanding. These areas qualify for greater concentration of police and other resources, since they are probably areas of high criminality or potential criminality, and they prey on fringe neighbourhoods—a phenomenon known as the displacement of crime.

Artificial means of non-conflict contact with police would have to be created, including police involvement in provision of activities such as recreational and training facilities including adventure playgrounds. The provision of police scholarships to outward bound type courses and the like for some under-privileged youths might help to create a modicum of tolerance which can slowly be built on in the future. The police in these areas must be seen as having a social as well as a legal function.

Edwin Chadwick, the great early nineteenth century reformer, applied his mind to the question of combating crime in the London of his time and in connection with the Metropolitan Police wrote: 'It would have adopted a varied system of patrol, by which every portion of road be traversed every quarter of an hour or within such short portions of, as must preclude the opportunity of committing a burglary in the intervals. It would thus restore safety to the lives and property of individuals within that district, and defeat every symptom of an attempt to recommence the career of depredation in adjoining districts. It would deem it an intolerable scandal that robberies could possibly be perpetrated night after night in the same district, until the inhabitants were driven to associate and exert their own unskilful and inefficient means to obtain that protection for which they paid so dearly.'

Today, of course, in our much more complicated and vulnerable cities the standards set by Chadwick are not always possible to maintain. We all know of high crime areas lacking adequate preventive patrols. It was therefore incumbent on the police to question professional attitudes which might hold back measures to restore safety to the lives and property of

133

individuals. A return to preventive concepts of policing was, I felt, long over-due.

In applying my mind to the subject I reached the following conclusions.

The 'Challenge of Crime' as expressed by the Police Federation in terms of an appeal to the citizenry was in keeping with the spirit of a thousand years of evolution of our police system. If, however, the spirit was to be carried into productive action it required that all who held positions of influence in these matters combine in fresh initiatives for the prevention of crime.

The police alone could not halt the rise in crime even if the community could provide additional resources.

The creation of community crime prevention schemes which in turn would coalesce to provide a concerted plan on the lines I tried to describe, should, I felt, be considered. Limited resources of a task force nature—highly selected, trained and orientated—could move into neighbourhoods showing a willingness to try mounting such schemes. The remaining areas where essential cooperation was not forthcoming would need to be the subject of initiatives designed to increase confidence.

Finally I fell back on the words of Sir Robert Peel when he set up the modern system of police in 1829. 'It should be understood at the outset that the object to be attained is the prevention of crime. To this great end every effort of the police is to be directed. The security of person and property and the preservation of a police establishment will thus better be effected than by the detection and punishment of the offender after he has succeeded in committing crime'.

I had high hopes that the message would percolate through the police service and be adopted as a strategy. However, it was to take some six years and the report of Lord Scarman on the Brixton and other disorders, plus one or two chief constables and a new Commissioner of the Police of the Metropolis in 1982 with similar ideas, to make a quantum leap forward.

Meanwhile I began to mark out a fresh model of community cooperation in the prevention of crime in the City of Exeter.

134

Community Policing

As policing is primarily a preventive activity, it can be described at three levels. Primary prevention involves not only the police but many other social agencies and the willing public. Secondary prevention is essentially a police activity of patrolling, both motorised and on foot. Tertiary prevention is the detection of crime and the correction of offenders.

It was the primary level which was being neglected in favour of the other two. I was determined to shift the accent from reactive to proactive policing. In addition it was my belief that the public voice was being given too little regard in police accountability. The police role was being defined more and more by the police and less and less by the consumers of police services. As a consequence the police were losing vital understanding and support. There were two main obstacles to overcome. I had to convince the officers in the force that a major shift in police practice had to take place and that we were in danger of losing our way. I had also to generate public understanding and sympathy. One was a challenge of leadership and management; the other was a public relations exercise.

With my deputy, Mr. John Woodcock (now one of Her Majesty's Inspectors of Constabulary), I appointed a selected team of officers under Superintendent Colin Moore, to form a special unit to spearhead the change. Roger Busby, the Public Relations Officer, was to carry the message to the people.

We began by carrying out surveys of communities which we described as urban villages. Crimes within the community areas were plotted and, with the aid of our graphs, we set up community meetings to discuss the whole question of crime and anti-social activities. We were pleased to find a positive reaction. With the social and welfare services, we began the long haul of setting up Community Policing Consultative Groups. This was the vital part. We now had the people, the police, housing, welfare, social services, education and voluntary agencies beginning to cooperate. The exercise aroused a good deal of attention from the media. The first year of the exercise, its tribulations as well as its progress, are well set out in a study by Ann Blaber of the National Association for the Care and Resettlement of Offenders.[2]

Police officers were taken out of cars and from other duties to work with the community representatives and the other agencies and volunteers. Others were assigned to duty with the Education Department. A great deal of initiative and freedom was given to the officers to develop the idea. Most of them did very well and in due course some 25% of the constables in the force were in one way or another assigned to these duties.

Reaction within the force was mixed. Some senior officers were fully supportive, others less so. The older specialist departments of C.I.D. and Traffic did not readily take to this new emphasis on the status of the preventive community police constables. The representatives of the Police Federation (inspectors, sergeants and constables) raised the issue with me through a formal resolution questioning 'the misdirection of police manpower'. I told them that nothing would deflect me from my purpose and of the reasons why. They were somewhat truculent as we left the meeting. Some months later, however, the constables' representatives called on me to say that the constables fully supported what I was trying to achieve. Somewhat wryly they told me that where obstruction, if any, did exist it was to be found among the middle ranks of the force! I was amused by this since I knew it to be true, and later informed the officers concerned. I was fortunate, however, that the assistant chief constables were with me and one of them, Brian Morgan, was given special responsibility for the implementation of the plans. We had many enthusiastic supporters in all ranks.

As crimes in those areas where community policing was well established began to recede, and the public approval to increase, I implemented the policy throughout the force. As might be expected much depended on the ability of the middle ranks and I am bound to record that their performance in this regard varied.

In 1977 at Ditchley Park in Oxfordshire I presented a paper to Home Office officials and chief constables. I called it *From Resources to Ideas*. I was at pains to stress that sooner or later a halt would have to be called on the pursuit of police efficiency through increasing resources and repressive activity. Sooner or later new policing policies would need to have more regard for the role of the public and other agencies and bodies in the achievement of effective and acceptable policy.

The subject of community policing as opposed to excessive reliance on reaction became a debating point within and without the police service. Other police authorities wrote for details and in one or two cases they pressed their own chief constables to implement similar policies. There was a little pique here and there. Some said they were already trying similar schemes and that John Alderson had 're-invented the wheel'. It is true that I thought that 'the wheel' had been forgotten or neglected.

Community involvement had been developed by the police in Scotland by Mr. David Gray while Chief Constable of Greenock and later, as H.M. Inspector of Constabulary in Scotland, he had impressed his views on his colleagues. I had examined the position but wished to take it a good deal further than the Scottish schemes. I was determined to make the principle of local accountability to the people meaningful, and for the style to become mainstream and not peripheral police activity. The Community Policing Consultative Group was to be the fulcrum for my plans. From it would eventually stem a whole battery of initiatives to change the emphasis in modern policing from reaction to pro-action. Policing was too complex and important to be left to the police. The matter was one of controversy among policemen. Speaking at the Police Staff College in 1974, David McNee, then Chief Constable of Glasgow, commenting on emphasis on the social role of the police, said. 'Those who talk of it, want to deflect as many police personnel as possible in the direction of their own special interests ... this new concern with police duty on the part of people who hitherto tended to shun it, is gratifying ... but it is a threat to overstretched resources ... it is further increasing specialisation at the expense of general police duty and thus further diminishing the status of the constable.' He was, of course, referring to Mr. David Gray's specialist community involvement teams, which I was not prepared to follow. Community policing was to be the foundation of the entire police organisation. In other words it was to be the essence of policing rather than the concern of a few specialist community involvement officers. When the crunch came at the Scarman Inquiry I found myself isolated in stressing the case for such a radical change and of its consequences.

137

But there lay ahead the problem of political apprehension. Some elected representatives were suspicious of police motives and on 25 January 1980, in an adjournment debate in the House of Commons, Alex Lyon, M.P. for York, launched what one newspaper described as 'an astonishing attack' on me and another chief constable. Referring to the development of community policing Mr. Lyon was quoted as saying, 'Mr. Alderson also regards himself as irresponsible. He believes he can create communities where police do the work of the social security department and housing department without overall control of local authorities. He complains when those councillors say that they should be properly consulted about work which falls directly within their remit.'

This was not the first nor the last occasion on which community policing was to be misunderstood, but the parliamentary outburst required an extra-parliamentary response. I decided to challenge Mr. Lyon publicly to substantiate or withdraw his remarks. To his credit, he accepted my invitation for him to visit the force and to debate the issue. The Chairman and members of the police authority met Mr. Lyon and assured him of the high quality of our relations and the practice of accountability. After his visit Mr. Lyon retracted his allegations and subsequently became a fervent supporter of the community policing idea. Meanwhile not only had he brought on himself considerable criticism but he had incidentally given a boost to the growing recognition of the importance of community-based policing. His comments had been founded on political objections which could not be dismissed out of hand. Others, both police and politicians, were often sceptical and hostile. I was concerned with the reasons for the failures of policing policies in some of our cities, and I feared that in some cases police were being directed into confrontation of a potentially damaging kind.

In 1978 I had accepted an invitation to speak on the subject to Mr. William Whitelaw M.P. and the Conservative Home Affairs Committee, then in opposition. I expressed my concern about the prospect of inner city riots unless some adjustments were made along community policing lines. I also expressed the opinion that excessive use of powers of arrest under the suspected persons ('sus') laws were damaging and that this law should be repealed. I was courteously received and heard.

During the 1979 General Election campaign, however, the Conservative Party made a great deal of political capital out of the 'law and order' debate, including the introduction of 'short sharp shock' regimes in detention centres, which were never likely to be effective and were acknowledged subsequently to be little more than an election diversion. Others pressed for the reintroduction of capital punishment. Only the Liberal Party stressed the urgent need for community-based police and a comprehensive strategy for the prevention of crime. With few exceptions, the police service was sceptical and believed that community policing was only applicable to areas such as Devon and Cornwall. I decided to press on with opening up the public debate.

It was during this period between 1977 and 1981 that the two competing philosophies of policing became polarised. The media joined in with relish, playing one against the other, and relationships between those propounding the community style and the advocates of reactive policing deteriorated. A coolness was noticeable at conferences of chief constables, and even police authorities became divided. The Home Office did not at this stage show its hand, although I believed that Sir Brian Cubbon, the Permanent Under Secretary, was sympathetic to my views. I urged my views upon the Chief Inspector of Constabulary, Sir James Crane. To push the debate along at a faster pace I published in 1979 a book, *Policing Freedom*,[3] in which I developed the theme of the need for radical re-thinking of the role of the police in the 1980s, stressing the need for greater community cooperation between the police and other elements in society if the police were to halt the slide towards alienation from the public.

London was at the centre of much controversy. Not only the racial minorities but many others from different walks of life pressed for change. The abolition of the 'suspected persons' law was finally recommended by the All Party Committee on Home Affairs who condemned it as undemocratic and its use as open to abuse. This caused great outrage among some police and the political far Right. William Whitelaw, the Home Secretary, only managed to push through its abolition in 1981 by introducing at the same time a new Criminal Attempts Act which gave back to the police some powers to arrest those suspected of attempting to commit certain types of crime, particularly of attempting to steal motor vehicles. It was a neat political ploy, however, which silenced the critics but gave little in return.

By this time the debate concerning policing styles had developed into one of police accountability. Some police authorities who wanted their chief constables to introduce fresh operational preventive and community policing methods came up against resistance. The chief constables stressed that they alone controlled the police—after all, had not the Royal Commission and the Police Act 1964 laid upon them such duties? Complaints of arrogance were voiced in Merseyside and Manchester, only to be countered by shouts about interference with the constitutional autonomy of chief constables. A continuous stream of complaints about the style of some policing in the Metropolis arrived on the Commissioner's desk but the Home Secretary loyally supported his police chief, Sir David McNee, Sir Robert Mark's successor, who must have wondered what he had to do to placate his critics. Having been appointed to head the London force by James Callaghan, the Prime Minister, and Merlyn Rees, the Home Secretary, from the position of Chief Constable of Strathclyde, he found himself facing an explosive situation for which toughness alone was not enough. The broadsword has its place but so does the deftness of the rapier. Having viewed the community policing system in operation in Devon and Cornwall, he felt unable to recommend its introduction in London where he believed the problem to be totally different. Nor did the new Home Secretary, who had also examined the system, feel that it was appropriate for Metropolitan application. There were those of us who differed and got little by way of understanding, for saying so. I believe we were regarded as interfering with the responsibilities of others.

It was in pursuit of further evidence to support the community policing style that I decided to seek permission to visit Japan, Hong Kong and China, under the auspices of the Police Bursaries Trust.

Chapter 7

East Asian Reflections

Crime, and anti-social behaviour generally, has increased in Great Britain and in other Western countries, especially over the last quarter of a century.

In Japan over the same period crime, particularly serious violent and acquisitive crime, has been contained and in some cases reduced.

Such reports which exist indicated that crime and anti-social behaviour in China had been contained, apart from the period of the Cultural Revolution.

Hong Kong, on the other hand, though populated mainly by Chinese nationals or people of Chinese descent, has exhibited the same tendencies towards the growth of crime as the Western nations.

Apart from having a unique opportunity to observe at first hand a communist totalitarian, a capitalist democratic and a colonial police system in the Far East, it was of the greatest interest to examine, albeit superficially, the cultural implications of crime control.

The Communist Totalitarian State

The Peoples' Republic of China is the classic example of a Marxist–Leninist political system. This is symbolised by the massive portraits in Peking of Marx, Engels, Lenin and Stalin. No sign of the anti-Stalin cult here! Everything I saw and heard during my all too short visit strengthened the impression of the totalitarian state.

It was stressed upon me that the problems of law and order thrown up during the cultural revolution had poisoned the ideological purity of the liberation and the machinations of the 'Gang of Four' had damaged the committee system of control.

141

The Policing System

The Minister for Public Security is appointed by the State Council. Public Security is one of 13 departments.

Public Security Committees exist at provincial, regional, city, county and commune level (Peking, Shanghai and Tientsin are regarded as provinces). In the cities there are sub-stations and police posts. In the rural areas the communes and production brigades exercise control. A public security committee is set up in every factory and enterprise and in each neighbourhood. Control by committee is total (see Appendix B). The system was set up in the early days of the Republic and must represent one of the most effective and simple devices ever fashioned to control people.

The neighbourhood and residents' committees register the movement of people in to and out of the commune. When changing residence, by permission, people must report to the police post. In the country such security administration is performed by the production brigades.

The prevention of crime is a paramount public duty as well as being of official concern. The prevention of attacks on the Republic (ideological crime), and crimes such as theft, arson and assault and of accidents are all the concern of the committees.

When a crime takes place the committee has to protect the scene and organise the people to provide clues and evidence for the police investigation. This is regarded as a collective responsibility and is reminiscent of the Anglo-Saxon hue and cry and collective responsibility known as the Frank pledge.

Criminal charges are approved by the Procurator and dealt with by Courts (neither of which I had time or opportunity to look into).

There are about one million committees of this kind throughout the Republic and it is the responsibility of the police to meet the commune committee every two weeks for political discussion and assessment of the behaviour and problems of the commune. The head of the police station and his men are always keen students of socialist ideology and follow the principles strictly. From time to time I witnessed political seminars being conducted in police stations and among prison staff.

Committees interest themselves in delinquents and their families and make rules for the good order of the neighbourhood. They also patrol the area when the workers are away in the factories or the fields.

People who commit wrongs are made to realise their mistakes and to understand their guilt, and they are required to mend their ways. The committee makes up the rules for the commune and can enforce them.

Juvenile Delinquency

So far as juvenile delinquency is concerned, I was informed that the situation is generally good, and it seemed to be, but the problem has increased somewhat of late due to the 'poison' of the cultural revolution. Violence and drug taking are not problems on any scale but when they do occur it is considered that ideological training is the main therapy. (My visit to a young persons prison is mentioned later.) Even prison is regarded primarily as educative.

Juvenile delinquents can be dealt with in four ways. First, by re-education by the people in the factories or neighbourhoods. Sometimes a team is made up of school-teachers, parents and committee members to analyse the causes of anti-social behaviour and to organise its prevention. Parents like this idea, and it is a fruitful way of making people realise their ideological mistakes. Secondly, juvenile offenders can be sent to special schools if they are out of control. Here they are set to work and to study under the Department of Education. Their studies follow the school pattern but there is more discipline and work. The staff are required to have a caring and affectionate pupil relationship. Thirdly, they can be sent to reformatory institutions, again with an accent on work, but this time in the fields and fruit farms. They have to study and mend their ways. After release they are under the supervision of the committee who can recommend them for this treatment in the first place or send them back again. Fourthly, juveniles who are unsuitable to be left in society are kept in reformatories for longer periods.

Although the age of criminal responsibility is sixteen, compared with ten in England, juveniles under that age can be dealt with by administrative devices similar to our own 'care' orders.

A Peking Reform School

I was told that I was the first foreigner ever allowed to visit this reform school. It had 1,200 inmates who were detained for periods of one, two or three years, depending on the nature of their crime; there was some remission for good behaviour.

51% were in for theft, 20% for violence, 11% for robbery, 15% for hooliganism and 3% for other offences. The guiding principle was re-education and reformation, and rules and regulations were on the lines of military routine. The inmates were divided into companies about 100- to 120-strong. One company was composed of females. Each company was allocated ten staff, three of whom were teachers. Education consisted of culture (two-and-a-half days a week), politics, languages and mathematics. Current affairs, morality and repentance were also taught. Three days a week were spent on manual labour, teaching the inmates skills to enable them to get jobs when they returned to society. They laboured in the fields and orchards, and built new dormitories. There was one day off a week, games were played twice a week, and they were allowed to read books, newspapers and magazines in their rooms, to write letters and to receive visits from their parents. Pocket money of $2\frac{1}{2}$ yuan a month (equivalent to about 70p) was paid, they had two suits a year and received free medical and clinical treatment.

When I arrived the staff themselves were engaged in ideological education. They were required to believe in the possibility of reform through education and repentance, to respect the personal integrity of the inmates and to understand their psychological condition. No beating or swearing at inmates was allowed. The staff had three roles to play: to be just and selfless in enforcement, to be tireless teachers and to act in the capacity of parents. They were also required to live with the inmates! I was told that the great majority of the inmates changed their habits through this treatment and some even came back to inform the staff of their progress. Most of the inmates were from the city and the staff visited family homes. I was informed that 80% behaved well after treatment, but 20% did not—almost the exact opposite of the rate of success in the U.K. This was a well-ordered though spartan regime, out in the country on the outskirts of Peking, and seemed to be no worse a condition than that of the average lower worker in society.

Adult Crime and Punishment

So far as adult crime is concerned, again the committee have their preventive and detective duties. Capital punishment for murder and offences akin to treason is by shooting, although the death penalty may be suspended for two years subject to good behaviour. I also visited an adult prison, which for foreigners was unusual.

The prison housed about 2,000 people, with about 100 females. People were interned for all crimes, from murder through to being enemies of the state. I was told that enemies of the state numbered only 3%. The prison held some of those responsible for murder during the cultural revolution. Prison regulations had been badly affected by it—prison staff had been accused by the revolutionaries of being revisionist. The prison governor told me that he was in hiding in the countryside for three years during the cultural revolution. The prison was only just settling down to its former regime. The guiding principle was to reform people by teaching them to work and to admit their guilt. They had political and ideological education to make them realise their mistakes and repent. They had lectures on the correct attitudes to be adopted in socialist morality and they were educated in cultural affairs. Lectures were given by wardens who also had discussions with prisoners. I found the thinking behind penal reform to reflect old Victorian ideas.

Staff members talked to prisoners individually to turn them away from 'being enemies of the people'. Families were sometimes brought in to advise and discuss, and former prisoners were invited back for the same purpose. There was a film once a week and access to magazines and booklets, and prisoners were encouraged to write plays and develop self-education. Most prisoners were in for periods of five to ten years. They could earn bonuses for good behaviour each

145

season and 80% did so. The main route to reform was labour, according to health and ability. From among the prisoners, fifteen inmates were selected to form a group and they, in turn, elected a leader to help manage the institution. They concerned themselves with production levels in the workshops and saw to the receipt and distribution of materials. They had to combine management with revolutionary humanism.

Each day they had eight hours' sleep, eight hours' work, two hours' study and one hour for sport. Each week they had one day's rest and they also had a rest during the National Festivals. I was informed that their board was provided free by the state. This amounted to three meals a day and they had the same amount of grain as other members of the community. They lived slightly above levels of the lowest people in society. They received $2\frac{1}{2}$ yuan (70p) pocket money a month and 3 yuan for females. Every 20 days they had a haircut, very short, and they were allowed to bath every two weeks, excepting in summer when washing every day was permitted. Every two months they could have a visitor. There were systems for praise and punishment: the good were praised and could earn some remission; the bad were criticised or punished by the withdrawal of facilities and privileges. Solitary confinement was retained for the worst cases. Some discharged prisoners became advanced workers and were thereby welcomed back into the communes by the people. The prison factories were old but able to provide a variety of goods, particularly socks and plastic sandals. Prisoners made much of their own machinery.

Social Control

There is no doubt that the control of human behaviour through the committee system and ideology is almost total. From dress to work-norms, and from food to property, much egalitarianism prevails. Disgrace falls readily on those offending against the people, and freedom as we know it is the heavy price paid for order. Judgment and comment have to be set against recent history, the difficulty of feeding and clothing a large population and a standard of living which would be regarded as very poor by Western standards.

The Capitalist Democratic State

The success of Japan in containing crime while emerging as one of the most successful capitalist systems has become of interest over recent years. Could it be that the police and criminal justice systems were so good, or were there underlying cultural, philosophical, historical and religious reasons? Why was Japan not plagued with the seeming crimogeneity of Western nations? These and related questions were and are of primary concern.

Their police system before the Second World War was centralised but, thereafter, the occupying forces created a decentralised system based on Anglo-American concepts.

Various Western observers (Gurr, 1978, and Bayley, 1976) had commented on the veracity of reports of successful crime control. The total of crimes known to the police had fallen over the past ten years.

Neighbourhood Police

I was interested to find that, whereas many Western police systems had favoured greater centralisation through the closing of local police posts and stations and the grouping of police resources at sub-divisional and divisional level, the Japanese had firmly strengthened their local neighbourhood police organisation. Every neighbourhood had a local post, even in Tokyo. The police are highly respected and are part of the daily round. To be seen and to be of service is regarded as a primary feature of policing strategy. There are 16,000 such posts in Japan, with 24-hour service available from a patrol strength of 76,000. This feature of the Japanese police system is of the greatest significance to Western observers. It reflects very much the British pattern of 30 years ago and is successful and highly regarded in a modern, heavily populated country (National population: 111,000,000; Tokyo population: 11,000,000; National police strength: 244,800).

To oversee the policing of Japan there is a National Public Safety Commission whose chairman is a State Minister. Each region also has a Public Safety Commission, members of which are local persons of standing, nominated by central government. A National Police Agency of civil servants and serving police officers provides a central service. The whole system testifies to the Japanese genius of adopting Western styles to its own traditions and of making them work.

It should be mentioned here that the police have a duty to maintain records on all citizens and residents. These are updated every six months by visits to homes and places of work. Patrol officers from neighbourhood police posts do this. This is a heavy burden and probably unacceptable in Great Britain, but its impact in Japan (as in the communes of China) is profound. When I asked what happened when people refused to give details, the question was received with some amazement. People just don't refuse! This provided at least one clue to the Japanese success in controlling crime, which is largely a cultural phenomenon.

A recent leader in *The Times* newspaper, 'Behind the Japanese Miracle', commented on this Japanese characteristic: 'Beyond the economic story there is a shared social creed that makes the warp and weft of Japanese society so much more secure than our own. This security is not simply the result of a discipline or conformism or hierarchy which Western democracy has long since outgrown. It is the legacy of the Confucian state system which dominated China's history and was imported by her neighbours.... (Japan particularly from 1615–1867)'. In seeking to provide an answer to the question of the relevance to the West of these cultural phenomena, the leader went on: 'Japanese are born into families as the basic group and loyalties must work upward from these or society cannot function. Against this is a western view of being born as individuals and seeking thereafter a fulfilment to which first the family and later society should contribute. The East Asian emphasises human obligations, the West human rights.

'Thus far East Asia has found the concept of individualism repellent or too difficult to digest. Thus far the West has found East Asia's conformism and consequent inhibition of original thought as no less undesirable. No good would be had by each pointing only to the faults of the other. Perhaps the West should now be more ready than in the past to take note of East Asian virtues.'

I have quoted this piece at length since it explains so much of what I observed in Japan (and China) and reinforces my preconceived ideas about our problem of anti-social behaviour, particularly of crime, and of the way to understand it. It is not the police system in Japan which is mainly responsible for crime control any more than our own.

The Colony

The Colony of Hong Kong, shortly to revert to China's sovereignty, is an anachronism in today's free world, but it works and seemingly works well. Colonial law and order can present problems of a kind different from both the totalitarian state and the democratic capitalist state. In many cases, colonial powers have had in the past to rely on strong and sometimes repressive police systems, backed up by considerable residual constitutional powers, although there have been many exceptions.

The first point of interest to me was the extent to which the characteristics of serious crime seemed to follow the pattern of Western democracies rather than that of either Japan or China. Robberies, hi-jacking, kidnapping, drug-trafficking indicated the level of both affluence and deprivation. Social cohesion was more fragmented, cultural contradictions greater, the problems unique.

Neighbourhood Watch

Efforts had been made to introduce Neighbourhood Policing Schemes very similar to, though less well established than, the Japanese system. I was told that the primary aims were: to help reduce the levels of crime in certain areas through joint police/community involvement; to establish good police/public relations and bridge the gap between the public and the force; and to capitalise upon community spirit for the reduction of crime by policing the same area with the same personnel over an extended period of time.

I found such schemes accepted and most effective in densely populated areas of high-rise buildings and flats. This refuted the assertion that such methods work best in rural areas, a view often expressed in England at the time. Use was made of Auxiliary Police (Specials) and Mutual Aid Committees (residential bodies who provided watch patrols).

In the densely populated city areas where very high-rise blocks of flats, shops and business premises presented crimogenic characteristics, the police developed special intelligence. Criminals' movements and activities were closely monitored—a scheme which is now paying dividends in parts of London. Military aid was a pronounced feature of illegal immigration control as well as providing a back-up for the police in extreme cases of disorder. The police commitment to riot control was an impressive and sophisticated example of quasi-military capability, commensurate with the need to govern a colony.

Corruption

Because of the nature of the economy of Hong Kong and its potential for corruption, the establishment in recent years of the Independent Commission for Corruption has shown the government resolve to police this aspect of crime in this economically successful colony. It not only polices the public aspects of corruption but also polices the police in this regard.

A Passing Phase

The policing of Hong Kong is *sui generis* since the conditions in which the task is carried on are probably by now unique. The traditions of Chinese culture which might lend themselves to secret societies and gangs may possibly sometimes be reinforced by an alien government. On the other hand, the observer can be witness to the important contribution of family and group loyalty to the policing function. Considering all the circumstances of Hong Kong, the acceptable system of policing and its success suggest something of the genius of government. What is likely to happen when the Peoples' Republic of China takes over in a few years time is a matter for speculation. There may be less crime, but also less freedom.

Confucianism

Cultures steeped in Confucian traditions will manifest one set of characteristics just as marked as those generated by the

150

Christian ethic. But there are clues to be found which are deserving of notice. If Confucian philosophy, stressing the link between the goodness of personal life and family and the national life, has been observed in East Asia as a main stabilising factor in maintaining social order, then the opposite effect can be anticipated if undue stress is given to a 'do your own thing' creed; and if the concept of the value of family and community in controlling human behaviour is ignored or undervalued or, worse, sacrificed in the pursuit of individualism as the supreme goal, then crimogeneity is likely to be produced.

In Western societies it might be said that much crime and social disorder stem from an exaggeration of individualism, the devaluation of the family, and disintegration of communities. When this happens, greater reliance has to be placed upon the formal controls of police, courts, prisons and other penal and reforming systems. If the informal controls degenerate to a sufficient extent, the formal systems will be overwhelmed and morbid crime levels will result.

On the other hand it may be said about the East Asian countries that informal controls, if too controlling, can inhibit a desirable state of individualism. China may manifest this to a greater extent than Japan where democracy and individualism at this point in time are more marked, though the crime levels are not morbid.

It seems that most Western nations need to encourage the pendulum of laissez faire in social behaviour to swing back a little towards a better balance with individual and group responsibility requiring some emphasis. This may seem to be too great a task to embark upon and many would prefer to wait for the forces of intertia to work in due time. It is suggested that those in positions of authority and influence need not wait and should not wait for the passage of time, but might with profit consider strengthening those elements of informal social control which are observed to be successful in controlling crime and disorder.

I concluded that the family as an institution should engender respect. It should be brought in a more central position in social and political philosophy. The role of the woman/mother should be revalued and the home should be seen as a cultural lynch pin.

151

Educational systems might also bring notions of social and moral responsibility into a more central position to balance the pursuit of individualism inherent in our culture. For example, in junior schools the morning assembly might be used in this social connection. A commitment to the need and desirability of social responsibility deserves to be seen to be critical to our progress as a civilisation.

The concept of community as an informal social organism needs to be nurtured to a much greater extent. The combined effect of individualism, neighbourhood reconstruction and the anonymous life style has virtually destroyed community in many places. The very vehicle which can allow people to express their social responsibilities and through which crime and disorder may be contained has become debilitated. Community affairs need to become the subject of social and political generation.

The idea of cooperative effort as a virtue needs to be highlighted. The many divisions in contemporary Western societies should be seen to contain the seeds of disorder and in Great Britain the industrial scene is testimony to this.

The fear of regimentation and the suffocation of individualism may lurk in the Western mind and cannot be glossed over in the search for improved social order. If the subjugation of individual liberties is a precondition of control of crimes then, in Western terms, the price is too high. The only route available to healthier prospects for social order in Western societies is the reconciliation of freedom and control.

My thoughts stimulated by this most interesting though all too brief visit included the following:

a) In a democracy the pursuit of order primarily through police systems is a mistake. 'Law and order' programmes should be based on moral, ethical, philosophical criteria suitable to our condition. The police system should be seen in its rightful place as operating on the margins.

b) The containment of crime should be the concern of the entire body politic and not be seen to be a side issue. When crime levels become morbid it is a manifestation of social malaise and not necessarily of a defective police. Conversely, an effective police is not necessarily responsible for low levels of crime.

c) In sheer practical terms, some form of social crime

152

prevention idea, based on communities, which can lend itself to the principles in (a) and (b) above, is called for. The concept of communal policing, involving caring agencies, both voluntary and statutory, working as a team and alongside community representatives, would seem to offer some possibilities.

Nothing observed during this visit caused me to doubt the viability of the path of community policing which I had chosen to develop. On the contrary it had strengthened my resolve.

Chapter 8

Riots: Causes and Consequences

It was during my visit to China that the first of our inner-city riots took place in the St. Paul's area of Bristol, an occurrence that was, to most people, totally unexpected. Bristol seemed to be the most unlikely place for the first manifestation of what was, in fact, almost inevitable. The China news agencies gave great prominence to reporting these riots, implying that British society was being destabilised by racial problems.

Ken Pryce is a West Indian sociologist whose four year study of the area in Bristol known as St. Paul's was a clear-sighted and objective report[1] singularly free of anti-police views. Referring to the 'ghetto' way of life, which for some took on an 'expressive disreputable orientation', he described the situation as 'characterised by wretchedness, sub-normal educational development, unstable family patterns and a heavy involvement in such predatory activities as violence, robbery, conning and living off one's wits.' He went on to predict that this way of life would most likely persist and the behaviour on which it is based would become permanent if job opportunities for West Indian men were not to improve or if the recession affecting the area worsened. He believed that the potential for revolution should not be under-estimated.

A year later the St. Paul's riots broke out.

To those whose curiosity about such events had led them to a study of riots in the U.S.A. in the 1960s it is well known that, where social conditions are of a tense and potentially explosive nature, the detonator is provided by some routine and proper action by the police. In the case of St. Paul's this was a police raid in daylight on a West Indian club called 'The Black and White Club' where illegal sales of liquor and marijuana were taking place. Looting, burning of police cars, and attacks on police officers finally drove the police, including reinforcements, out of the St. Paul's area. The Chief Constable, Mr. Brian Weigh, gained support for his action in removing his outnumbered police until tempers cooled and reinforcements arrived. Considerable damage to shops and offices resulted during the absence of police on the streets. The latent anger of the alienated coloured population had exploded. Within a few hours it had subsided.

A statement, however crude, had been made, but had it been noted elsewhere? Timothy Raison, M.P., the Home Office Minister, who visited the scene was quoted as 'fervently hoping that the riot had been a "one-off" event.'[2] St. Paul's, however, was merely an advance warning. The omens for the Metropolitan Police could hardly have been clearer. The graffito ST. PAUL'S TODAY BRIXTON TOMORROW which appeared on some of London's walls said it all.

Some move towards a programme of community policing was a matter of urgency. But it was not to be. And, as relations between the police and the inner-city underclass (predominantly black) deteriorated further, the outbreaks of riots in 1981 became almost inevitable.

The report of the President's Commission on law enforcement and administration of justice in the U.S.A. recorded: 'The studies show that the rioters were not preponderantly wild adolescents, hoodlums, racial extremists and radical agitators, as is sometimes asserted [and was also to be asserted in London and elsewhere] although such people undoubtedly did take part. They were more or less a representative cross section of the negro community, particularly of its young men, many of whom had lived in the neighbourhood for many years and were steadily employed. The studies show further that many of those who participated in the riots, when questioned subsequently about their motives, stated quite explicitly they had been protesting against, indeed trying to call the attention of the white community to, police misconduct, commercial exploitation and economic deprivation, and racial discrimination.'[3]

Those of us pressing the case for community policing were dismayed that the sense of urgency in these matters seemed lacking. The main reaction of many on the Right of the political spectrum, both in and out of government, was to

155

demand further use of aggressive police tactics. The National Front and other extremist groups gained ground. The smear of 'soft' policing began to appear in interviews when the subject of community policing was mentioned and new phrases such as 'aggressive' or 'positive' and 'offensive' police tactics became quite popular within and without the police service. This is not to concede that the 'community thinking' school ever denied the need for police toughness at the right time. What we did deny was that 'hard' policing as a universal and basic philosophy would bring peace to our city streets. In the event, the government of Mrs. Thatcher—elected in 1979 largely on its claim to be the party of law and order—was to preside over the worst riots in England within living memory.

There had been no reluctance to spend money; on the contrary, we had more and better paid police than at any time in history. The cardinal error was to believe that, simply by pushing in resources, without radical changes of thinking and direction, order would follow automatically. Canute's lesson had not been remembered: the resistible force was to meet the immovable object.

The Brixton disorders broke out on 10 April 1981 and lasted for three days and shocked the Home Office and the police establishment into action.

After visiting the scene of devastation with the Commissioner of Police of the Metropolis (Sir David McNee), the Home Secretary William Whitelaw moved with speed to set up an inquiry using his powers under Section 32 of the Police Act 1964 to 'inquire urgently into the serious disorders in Brixton and to report, with the power to make recommendations'. It was Lord Scarman who insisted on having the clause 'with the power to make recommendations' included in his terms of reference—a wise move by a wise man. His appointment was a brilliant choice.

No sooner had Lord Scarman set to work on his inquiries than further riots were breaking out in Merseyside at Toxteth (4, 6, 28 July and 15 August); in Manchester at Moss Side (8, 9 July); and to a lesser extent in Birmingham and at Handsworth, Wolverhampton and Smethwick. Even the sedate City of Leicester felt the shock of riotous behaviour; and in Southall, London (3 July), skinheads and National Front clashed with Asian youth, and more police were added to the growing list of casualties. Not that all the riots arose from exactly the same causes, though there were similarities in many cases. Those in Brixton and Toxteth were particularly savage and took the terrifying form of large-scale assaults on the police.

One of the immediate responses of the Home Office Police Department was to advise on the procurement of C.S gas, plastic bullets, dischargers and protective equipment, as well as better training. I argued against (and still do) the use of plastic bullets and C.S. gas. C.S. gas because it merely inconvenienced rioters—and sometimes the police if the wind was in the wrong direction—but nevertheless could harm the lungs of innocent people. Plastic bullets because they had proved so deadly in Ulster killing young innocent children. Also I believed that such use would bring deep hatred upon the police at a time when a good deal of patient healing on both sides was called for.

I believed that Lord Scarman would produce a positive report (which he did) and that meanwhile every effort should be made to cool the situation. My own officers from Devon and Cornwall—who had performed duty at St. Paul's, Bristol, and in Toxteth, particularly the latter—found hatred of the police highly explosive but less so towards reinforcement from other areas. The problem, it seemed, was to contain the situation until Scarman reported.

The differences of opinion and controversy concerning the nature of policing, both inside and outside the police service, were now being forced to a head.

My own sympathies lay, of course, with the junior officers who were having to bear the brunt. Politicians and administrators were generally at a loss to know what to do, as reflected in the evidence submitted to Lord Scarman's inquiry. There was little straw for him with which to make his bricks.

So long as the Scarman Inquiry had been limited to the Brixton affair I chose not to submit evidence for, although I had experience of some of the underlying problems, it was not professionally appropriate to intervene in that way. However, as riots began to break out in various provincial centres and my own officers became involved as reinforcements, the position changed. We were all in it together. In addition, on 3 August 1981, I received a message from one of the parties represented at the inquiry asking me to submit evidence during Part II (focusing particularly on policing arrangements). This I agreed to do. The evidence which I submitted is set out in Appendix 'A'.

Meanwhile evidence had been submitted by the Commissioner of Police of the Metropolis, the Association of Chief Police Officers, the Police Superintendents' Association, and the Police Federation, as well as the Home Office, and one or two individual chief constables. The evidence of Sir David McNee, Commissioner of Police of the Metropolis, illustrates the dilemma in which he found himself.

In the first place, as he revealed in his memoirs,[4] the Scarman Inquiry was set up against his wishes. There was clearly considerable disagreement about it and he refers to 'an acrimonious' meeting at the Home Office. He was at odds with both the Home Secretary, Mr. William Whitelaw, and the Permanent Under Secretary, Sir Brian Cubbon. He suspected that he was being got at for political reasons. It appears that he wanted a wider inquiry where blame, if there was to be any, would fall upon others for their policies rather than singling out the police. He was conscious of the price which had been paid by the police both physically and psychologically. But then if policies go wrong in this way, whether in war or in peace, the poor bloody infantry or the foot-slogging constables sustain the casualties. In the event, the kindly and wise Lord Scarman paid a handsome tribute to the police virtue of courage. He also was at great pains to highlight the issues which Sir David felt might be overlooked, namely the social background which had set the scene for the eruption.

Sir David declined to give his evidence personally—that was done manfully for him by one of his assistant commissioners, Mr. Wilfred Gibson. The evidence to Part Two of the inquiry reiterated the traditional police virtues and the determination to maintain them. He was not in favour of setting up statutory Community Policing Consultative Groups, preferring to rely on 'good will'. But good will was by then in shorter supply. 'This cannot be attained by a statutory body, meeting not because it wishes to do so, but because it is required to do so,' were his feelings.

I felt otherwise, believing that the setting up of statutory consultative groups was the better way of ensuring both police accountablity and public understanding.

When it came to the presentation of Sir David McNee's evidence, Mr. Gibson on his behalf was of the opinion 'that on the whole we have not found anything that is dramatically wrong with our present (policing) policies'. We also differed on the issue of racial prejudice in the police, which I knew was there, and which the Policy Studies Institute Report on the Metropolitan Police in 1983 confirmed. The Commissioner was opposed to my proposal that racial discrimination in police duty should be made a specific disciplinary offence.

The Commissioner's evidence concluded: 'Therefore to sum up this submission it is my intention to maintain the concept of policing where the officer is the servant to all, a friend to many, and is a respected member of the community in which he serves. I see the way to achieve this as a continuing dialogue between the community and the police in order that both parties can recognise and eradicate the influence of those who have much to gain from a break in relations so that all sections of the community can live in the area without fear of crime or disorder. On the police part we shall give even greater emphasis in training to the importance of proper attitudes to the public.' Training apart, the evidence did not tackle essential changes in consultative machinery, nor improved accountability of police to public, nor the establishment of community policing systems. Sir David McNee does not describe his evidence in his memoirs, though it is clear that he disagreed with many of my own views.

The evidence of the Association of Chief Police Officers also failed to come to grips with some of the more contentious issues surrounding policing patterns and tactics. It made clear, as it had to do, that it did not necessarily reflect the views of all chief constables. Headed 'General Involvement of the Association in Matters Affecting Police/Community Relations', it covered the relationships between the police and multi-racial communities, and the search for improvements in training, recruitment and dealing with the problems of ethnic minorities and current racial difficulties. The arrangements for maintaining public order after a recent review were mentioned and the following conclusions reached:

'Although undoubtedly examples do exist where the relationship between the police and some members of ethnic

159

minorities is bad, we would wish to emphasise quite emphatically that generally this is not the case. We certainly do not see members of ethnic minorities as being more inclined to lawlessness than any other representative group within society given the circumstances which often prevail in the socially deprived inner city areas they frequently live in. It may well be that in certain parts of the Country some categories of crimes, particularly street robberies or muggings, would seem to be more prevalent to black youth, but this is not necessarily analogous overall.

'We also feel that we should bring to the attention of this Inquiry the view often held by chief officers that all too frequently a generalisation is made by ethnic minority groups that certain categories of crime, particularly crimes of violence, committed against them are motivated through racism. Even though subsequent police investigations may dispel or entirely rule out any racial connotation, the generalisation persists. This serves to give credibility to the quite erroneous belief that the police are unwilling to accept that crime motivated purely through racism exists. We do, of course, accept that examples of racial crime take place. But overall, we see violent crime, including mostly that committed against ethnic minority groups, as being examples of the unacceptably high level of violent crime generally within our society, to which all chief officers have frequently drawn attention.'

The Home Office study[5] on racial attacks published later in the year proved conclusively, however, that this evidence was either too complacent or had failed to grasp what was happening in the area of racial violence. Asians and blacks not only suffered more from physical attacks than whites, but far too many of these crimes went undetected; and the feeling was growing, rightly or wrongly, that the police in some areas failed to recognise the problem to be as acute as it was. The ACPO evidence concluded:

'Chief Officers of police also sadly reflect that too often ethnic minority groups attribute failure of police investigation to show positive results as being synonymous with a lack of real commitment. Yet this is not the case, and the efforts of police are directed towards safeguarding all sections of society through the prevention and detection of crime. It should also be mentioned that the duty of police to safeguard the rights of people to visibly parade on our streets in pursuit of often the most extreme political beliefs cannot serve to increase the understanding of the police role.

'In conclusion, therefore, we feel that a greater degree of understanding would be achieved by the wholehearted acknowledgement of society generally, and the more extreme members of ethnic minority groups in particular, to appreciate that the prevention and detection of crime is a responsibility of the whole of the community and cannot be abrogated in isolation entirely to the police.'

This evidence was very cautious and failed to offer the radical changes required to improve the deteriorating position in which the police in many parts of the country were finding themselves. The way was clearly open for submission of more drastic proposals which might have been expected to come from the Home Office but, since the Home Secretary is the police authority for London, it was only to be expected that what it had to say would be bland and non-commital as indeed it was.

Again the evidence offered few new ideas to the inquiry. After setting out the Home Office role in race relations, it went on to describe the Home Office role with regard to the police. 'Successive Home Secretaries have emphasised the importance of establishing and maintaining good relations between the police and ethnic minority groups', it said and described what they had done to achieve those objectives. Training and efforts to recruit candidates from ethnic minorities were reported, along with other features of this policy, but, wide ranging as the evidence was, it included nothing radical or even mildly different in the way of reform, presumably leaving Lord Scarman alone to tackle such matters. The call for better police training and improved protective clothing had been stressed during the inquiry by the Superintendents' Association and the Police Federation but the fundamental policing issues had been given scant recognition. The way was open for evidence which would deal with some of these issues and that evidence was to be found among the topics which had fuelled the debate over the preceding decade or more.

First, it was important to understand what forces had

motivated the riots. Many theories were advanced before Lord Scarman had received all the evidence, which he was to set out in his report with great clarity.

Riots may arise from among the following causes:

1) *Political:* There was no evidence of riots beng inspired by political factions although there was a limited amount of political opportunism as the riots developed.

2) *Social:* The riots took place mostly in the poorer inner city areas: in a large part they resulted from social conditions.

3) *Moral:* Although there have been protests on moral issues (for example, anti-nuclear demonstration or protest about rights of minorities), these have been of a non-violent nature so far; but they could develop violently if mishandled or misdirected.

4) *Religious:* Although the problems of Northern Ireland have (among their many causes) a religious basis, none of the riots in Great Britain was of a religious nature.

5) *Racial:* Generally the riots were of a mixed race type. Only one had a racial cause and that took place in a predominantly Hindu neighbourhood when white extremists paid a provocative visit. The police were also attacked by the Hindus when perceived to be unable to protect the minority.

6) *Anti-police:* The predominant motivation appeared to be anti-police in the culmination of riot. Although social conditions may have caused frustration, it seemed that violence was detonated by police action regarded as hostile and unsympathetic.

7) *Excitement for its own sake:* Interestingly, the heavy coverage given to early riots by the news media (particularly television) resulted in a wave of riotous behaviour with little motivation other than imitation for excitement.

Riots designed to overthrow institutions of democratic government, for example, have to be put down firmly and prosecutions for serious crimes considered. Anti-police riots, on the other hand, may call for little more than sensitive police action. The police, therefore, have a vested interest in helping to reduce tensions and fears. Persons who are afraid of crime suffer a diminution of their human rights since one of the rights is said to be freedom from fear. Although this may appear difficult and beyond the capability of the police, this is not necessarily so. By working closely with all sections of society the police can influence social attitudes particularly where they have gained the respect of the public. The police can reassure nervous minorities by indicating their will and ability to protect them. If this is not done, the danger of unorthodox vigilantism may develop, further heightening the prospects of communal violence. These are often very complex situations and require much thought and understanding if the police are not only to control violence through repression but also to prevent its escalation in the first place.

In the event, my own evidence centred around theories of policing a plural multi-racial and liberal democracy which differed in many ways fundamentally from the modern reactionary policing which had been developing over the preceding 15 years. There was a growing need to establish some form of police accountability at community level which might conceivably generate greater sensitivity in day-to-day policing. The greater understanding accruing from these new arrangements would provide the police with a sound basis upon which to investigate and detect crime, given that members of the public would participate with the police in their essential measures for preventing street crime in particular.

Delivered on the day before Part II of the inquiry (see Appendix 'A') my evidence was admitted by Lord Scarman with the following comments: 'I propose just to mention one written submission which reached me in fact only last night; of course way out of time. It is, of course, not in any sense controversial in that it does not deal in personalities or with these disturbances but it is an interesting contribution by a very senior chief constable to thinking on the subject of the principles of policing. I am, therefore, even at this late stage, circulating that document. It is quite short and I hope that represented parties will be able to study it before we have concluded the police representation.'

Other police evidence had been reported in the press to stimulate public debate and I followed the same course. Some of my comments were admittedly tendentious and I was not surprised to find myself the subject of some attack.

The Times in its leader commented, 'The ideas of Mr. John Alderson, whose presentation his fellow chief constables find so irritating, should not be dismissed as the idyll of a west country policeman with nothing heavier on his mind than Clovelly and the Exeter by-pass. Mr. Alderson has a firm grasp of an essential principle of English policing: that they are the police of the people and not of the prince: that they grow out of the community in which they work and are not apart from it: that they engage to the fullest possible extent with other social agencies for the prevention of crime and preservation of the civil peace'. The same leader added; 'Community policing is not simply a technique for policemen but a prescription for society.' In a sentence this summed up much of what I had for long been trying to get across to the public and politicians as well as the more understanding of my own colleagues. And when the same leader added that 'equipping and training police forces to be in a position to quell riot, arson and looting of ferocity for which they were found not to be prepared this summer' was an essential counterweight to community policing I found myself in accord.

Meanwhile we awaited the outcome of Lord Scarman's inquiry, which was to become as important to Britain as was the President's Commission to the U.S. police in 1967.

Lord Scarman's report was published on 25 November 1981. It found that social conditions had produced the explosive, and heavy and insensitive policing the detonator. Politicians and their departments had failed to bring about improvements in inner-cities which might have given the police a better prospect of performing their own role with greater success. On the other hand, there had been failure in adjusting policing policies and styles by the police managers.

Lord Scarman's recommendations on the police included some which were crucial for desirable change.

After stressing the need to recruit more police from ethnic minorities, and to improve police training and supervision, he turned his attention to the vital questions of methods of policing and the crucial issue of consultation and accountability. It had become obvious throughout the inquiry that saturation policing had exacted a heavy price and since then both senior politicians at the Home Office and senior police officers had admitted that 'We had got it wrong,' as one said to me. On the other hand, the community or home beat constable had been undervalued and, where he existed, often ignored. Lord Scarman recommended that the manner of policing neighbourhoods should be reviewed in consultation with representatives of the community in question. This was the keystone to it all. The setting up of community policing consultative groups should become a statutory duty! To my mind, that recommendation pointed the way to a new form of police accountability with far reaching consequences for the future of policing in England. I had made a strong point on the subject in my own evidence, for in my own experience reliance on voluntary consultation by the police would not produce the desirable results, and in Brixton the consultation had broken down before the rioting took place.

At first the Home Secretary appeared hesitant about making consultation a statutory obligation on police authorities and chief constables, but such a provision was provided for in the Police and Criminal Evidence Bill laid before Parliament in 1983.

I supported Lord Scarman's recommendation that racial discrimination in police work should be an offence under the Police Discipline Code and had included it in my own evidence. I was disappointed when the Police Federation and the chief constables resisted this provision and when the Home Secretary decided not to enact it. The opportunity for the police to register their abhorrence of such practices was unfortunately missed. The police objections were based mainly on two grounds—first that the existing provisions of police discipline could be made to fit racial discrimination and, secondly, that it would be a difficult clause to draft. I believe that neither of these arguments can be sustained, any more than the police themselves believe that criminal laws should be based on similar principles. When there is a problem, as there is, of racial discrimination in any branch of government or other powerful bureaucracy, racial discrimination has to be seen to be outlawed.

The police service generally accepted the remainder of Lord Scarman's report with enthusiasm. Here was an opportunity to go back to the drawing board and build afresh, a time to put the past behind and work for a new understanding, or, as the Chairman of the Police Federation, Mr. Jim Jardine, put it, 'an opportunity for a new beginning'. For the sake of both police and public it marked a very important date in the annals of the history of the police in England. Only the Right Wing press was grudging.

Mr. Whitelaw and his department set about implementing the proposals on consultation within weeks of the report coming out.

Within a year Sir David McNee announced his retirement. He had experienced a hard time in London as he makes clear in his memoirs, and I felt much sympathy for a man of great charm and integrity; but those of us who know the problems of commanding that almost unmanageable force saw it as something of a 'bed of nails' for a Commissioner. The Metropolitan Police Force is the most important police organisation, and the most professional, in the country. Furthermore it is directly administered by the Home Office. It is expected to set the standards.

I have long held the view that its size warrants some fresh appraisal. The senior management structure has barely altered since the nineteenth century and, given the stresses and strains placed upon the Commissioner and the higher echelons, it could well take on a new top structure. The river divides the area conveniently so that the northern and southern parts could, I believe, have their own Commissioner accountable to a Chief Commissioner relieved of many of the day to day issues. The central area containing Parliament, Royal Households and diplomatic enclaves would be a special command under a Deputy Commissioner accountable to the Chief Commissioner. In this way the burdens may be eased. That however is for future debate, or for a Royal Commission when the time comes.

Meanwhile new policies were required and, since the Metropolitan Police should normally act as 'flagship' for the British police service, its example is important.

In October 1982, Sir Kenneth Newman became the new Commissioner of the Police of the Metropolis. I had known him as a student at Bramshill in the early 1970s and regarded him then as having an intellectual capacity above the ordinary. I had no doubt that, having served from constable to commander in the Metropolitan Police, he would understand the uniqueness of the organisation. It was an indication of the difficulty of the task before him when, on his first address to the Police Federation of his force, some barracked when he spoke of the need to improve public relations and some applauded when he said they would be issued with plastic bullets and other anti-riot gear. This was the mood of the force. At the same meeting the Home Secretary, then Mr. Whitelaw who had done so much for police pay and conditions, received a hostile reception. Even Mrs. Thatcher was moved to express her disgust about the behaviour of some police officers to the Minister, who is also their own police authority. All in all, this first meeting with the new Commissioner and his police authority did the Metropolitan Police little credit. Newman had written an article in *The Times* on 14 June 1982 in which he pledged himself to Lord Scarman's recommendations. About community style policing he wrote, 'It is a potentially rewarding activity if it leads to enhanced public co-operation because research has demonstrated beyond any doubt that police effectiveness is almost totally dependent on public co-operation.' Those of us who had been propagating the same message over the years were delighted to read this kind of comment. Now we awaited the outcome of new policies based on these principles.

We had not long to wait. Within months of the introduction of the new Commissioner's policies, results became promising. Not only was consultation beginning to show dividends from better public understanding but the system of beat patrols coupled with proper intelligence gathering and targeting of suspects provided results. In August 1983 New Scotland Yard reported a dramatic fall in street crime. Robbery (mugging) and theft fell by 39% over the year before. It was reported in the *Guardian* of 17 August that the police figures disclosed that in Lambeth crimes of violence fell by 20%, auto crimes by 13%, and burglary by 5%. Complaints against the police fell by 53% in the first quarter of 1983, compared with the same period the year before, a clear sign of improving police attitudes and public response.

Chapter 9

1981: Seeds of a Para-Military Response?

A senior French police official has said, 'The French have a tradition of strong central government. This is the country of the revolution, we have to maintain a strong repressive police arm.' Absolutely right. When revolt and large scale violence are anticipated, strong repression is the necessary police response. In recent history, the social order in Britain has not required creation of para-military police. By para-military police we understand the term to mean specially trained and equipped cohorts of police with a repressive capability which places them mid-way between the traditional peace-keeping police and the military. Northern Ireland and Hong Kong provide good examples of a social order which has a need for this, as traditionally do most European countries. A society acquires the police it deserves.

Ireland and the Colonies

Since the early 1970s the possibility of Britain acquiring a para-military police has been discussed at great length in both police and military staff colleges. The general view of the military is that, having been sucked into a peace-keeping role in Northern Ireland from which there is little sign of their being extricated, they have no wish to find themselves playing such a role in Britain. Many have argued for the creation of a third force, a kind of mobile gendarmerie, to play the more repressive role which we in the police would seek to avoid at almost any cost, and from which the army wish to remain free.

The policing of Ireland over the years of British rule was at times in the past no easier than it is today in Northern Ireland. The 1814 Act for the Better Execution of the laws in Ireland stated; 'Disturbances have from time to time existed in different parts of Ireland, for the suppression whereof the ordinary police hath been found insufficient.' From this Act can be traced the para-military police of Britain's other colonies and of British Ireland down to the present day.[1]

When does an ordinary police force become inadequate?

Clearly a colonial government as an alien force requires a strong repressive police capability and the power and the will to use it. Although the imperial British recognised this need for the control of their possessions overseas, their own domestic model for police became one of the least repressive in the developed countries of the world. As in the case of slavery, which was exploited in the colonies but illegal at home;[2] the British Empire had its two moralities and systems of law. From its foundation in 1829 the modern British police system (through deliberate political choice) has remained unarmed. Throughout all the many disturbances, riots and public disorder of the nineteenth and twentieth centuries, Britain has avoided the creation of a para-military police. True, the army has been called in to assist the civilian police from time to time. It was deployed in 1911 to support the police in Liverpool during a period of industrial unrest and again (the most recent occasion) during the police strike of 1919. Since then an unarmed civilian police force—often under great difficulties and provocations—has retained its own unique character.

The late Sir Arthur Young, Commissioner of Police for the City of London, who was appointed Chief Constable of the Royal Ulster Constabulary in 1969, recounted to me some of the difficulties which he had in trying to implement the recommendations of the Hunt Report in bringing about the creation of a British-style police in Northern Ireland. He believed that he had been forced upon the government in Stormont and the Royal Ulster Constabulary, which made his task very difficult. He said, 'One of my problems was the fact that extreme Protestants saw that I wasn't re-establishing the police by force of arms. And because when talking in their area I used the expression, "We are coming in softly, softly," Mr. Paisley and Mr. Craig, both leading politicians in the Stormont government, described me as a traitor to the constitution and the sooner I was sacked the better.' He even found it difficult to appear in public in some Protestant areas because stones and bottles were thrown at him, and in one of them he was burnt in effigy. He undoubtedly did much good work for the Royal Ulster Constabulary but to change the fundamental model of the police from an armed para-military to an unarmed civil force on British lines was impossible.

Social Disrepair

In a society where communal violence represents divisions which are deep-seated, and where police are vulnerable to violence of an extreme kind, it is just not possible to bring about such change. Only when society changes can the police change. But just as a society can change so that the police can play a more gentle role, so it can change in the opposite direction. What was a moderately tranquil social order can become a more violent one. The police must never lead the escalation—this is the big challenge. It requires high police morale, calibre, training and leadership on the one hand, while government has to be active in reducing festering social discontent.

The riots which took place in London, Liverpool, Manchester and elsewhere in 1981 once more raised the issue of whether an 'ordinary' police force would, alone, be adequate in the long term.

These disturbances were not insurrections: it was not that the government of the day was faced with an attempt to overthrow its political authority. The riots were in the main directed against the police and sprang from rioters' many frustrations, some caused by destructive social situations and some provoked by insensitive police actions over a number of years. If, in future, such frustrations are not to be met by social, economic and political remedies, then a case could be argued for the creation of a para-military police out of necessity. The British police will have crossed the Rubicon. Some areas of our society will be policed from time to time by a para-military response. These areas are of course likely to be those where social order has broken down, where poverty, unemployment, bad housing, and urban decay have produced an under-class to whom normal standards of behaviour had ceased to have any meaning. These will be the areas where crimes of theft and violence will be endemic.

Even today the police in inner-city areas such as these have to maintain a kind of uneasy state of order, sometimes under extreme provocation. They are trapped: some see their role as that of an alien force; while others (such as the victims and potential victims of crime) plead for their protection. Yet the police service cannot change the context within which they operate; that is for others, particularly government both local and central.

Difficult though the task may be, it is in the interests of all people that we should avoid the trap of regarding a strong repressive police arm as a substitute for greater social justice and the amelioration of conditions which contain those destructive social forces for which a para-military police is wrongly seen as the only answer. It may well be that seeds of para-military police were laid in England after the riots of 1981. If so, it will be an historic step. Writing in 1978, the police historian T. A. Critchley[3] said, 'If the police were to lose public support and goodwill on any significant scale it seems clear that their traditional character would not long survive. Britain could then expect what she has long resisted—a tougher, more authoritarian, more oppressive system of police; and public confidence, once lost, would be hard to regain. The price, ultimately would be to set at risk liberties that have been cherished for centuries.'

It has to be stressed, however, that although the police themselves have to discharge the burden of retaining public confidence, they have but little choice in using force to put down disorders, and if those disorders arise from unacceptable social conditions then only a change in those social conditions is likely to put the police in a better relationship with all the people.

Plastic Bullets

In the event, after the 1981 riots the Home Secretary agreed that chief constables could have at their personal disposal a supply of plastic bullets and C.S. gas. I opposed the issue of plastic bullets and C.S. gas for use against crowds (although not for armed besieged criminals). This was in my view an

171

unnecessary escalation of the threshold of police counter-force, the use of which would one day rebound on the police. In all cases where police have embarked upon the use of weapons which can have deadly effect against non-deadly force, hostages are given to fortune. Death on the streets of English cities caused by police, when not themselves the objects of deadly force, was too high a price to pay. No police officer in Britain in recent times has yet been killed while containing riots. These are among the weapons of para-military police in Ulster and Hong Kong, but few if any European countries accept the use of plastic bullets.

Plastic bullets are known to have a deadly effect. 'Fourteen people have been killed (in Northern Ireland) seven of them school children and hundreds have suffered a wide range of serious injuries to bones, flesh and organs.'[4] The weapons and their missiles were developed in the U.S.A. and Britain, and brought into use by the army in Northern Ireland and Hong Kong. Is it just a matter of time now, before the British public witness the escalation of violence on the streets of English cities comparable with that in former colonies?

At the annual conference of the Association of Chief Police Officers at Preston in the autumn of 1981, senior police advisers from Northern Ireland and Hong Kong were invited to advise on the deployment of police and such equipment. It was as if time was being reversed. The British police—so long looked to as an outstanding example for their stoic, patient, brave handling of urban violence—were now turning to police methods long regarded by them as only fit for colonial use. I thought it premature and said so, for we had not yet exhausted the alternatives of well drilled, well protected and well led anti-riot squads. Nor had we instituted the necessary police information-gathering to help forestall the outbreak of riots.

It came as no surprise to me that some of my colleagues should criticise me for saying that 'we were tooling up to declare war on the public' and that 'a hundred and fifty years of police heritage would go down the drain for the sake of a few hours of madness on the streets'. *The Times* commented, 'It was also a mistake on Home Secretary's part to authorise the issue of plastic bullets. They may kill, though they are not intended to. Bad as the disorders were this summer things have not deteriorated so far that the police yet need a riot weapon as close as that to being lethal.' The *Sunday Express*, on the other hand, published an article by Sir Angus Maude, M.P., in which I was described as 'this sanctimonious officer of the law' and went on to recommend that the Tory government should take an even harder line.

I had certainly never believed that the police should not be tough in dealing with riotous behaviour once it had broken out. But I did not and do not think it prudent to encourage the police to escalate their own violence to deadly proportions when the exercise, though violent, is not of a deadly nature. Politicians may not always see the point, though they should, but most thinking police officers certainly do.

If British government approval of the supply of plastic bullets and C.S. gas for use in 'the last resort' may have sown the seeds of a para-military police response, it is likely that the ground from which its fruit springs will be provided by our decaying city enclaves where ordinary social values are fast diminishing. A suitable strategy for the prevention of riots should therefore begin in as ambitious a 'new deal' for these areas as we can genuinely afford. As for the police, they will need carefully to monitor such areas for tension, and report their findings to the government. The potential for disorder is too great to be left to the police alone. There is a need to manifest much sympathy and understandng along with fairness, and if—in the final analysis—the police are required to act, then they have to put down disorder early through well trained and controlled squads, properly protected but with minimum force. After all, they have to go back the next day and start all over again in trying to help repair community relations. As Richard Clutterbuck comments on British genius in avoiding excesses of social violence: 'The tradition of non-violence has taken one and a half centuries to build. It could be much more quickly destroyed.' It would be a tragedy should its destruction arise out of policing.

In May of 1982 the European Parliament passed resolutions calling on member states to ban the use of plastic bullets. It was a misjudgment, I believe, for Lord Scarman in his report on the Brixton and other disorders of 1981 to accept the inevitability of the supply of plastic bullets for use on the streets of English cities—even though 'only as a last resort'.

Chapter 10

Operation Countryman

The criminal most hated by the police is the criminal police officer.

Though they are relatively few, the damage which they cause to the criminal justice system and to the police in particular is out of all proportion to their numbers. Honest police are faced with suspicion and hostility by association: their reputation is put at risk; their own conduct is questioned both internally and by the press; and their evidence in court is regarded with scepticism. Criminals learn to exploit their corrupt police associates by threats of disclosure—threats which are countered by the fabrication of evidence by their police adversaries. The criminal police officer is able to exploit his official record of honesty against the criminal's record of dishonesty. In assessing the allegations and counter-allegations which are brought out in court, it is only natural for juries to hesitate to convict police officers on the word of a known criminal, though naturally the converse does not apply.

Because it is easy for criminals to make allegations against police officers as a means of defence or revenge, it is important that everything reasonable is done to protect police from malicious prosecution. Prosecutions of police officers are decided by the Director of Prosecutions, and the present holder of the office, Sir Thomas Hetherington, has made it known that his policy is to ensure that at least 51% of the available evidence points to guilt before authorising such prosecutions. The criminal police officer, therefore, is able in many instances to exploit the reasonable safeguards which are provided to protect his honest colleagues.

The internal investigation of criminal police officers is one of the least popular of all police tasks and it is often one of the most difficult. The activities of the investigators make other police officers jumpy, since in the course of the investigation they may come across administrative and procedural misdemeanours which render their colleagues liable to disciplinary charges. One of the side effects of a major internal criminal investigation may be that the pace of operations becomes slower, as other police officers cease to take shortcuts and begin to pay more meticulous attention to detail, while at the same time concentrating on covering their own tracks. Old loyalties come under strain; past friendships and complicity in breaches of orders stand in the way of impartial investigation. For all these reasons, when a serious allegation of criminal activity by police is made, it is the practice to call upon the services of investigators from other police forces whose personal loyalties and future careers are less likely to become an embarrassment and impediment to efficient enquiries. It was one such case which led to the setting up of what became known as 'Operation Countryman' in August 1978. Many of us were to become directly or indirectly involved in what turned out to be an unhappy experience.

It happened that, during routine criminal investigation of major crime, a senior officer of the Metropolitan Police had misgivings and suspicions concerning the activities of a few senior detectives in the City of London C.I.D. An earlier armed robbery at Williams and Glyns Bank in the City of London had netted some £250,000 and there were allegations that corrupt detectives had received as much as £121,000. Mr. Peter Marshall, the Commissioner of the City of London Police, took the right course of action in asking the Home Office in the person of the Chief Inspector of Constabulary, Sir Colin Woods, to provide a number of detectives led by a senior officer from another force to conduct the inquiry.

The chief constable of Dorset, Mr. Arthur Hambleton, was asked to supply the team. It was regarded by some of us as an unusual choice since the the Dorset C.I.D. was small by comparison with some of the larger Metropolitan forces and its range of officers with relevant experience was limited. However, the officer chosen to lead the team, Mr. Leonard Burt, was a man of strong character, determined and with experience in regional crime squad activity as well as having played a leading role in the break up and conviction of the notorious Portland spy ring in 1961. As Burt began to assemble his team it became known to the Deputy Commissioner of the Metropolitan Police, Mr. Patrick Kavanagh, that inquiries relating to officers in the Metropolitan C.I.D. would, of necessity, take place. Hambleton and Burt agreed to take on responsibility for the operation in both City and Metropolitan areas. It is unlikely that they foresaw the morass in which they were to become entangled over the next two years.

The world of professional criminals (particularly bank pay-roll and bullion robbers) in which Metropolitan detectives operate is rightly termed 'the underworld'. Its nature has been starkly portrayed on cinema and television screens through popular series such as *The Sweeney* and *Law and Order*. The London scene is unique and its nearest (though more violent) counterparts are Paris, Rome, and some American cities such as New York and Chicago. For these reasons, provincial detectives without experience in London or a large city require time and opportunity to adjust. Burt and his team found themselves in the web of intrigue, plot and counter-plot, allegation and counter-allegation, which characterises the London underworld, the home ground of the London detective. Even the jargon is different. I remember when first going to London as a deputy commander in 1966 having to ask a Metropolitan police officer to draw up a glossary of terms before I was able to make sense of some of the phraseology in reports and statements.

The battle of wits which goes on, day in and day out, between the London detective and his quarry is sharp and can be deadly for the unwary and more orthodox detective. Each plots the downfall of the other and each learns the nature of the contest as they develop and mature, either in the ranks of the C.I.D. or in those of the criminal network. A professional reputation is to be made on the one hand and large pickings on the other. The officers of 'Operation Countryman' were walking into a hornets' nest. I knew most of them as men of unswerving loyalty and integrity and I watched their perplexity and disillusionment grow.

The operation began with some 30 officers involved: two years and two million pounds later it numbered 90. Ten of them were from my own force in Devon and Cornwall and many came from the South-West region.

Burt soon asked to locate his headquarters outside London to safeguard the inquiry and its records from interference. It is not unknown for the criminal police network to destroy records by breaking into offices of investigating teams. Nor is it a novel experience for provincial detectives to experience non-cooperation and even obstruction from both corrupt and non-corrupt Metropolitan officers. Mr. Frank Williamson, one of the inspectors of constabulary who from 1969 to 1972 headed the enquiry into what were known as '*The Times* disclosures' of police corruption, complained throughout of obstructive tactics by some senior officers in the C.I.D. at New Scotland Yard. His frustration was such that he resigned in protest. Burt and his team were to encounter similar difficulties.

Of course, neither the Commissioner, Sir David McNee, nor his deputy, Mr. Patrick Kavanagh, nor the vast majority of senior officers were in any way involved in impeding this inquiry. The Metropolitan Police, however, is a vast organisation, difficult if not impossible to control from the centre. On the other hand the City of London Police is a compact force numbering less than a thousand officers with few of the problems of its massive neighbour. Had the Countryman inquiry been confined to the City of London few of the complexities which eventually beset it would have happened.

The allegations against the detectives came from persons who in the past had been convicted of or were awaiting trial for charges involving robbery, often involving firearms, in which large amounts of money were stolen. They alleged that officers were paid substantial sums to weaken the evidence during their trial and to secure their bail. Unfortunately for the inquiry and the police generally, there was widespread news coverage of the setting up of the inquiry and its activities. Hardly a week passed without the operation being mentioned by the news media, and this resulted in numerous allegations being brought to the attention of Burt and his men. Criminals, both in custody and at large, could hardly wait to try to settle old scores. What had started as an investigation into the handling of a major crime became an inquiry into much of the work of various police squads over many years. The allegations spread to touch upon some 70 officers of both low and high rank, while the inquiry team grew. It was swamped with work. Its commitment to clearing the names of honest officers unjustly defamed as well as securing the arrest of the guilty demanded long hours of patient dedicated effort. Furthermore, much of it had to be carried out without help from local officers. Secrecy was essential.

Staff from the office of the Director of Public Prosecutions and even the Director himself were drawn into the inquiry, particularly when there arose the question of granting immunity from prosecution to criminal informants. As the months went by and no prosecutions had taken place, the inquiry team felt the backlash of criticism from many quarters. Their perplexed feeling was noticeable to those of us who had maintained contact with seconded officers. Mr. Merlyn Rees, who was Home Secretary when the inquiry was set up, wrote later in *The Times* that he had made a mistake and in future would not agree to bringing officers in to London from the provinces unless they had wide experience of metropolitan criminal investigation.

Arthur Hambleton's impending retirement in February 1980 raised further problems for the inquiry team as to who their new manager would be. One of the last acts Hambleton was to perform took place in a meeting at New Scotland Yard involving the Deputy Commissioner and the Director of Public Prosecutions. Hambleton later said that he had complained vigorously on behalf of his officers about the procedural delays, frustrations and obstructions they had encountered. Others have said there was no such obstruction. At all events, Hambleton agreed that Burt should sign a press statement including the following passage: 'Suggestions that the Countryman investigations have been obstructed are completely without truth. I and my officers have received the fullest cooperation and every assistance from the Director and the 2 Commissioners. In particular the Director has acceded to a request I made concerning the giving of certain limited undertakings to persons helping our inquiries, and I unhesitatingly accept that, when criminal proceedings against police officers are being considered, there can be no departures from the evidential requirements which apply to civilian suspects.'

The latter part of this statement reflects the reluctance of 'Countryman' to use the testimony of 'supergrasses' against suspect police officers by offering immunity from prosecution for their own crimes. However, the fact is that the inquiry was obstructed, not at the very top, but at the intermediate levels of the C.I.D. It was felt by the seconded officers that a small number of their own professional colleagues had let them down and that a number of corrupt police officers were escaping prosecution through default at these intermediate levels and through lack of sufficient evidence to warrant successful prosecutions.

Hambleton's retirement provided an opportunity to run down the inquiry team from the provinces and to hand over the bulk of the inquiry to the Metropolitan Police. Sir Peter Mathews, Chief Constable of Surrey, was given this task. My own officers were peremptorily returned to normal duties, feeling that their mission had not been completed; and I informed Sir Peter accordingly. Both Hambleton and Burt were frustrated and, despite requests both in Parliament and the press, the Home Secretary, William Whitelaw, refused to set up a full inquiry into the affair.

The whole 'Countryman' saga pointed to the need for an independent body of a permanent nature to carry out inquiries into serious allegations against police officers. This must be an organisation to which both selected police officers and investigators from other government services can be seconded—where the necessary experience will be developed in order to avoid the many and embarrassing pitfalls into which the 'Countryman' inquiry fell.

The Police Complaints Board is an independent body whose chairman (a layman) and members are appointed by the Prime Minister and the Home Secretary respectively. In its first triennial review in 1979 the Board recommended that complaints of serious injury inflicted by police should be investigated by an independent body of police officers seconded for that purpose. This followed controversy surrounding the death and injury of a number of prisoners in police custody. There was no mention of serious police corruption, and in any case the 'Countryman' saga was yet to be enacted. A Working Party appointed by the Home

Secretary, William Whitelaw, in 1980 considered the setting up of such an independent body of investigators but came out against it. They reported, 'We argue that to establish a central team of investigators would not be the best course, but draw attention to the possibility of developing the existing arrangements under which an investigating officer is appointed from another force.'[1] Yet this is precisely what had happened in the 'Countryman' case with such important consequences and dissatisfaction.

Since this Home Office Report was published, both the Police Federation and a number of chief constables have expressed the view that an independent body should be established to inquire into serious complaints. The matter is in any view one of urgency and the Home Secretary has undertaken to act.

The Countryman investigation resulted in the prosecution of eight Metropolitan officers, all of whom were acquitted, but the subject of their original brief in the City of London resulted in the conviction and imprisonment of a chief inspector.

Chapter 11

Contentious Business

In the middle of May 1981, 31 people, marching behind the Lostwithiel Silver Band, left the scene of a protest against nuclear power taking place in the field of a farmer, Mr. Rex Searle, at Luxulyan in Cornwall.

They had been served with injunctions restraining them from obstructing workmen of the Central Electricity Generating Board. The Luxulyan case, as it came to be known, was to find a significant place in the law books under the title: 'In the Matter of the Queen v. Chief Constable of Devon and Cornwall. Ex Parte Central Electricity Generating Board (C.E.G.B a corporate body) v. John Cottingham Alderson (Chief Constable of the Devon and Cornwall Constabulary), Tuesday, 20th October, 1981.'

Luxulyan, a quiet little Cornish hamlet of a few hundred people, was an unlikely place to become the scene of a legal impasse. But the C.E.G.B. had been conducting investigations, including seismic surveys, in the south west, to find a suitable site to build a nuclear power station and, unfortunately for Mr. Rex Searle and his wife, the eyes of the Board's surveyors had fallen upon their farm.

Now, the Board has a statutory duty to develop and maintain an efficient, co-ordinated and economical system of electricity for England and Wales. Its powers lie in the Electricity Acts of 1947 and 1957. Furthermore, it had the approval of the government's policy. On the other hand, Mr. and Mrs. Searle and their neighbours were worried about the possible threat to themselves and society in general should an accident, such as the celebrated one at Three Mile Island in the U.S.A., take place. There were other strong and well organised pressure groups to lend support.

The Board Moves

Due notice was given to Rex Searle that the Board were going to operate on his land and near his house. His protest to the Board was backed up by a flat refusal to allow them to do so. He was strongly opposed to the plans and set to work to frustrate them. On 24 February 1981, the Board's surveyors and their contractors arrived at the scene, only to find their way blocked by some 60 protesters under the banner, LUXULYAN AGAINST NUCLEAR DEVELOPMENT. Trelawney, the Cornish hero, would have been sympathetic to this cause, no doubt. The officials of the Board retreated, to the boos of the protesters. Neither the Board's men nor the protesters used any violence or force. Round one to Luxulyan.

Round two opened on 4 March 1981, when the C.E.G.B. issued writs against Farmer Searle and his neighbour, Farmer Lawton. Injunctions were granted to restrain these two farmers and their families from interfering with the operation. Being law-abiding citizens, they obeyed. But Farmer Searle declined to remove the protesters from his land, arguing, quite rightly, that they were not included in the injunction, though some of them were his friends. The result of this ploy was that the protesters were not trespassers on his land and for that reason at least could not be forcibly removed. This round seemed to be a draw.

On 26 March, the Board carried out some drilling on the farm without obstruction. By the middle of May, however, several local objectors appeared and blocked gateways with motor vehicles. The Board tried to move drilling rigs in to carry out seismic tests. Some protesters lay down on the ground to block the way, and two middle-aged ladies chained themselves to a rig! By this time, some of my police officers were on the scene and persuaded the protesters to remove obstructions to the highway, taking some names and addresses in the process. Several protesters, invoking their belief in the ancient stannary rights freely to dig for tin, began to dig ostensibly for the precious metal. They dug down a few feet and burst a water main! A touch of farce enlivened the proceedings which ended in defeat for the Board, who still declined to use the force which, it was contended, they might lawfully have employed.

Having identified the protesters, the Board obtained 31 injunctions against those responsible who, again obeying the law, did not continue physically to obstruct the operation.

It was then that they left the site, marching, behind the Lostwithiel Silver Band.

Peaceful Protest

Hardly had these protesters left, than reinforcements arrived to take up position on Farmer Searle's land. It was alleged by the Board that they came from all over the country, even from abroad, but the police information was somewhat different. New people certainly appeared, but most of them were from Cornwall and a few from Devon. The protests continued in a passive way—lying on the ground and standing near intended explosions and sitting on bore holes before charges were put in. The demonstraters concealed their identities and neither the police nor the Board had powers to require them to reveal them. They placed tents, caravans and vehicles at the five entrances to the field. Meanwhile, the good Police Constable Penderick, the local community police officer, kept a benevolent eye on the proceedings. As a good police officer should do, he had built up an excellent relationship with both sides in the dispute. Neither inclined too readily to the use of force nor to permit excesses, he had been present as and when necessary. Reinforcements had been requested to clear the highway and generally to prevent the likelihood of a breach of the peace.

From time to time the protesters assured him that this was a passive protest, of which Gandhi himself might have approved. They even issued a Code of Non-Violent Practice to each demonstrator. The sturdy and watchful figure of Chief Inspector Bradley was to be seen perambulating at the scene, but he too came to the conclusion that no breach of the peace was threatened, and that the protest was on private, not public, land. There was no further role for the police to play.

Correspondence

On 1 June, I received a letter from the Board asking for police assistance in enabling the Board to carry out its statutory duties by preventing further unlawful obstruction. After seeking legal advice, I replied at length. 'I am sure you will appreciate that although the Town and Country Planning Act 1971 does create an offence of wilful obstruction, it does not give any power of arrest. This legislation is one not normally prosecuted by the police and even if prosecution were undertaken by summons, those initially reported would not immediately appear before a court and could be replaced by others causing obstruction at the site.

'The dispute is one of a quasi-private nature made more complicated by the reluctance of the owner of the land to co-operate thereby hindering any assistance under the common law right for trespass.

'I realise that the issue is one of national importance, and accept that until exploratory work is successfully completed, the Board cannot perform its statutory function. The local protesters have complied with the injunctions obtained by your solicitor and, happily, that phase in the protest has passed without serious disturbance. The present protesters are a small part of a growing body of opinion whose aim, amongst others, is to obtain public and political support for a general cessation of various applications of nuclear power.

'I accept that the power given to the police under common law is supported by Thomas v. Sawkins (1935) and preserved by the Criminal Law Act of 1967, section 2 (7). Police have remained on private land during demonstrations at Luxulyan expressly to ensure the preservation of the peace. The demonstrations so far have been of such a nature that possible breach of the peace and instances of criminal damage have not occurred. Had they done so, there would have been a clear opportunity for police to act and they would have done so.

'I am sure you will appreciate that contentious issues such as the work at Luxulyan place the local officers in an unenviable and sensitive position. We have endeavoured to give the Board every possible assistance and we will continue to do so. The legal position is complicated and the public opposition genuinely and vociferously expressed. Against this background, without a more definitive mandate, the police must inevitably maintain their low-key presence to preserve the peace.'

I awaited the Board's next move, for their work had been

frustrated for some three months and I was conscious of their feelings that the police were taking too lenient a view of the protesters. In our view, it was a case of vagueness of the law and an exercise of the resulting discretion in favour of no criminal procedure unless a breakdown of the peace was apprehended. Had the Board sought to move the protesters, as I believed they would, the police would most certainly have acted to prevent violence on either side. As it was, the position was stalemate.

The High Court

On 23 June, at a meeting at Police Headquarters in Exeter, the Board indicated their intention to make an application to the Divisional Court seeking an Order of Mandamus to command me to instruct my officers to remove, or assist them in the removal of, protesters from the Luxulyan site. No chief constable would wish to find himself ordered by the High Court of the land to perform a task which, in his judgment, was undesirable and doubtful in law.

The application was heard on 27 and 28 July 1981, by Mr. Justice Hodgson and Mr. Justice McCullough, and was refused.

Mr. Justice Hodgson said, 'A policeman has power to use force to prevent a breach of the peace which he on reasonable grounds apprehends. There are thus two ingredients, one objective and the other subjective. There must be reasonable grounds and on those reasonable grounds the policeman must think a breach of the peace is likely. If the view of the chief constable be correct then the police clearly have no power to arrest these demonstrators... The opinion formed by the chief constable is far more likely to be correct than any view of the matter which this court might take and I think it would be wholly wrong for this court to tell the chief constable to do something which, if he is right, would amount to wrongful arrest by his men.'

Mr. Justice McCullough said, 'By far the most important reason for refusing this application is the consideration that policing is essentially a matter for police officers, not for Judges.'

The Divisional Court had vindicated our action and their

185

decision left the Board with one of two courses open. They could have gone to Luxulyan and removed the protesters from the site, whereupon the police would have assisted in protecting them from any violence and arrested any protesters who caused a breach of the peace; or they could have gone higher in pursuit of the order compelling me to order my officers to carry out arrests and removals. They chose the latter course.

On 7 August 1981, the case came before the Vacation Court of Appeal where it was decided that it involved such important issues, some of constitutional significance, that the matter must be heard by the full Court of Appeal.

The Court of Appeal

On 27 September, the case came before the Master of the Rolls, Lord Denning and Lords Justice Lawton and Templeman. The case was argued for four full days and it took their Lordships almost four weeks to deliver their judgments. It was not a simple issue for the court, any more than it had been for the police. On 20 October, the reserved judgments were delivered. The Court unanimously dismissed the appeal and refused to make an order of Mandamus against me. But we still awaited some pronouncement on the issue of whether the protesters were committing any offence for which the police could arrest them. We were not to be disappointed. (The full judgment appeared in *The Times* Law Report, 21 October 1981.)

In his inimitable way, Lord Denning began by saying that the coast of Cornwall was beautiful. Much of the inland was ugly and despoiled by china clay workings. Not far from them was open farmland with small villages. It was pleasant but not outstanding. As to moving the demonstrators, 'The Chief Constable felt that he could not use his force for this purpose. It would put his men in a bad light with the local inhabitants.' Well, there was more to it than that, of course—a matter of whether the police had the power to do it. After a lengthy review of the circumstances, Lord Denning said, 'I cannot share the view taken by the police.' He went on to ask, 'Is the law powerless to stop them (the protesters)? I think not.' And later: 'The arm of the law is long enough to reach them.'

The apparent effect of his judgment was that the conduct of the protesters and their criminal obstruction of the Board was itself a 'Breach of the Peace'. That this is so 'whenever a person who is lawfully carrying out his work is unlawfully and physically prevented by another from doing it'. To many police and lawyers this seemed to stretch the law on breach of the peace. Previously, a degree of violence or its threat had been looked for. Lord Denning went on to say, 'Notwithstanding all that I have said, I would not give any orders to the Chief Constable or his men. It is of the first importance that the police should decide on their own responsibility what action should be taken in any particular situation.' He continued, 'The decision of the Chief Constable not to intervene in this case was a policy decision with which I think the courts would not interfere. All that I have done in this judgment is to give the "definitive legal mandate" which he sought. It should enable him to reconsider his position. I hope he will decide to use his men to clear the obstructors off the site, or at any rate help the Board to do so.'

We had sought a legal mandate, but still thought the Board should take the first step.

Lord Justice Lawton said, among other things, 'On the evidence, it seems likely that the Board will have to use self help if it is to perform its statutory duties at Luxulyan. Civil proceedings have been ineffective. Prosecutions for offences under sections 280 and 281(2) of the Town and Country Planning Act 1971 would serve no useful purpose. When it does decide to use self help and fix a day for doing so, it should inform the local police who will no doubt be present in sufficient numbers to ensure as best they can that breaches of the peace do not occur, and that if they do, that those responsible are removed from the site.'

We would have agreed with that arrangement from the beginning had the Board accepted that course.

Lord Justice Lawton went on, 'In my judgment this is not a case for making an order of Mandamus against the Chief Constable. It is a case for co-operation between the Board and the Chief Constable and the use of plenty of common sense by all concerned, including those who are on the site obstructing the Board's functions.'

Well, we were ready to co-operate and had said so to the

187

Board in my letter of 11 June, and would certainly do our best with common sense.

Lord Justice Templeman said, among other things, 'This court can and does confirm that the police have powers to remove and arrest passive resisters in the circumstances which prevail at the site when the Board resume their work to complete their survey.'

The Luxulyan affair was entering its final stages.

A Peaceful Affair

It was now 20 October and the protesters had been on the site for some six months. The Board was, no doubt, angry and frustrated that the Court of Appeal had declined to order any arrests, though they had strongly indicated, at least in part, that the protesters were committing breaches of the peace. At all events, we were given the go-ahead if necessary. My own view by now was that the issue could be solved without the use of force, though the Board were now pressing me for a show of police strength at the site.

I decided to ask the protesters to agree to meet me on the site and I took along the local community constable, the faithful Penderick. We were greeted with great courtesy and understanding. 'You and your men have been very fair with us and we would not wish to cause you trouble. We do not want to embarrass you,' were among the sentiments being expressed. I asked the protesters if they would go peacefully by 2.30 p.m. that day, and they agreed. After a meeting and a sing-song they quietly left the site, having cleared away all their belongings, tents and rubbish. Lower Menadue Farm returned again to its unimportant self and the Board were now free to complete their work. Nobody had been manhandled or arrested.

Nuclear Demo Ends Gracefully and *Nuclear Protest Ends for 'Fair' Police Chief* were headlined in the Sunday press. But perhaps the most apposite comment appeared in the *Justice of the Peace* of 21 November 1981, under the name of Leslie James, 'Although the recent judgment [in the Luxulyan case] will have potentially strengthened the Chief Constable's arm in dealing with those who are obstructing the Board in carrying out its survey work on a farm in Cornwall, it has not necessarily transferred the onus of taking action from the Board to the police. It is still within the discretion of the Chief Constable to require the Board to take initial action and it would be consistent with his commendable anxiety to maintain a harmonious relationship with the community he serves if he did so... It would seem that Mr. Alderson has been substantially vindicated in his efforts to avoid confrontation between his officers and the members of the public taking part in the obstruction and charges in the media of naivety on his part have not been justified. At a time when the police image is not everywhere free of criticism, we hope his courageous stand for a close identification of interest between the police and public will not be undermined.'

The sheep and cattle have now taken over the farm in Cornwall and the Central Electricity Generating Board, at least for the time being, have transferred their interest elsewhere. A community and their policeman carry on as before—so far without the trouble or benefits of a nuclear power station.

Part Three

THE SOCIAL ORDER:
A COMMUNITARIAN BASE

Chapter 12

Policing Ourselves

I have sought to argue throughout the preceding chapters that many of Britain's problems of crime and public disorder are not only inevitable but stem also from the nature of the social structure and the cultural and social changes taking place. However, what has been said about Britain can, pari-passu, be said about Western countries generally. Conversely, the social structures and culture of both China and Japan, the one totalitarian, the other democratic, show a greater ability to contain crime, at least superficially. The contrast supports the view that containment of criminal behaviour is achieved (or not) as much through cultural and social characteristics as though political and police systems.

As David Bayley points out in his comparison of Japanese and United States police[1], 'Searching for an explanation of the remarkably different crime rates in Japan and the United States, it is a mistake to write off as fortuitous the fact that Japanese, compared with Americans, are less combative in confrontation with authority; that offenders against the law are expected to accept the community's terms for resocialisation rather than insisting on legal innocence and bargaining for the mitigation of punishment; that individual character is thought to be mutable, responsive to informal sanctions of proximate groups; that government intervention in social life is more acceptable and that individuals feel a moral obligation to assist actively in preserving moral consensus in the community.' As he so rightly points out, if social context is crucial for understanding how the police behave, it is unlikely to be less important for understanding criminal deviance.

The kernel of the argument therefore is that, for our problems of crime and disorder to be diminished, the social structure in which people grow up and live out their lives requires adjustment. The idea to be exploited, which is by no means new (though the social context is new), is that an extension of democratic activity and participation must be sought and encouraged, since chaos or repression are the unattractive, but probable, alternatives.

'It may be that the evolution of the structures of representative government which has concerned western nations for the last century and a half is now entering in a new phase. There is a growing demand by many groups for more opportunity to contribute, and for more say in the working out of problems which affect people, not merely at an election but continuously as proposals are being hammered out, and certainly as they are being implemented.'[2]

The Skeffington Committee's observations, made as early as 1969, anticipated impulses for participatory action which have increased and will no doubt continue to do so, until they become irresistible. They may also represent the genesis of another lurch forward in the evolution of Western society.

Sir Henry Sumner Maine's famous aphorism that the movement of progressive societies has hitherto been a movement 'from status to contract' expresses the growth of the idea of individualism. The contrast between primitive and developed societies, he declared, 'may be most forcibly expressed by saying that the unit of an ancient society was the Family, of a modern society, the Individual'.[3]

The legal notion that each adult individual is capable of making a contract, binding upon him until it is breached or completed, has undoubtedly permeated political thought and provided the theoretical basis for the progress of democratic government since at least the seventeenth century. Bertrand Russell, commenting on the great philosophical protagonists of this theory as a basis of government, explains, 'Some writers regarded the social contract as a historical fact, others as a legal fiction; the important matter for all of them was to find a terrestrial origin for governmental authority. In fact they could not think of any alternative to divine right except the supposed contract.'[4]

More recently in Western society, the rise of individualism has placed considerable strains on the social order as people have asserted their human rights, their rights to choose their own moral standards and their often idiosyncratic way of life. This weakening of consensus has often elevated the status of the individual in the social order, but at times has diminished it. The plural society has its great merits, but it is not easy to control.

However, 'man is not a solitary animal, and so long as life survives, self-realisation cannot be the supreme principle of ethics.'[5] The reconciliation of man as an individual and man as a member of society is central to considerations of social order.

I have argued elsewhere (see Appendix A) that, when people talk of policing by consent, they are in fact referring to some notion of a social contract between the police and public in general as well as at the individual level. In the most basic sense, this means that 'If you, the police, perform your function fairly, I will submit to the authority vested in you, and indeed will help you in the discharge of your task.' This is not a written contract, nor can either of the parties to it opt out. If the policeman opts out of enforcing laws or applies them unfairly or illegally, he is in dereliction of his duties and can be disciplined. Similarly, if individuals or groups seek to opt out of complying with the laws, they will soon be made to realise that there are penalties involved. The 'contract', however, is basically not one between police and public but between government and public. The contract can be changed to a limited extent through the ballot box but the Constitution of the Crown in Parliament, the legislature, is binding on all.

Modifying the fictional social contract through the ballot box is, however, a fairly recent development in Western Societies. In Great Britain, universal franchise only came about after a prolonged and sometimes painful struggle. Women in general secured the vote on an equal footing with men only as recently as 1928, and persons of 18 only secured it in 1969.

As the Skeffington Committee commented, however, the idea of representative government may require some reconsideration in the light of social advances. The advent of the Welfare State was, in contractual terms, the promise that governments would provide health care, education and social security for all people irrespective of their social standing. It has long been accepted that one of the obligations of all

195

governments is to maintain law and order and to defend the realm, but the idea that they should relieve people of the need to care for much of their own social welfare is fairly modern.

Governments are now finding it increasingly difficult, in economic terms, to maintain existing levels of social welfare, much less to plan for its desirable extension. Mrs. Thatcher and many of her closest supporters refer to themselves as old-fashioned liberals with a belief in self-reliance and the discipline of the market place—a reversion, it seems to many, to the tenets of laissez-faire. The growth of unemployment and the subsequent loss of tax revenue and the high cost of unemployment benefits may well provide an excuse and an opportunity to reduce commitment to the idea of the Welfare State. Should this happen on a large scale, the consequences for the social order would be considerable. Not only would the nation divide on economic terms—with legions perpetually dependent on the charity of the state and others benefitting from smaller yet more profitable industrial and service sectors—but it would also divide in political terms more acutely than at any time in the recent past. One party would maintain the values of those doing well out of the new social order while others polarised in fighting for the cause of those doing badly. A sense of grievance would fester and it would become impossible to achieve change through the ballot box. (However large the minority of the disadvantaged may grow, they will remain a minority.) The tyranny of the majority will prevail, and high levels of crime and political violence will become probable.

In such a situation, many people would abandon the social contract. The police and the criminal justice system would be out of harmony with perceived social justice. Society would become more unattractive, discriminatory and brittle.

I want, however, to suggest a way out of a number of dilemmas, doubts and uncertainties, for those whose professional concern or civic awarenesss leads them to seek better alternatives to our present social system. It would be absurd to invent and elaborate some Utopian ideal unattainable by twentieth century man struggling in a complicated and often hostile environment. Nor would it avail any of us concerned with practical issues, such as crime and public disorder, to embark on a grand plan or theory to create a new society of an ideal nature. The issue before us is simple—we take what we have with all its imperfections and do the best that we can to make it work better.

I suggest that experience in human affairs, in the administration of justice and in the control of organisations, provides opportunities to envisage a step forward in the general scheme of things. The step in this case is the further development of a communitarian base for the existing social order. If any inspiration is required, let it come from the cradle of democracy. 'Moral ideals—the sovereignty of law, the freedom of equality of citizens, constitutional government, the perfecting of man in a civilised life—are always for Aristotle the ends for which the State ought to exist. What he discovered was that their ideals were infinitely complicated in their realisation and required infinite adjustment to the conditions of actual government. Ideals must exist not like Plato's pattern in the heavens, but as forces working in and through agencies by no means ideal.'[6]

Chapter 13

Communitarianism

The Social Superstructure

The superstructure of our society, though undoubtedly imperfect, continues to function reasonably well. In other words, our institutions have stood up to the immense strains placed upon them in recent times. There are cracks appearing, however, which will demand attention. The racial issue remains a stain on our traditional tolerance of strangers, and our political institutions require the introduction of electoral reform and a Bill of Rights. There are acute tensions and conflicts between central and local government and between unions and employers (including the state in its role of employer).

It is not only the superstructure, however, which should and does concern us, but conditions in many of our communities where social cohesion has broken down or is disorganised. The power and resources at present deployed in an attempt to deal with many of the problems of social order, particularly in the urban areas, are vested, of course, in the superstructure. That is where the decisions are made, that is where the bureaucracies of state are to be found.

In the past, it was popularly believed that much crime and public disorder would disappear from society once abject poverty was eliminated—and yet despite the Welfare State no such thing has happened. Others have argued (and do so still) that the key is to be found in the criminal justice system. More police, more courts, more penal institutions and harsher punishments would provide the answer—yet in British experience this has not happened either.

'But we have no evidence to demonstrate that advances in prosperity, welfare and education have reduced its incidence or even restrained its rise. Nor has it been shown that more elaborate devices in the classification and treatment of offenders have made any impact on the rates of recidivism.'[1]

The conundrum of crime is posed by Sir Leon Radzinowicz when he asks the question, 'Why should it be that a century of theorising and research should have made little or no apparent impact either upon the trends of crime in society or upon our ability to modify criminal tendencies in individuals?' He is forced to conclude, 'It is easy to ask for general explanations or expect straightforward remedies. But the more we learn and experiment, the more we are driven to recognise the limits of our power to control either society or individuals.'[2] With his co-author, he concludes a tour de force of criminological theory and a career dedicated to international enquiry with this observation about the growth of crime; 'So far there has been no reversal, even stabilisation, in the trends of crime. For the time being we have to live with it and try to contain it.'

The Social Substructure

If the political and bureaucratic superstructure of modern Britain works, with all its imperfections, the same cannot be said of the social and political substructure.

As both government and state bureaucracies strengthen their power over people's lives, consensus withers away and social apathy and alienation at community level increase. If power at 'establishment' level is firmly moored, the spirit and reality of community in many places can be said to have slipped their moorings. In this context, three recent important reports highlight a paradox—recognising the absence of community while at the same relying on community to solve their problems.

Lord Scarman's Report[3] on the Brixton and other disorders of 1981 refers to consultation with the community. 'Consultation and accountability are the mechanisms—in part administrative and in part legal—upon which we rely to ensure that the police in their policies and operations keep in touch with, and are responsible to their communities.' Yet the same report emphasises that some of those most in need of dialogue and understanding feel themselves to be outside the community. He says, for example, 'Some young blacks [and

199

we may add some young whites] are driven by their despair into feeling that they are rejected by the society of which they rightly believe they are members and in which they would wish to enjoy the same opportunities and to accept the same risks as everyone else.' He also spoke of the breakdown of relations between the community in Brixton and the police and, it could no doubt be added, between other officials of local government.

David Donnison, Professor of Town and Country Planning at the University of Glasgow, comments,[4] 'We are witnessing the exclusion from the life of the city of whole groups and neighbourhoods. Unemployed people are more likely than most to have been out of work in the past. Their spouses are less likely than most to be at work. The unemployed are less likely than most to participate in public meetings, and—despite their long hours of leisure—in recreation of nearly every kind. They are less likely to have contacts with working people who would put them in touch with job opportunities. It is in neighbourhoods like this that the credibility of British government and its capacity to maintain the conditions for civilised order will ultimately be tested.'

I believe that Professor Donnison is right. He does not doubt, I suppose, the government's capacity to maintain order. After all, they have the police and even the army at the end of the day. He challenges the government to maintain 'civilised order'—and that is another matter altogether.

In 1980, the Barclay Working Party,[5] set up at the request of the Secretary of State for Social Services to report on *Social Workers—their Role and Tasks*, also reflected much concern for community. They reported, 'We defined community as a network, or networks, of informal relationships between people connected with each other by kinship, common interests, geographical proximity, friendship, occupation, or the giving or receiving of services—or various combinations of these.' They spoke of mutual aid and the capacity of a community to 'mobilise individual and collective responses to adversity'.

In 1982, the Thompson Committee on Youth,[6] set up in 1981 by the Secretary of State for Education and Science, reported on its findings. It refers throughout to the community, stressing the social therapy which community service provides for youth. In a note on the challenge of special community needs, it comments that 'every environment or locality will have its peculiar character and associated problems', and makes particular reference to the different and special nature of community problems in inner-city and rural areas. Among other recommendations, the Committee urges that community involvement should be made available to all young people and (more strikingly) that the provision of political education should be a normal part of the Youth Service curriculum, pursued in such a way as to involve maximum participation.

The accent on the growing importance of community and participation in its affairs is strongly reflected in the increasing activities and influence of the National Council for Voluntary Organisations. Commenting on this, their director, Nicholas Hinton, said, 'Among the less well-recognised changes that have taken place in the last decade is the increase in the activities of voluntary organisations. Whether in the sphere of personal social services, housing, services for offenders, advisory services, or the provision of assistance for the unemployed, voluntary action continues to grow.' He could well have added support groups for the victims of crime, the use of community service orders for the less serious juvenile and adult offenders, and the long and growing catalogue of voluntary action in the social infrastructure.

The National Association of Victims (of Crime) Support Schemes reported that in 1981 at least 27,521 people were referred to them for help; and that local groups joining the association number 114 and are still increasing.

The National Federation of Community Organisations which separated from the NCVO in 1982 reports that community groups now number over 800 and are growing fast and that, for millions of people, voluntary neighbourhood groups are a significant feature of local life, promising educational, recreational and social facilities with a local community focus. They are campaigning for the appointment of a Minister of Community Affairs and community affairs committees in local government as well as improved use of powers under the Education Act 1944 for adequate facilities for further education and leisure time occupation. As unemployment for many becomes a permanent prospect, the

201

importance of this work speaks for itself.

In some areas, women have come together to form Rape Crisis Centres to help those who suffer from the exceptional effects of this type of crime. To the contemporary developments of mutually supportive groups of one kind or another to meet novel situations might be added a long list of existing bodies too numerous to mention. As central and local government falters, or runs out of resources, initiative and impact, it seems that there is already a powerful force for community activity poised to fill at least some of the vacuum.

All this is very well as far it goes, and some would say that it has gone far enough. When ordinary citizens begin to seek accountability of their professional public servants and when they are excluded from the distribution of power and its effects, they need more than the opportunity to engage in voluntary tasks to keep them from asking awkward questions and seeking to influence the policy working and implementation which so many carry out in their name, but not always in their interests. We are concerned here with more participation and less government.

Concluding his comments in his BBC lectures *On Britain*[7], Ralph Dahrendorf, Director of the London School of Economics, said of the people themselves, 'They may join forces, create organisations, build localities, set up enterprises, but they must not wait for anyone else to tell them what to do. On the contrary, the leash of government has to be pulled and pulled until it gives. A network of relationships which holds people, and a full life of activity which gives them satisfaction, are two objectives of which sight must not be lost.'

The growth of voluntary organisations is only the tip of the iceberg—new ways have to be found to release 'people potential' in dramatic form for everyone, not just for the socially able, articulate and well organised middle classes. People power is a nation's last resource.

I have been convinced, from experience and inquiry, that it lies within the capacity of the community itself to solve many of the social problems that give rise to delinquency. The setting up of the Exeter Community Policing Consultation Group[8] in 1976 was the practical application of this belief. It was a modest attempt to solve problems within a community instead of attempting to impose solutions upon it. The original aim of the experiment was to reduce crime. It was started by the police. It was stimulated by a cutback in resources and by the realisation that alone we were unable to make a lasting impact on crime, and nor could it be done by traditional means. Crime is encouraged by factors which are clearly not the responsibility of the police, but of other agencies. As these other agencies become involved, the focus shifts from crime to other social problems such as housing, planning, welfare, education. Thus a consultative group finds itself tackling a much wider range of problems than was originally foreseen. This movement not only provided the model for policing within the community recommended to Lord Scarman in his inquiry following the 1981 riots, but it has now been implemented as standard procedure by the Home Office and will be a statutory obligation when the Police Bill, presently under consideration, becomes law.

The implications are, however, much wider than its effect on the police, for it reveals that there is a much greater need to tap the energy, imagination and initiative of communities through an extension of democratic political activity. The social substructure lies largely untapped.

R. H. Tawney expressed it well when he said, 'A local community of one kind or another is, in the first place, the normal environment of man, and the quality of his life depends in no small degree on what he makes of it, and what it makes of him. In the second place, the local units are the primary cells of a larger organism, in Europe usually the nation state. As the vitality of the former is, so will the health of the latter be. And, finally, many issues often described as of national importance are of their nature such that, unless grasped in terms of their local setting, they cannot be effectively grasped at all.'[9]

We are once more drawn to the inescapable conclusion that the vitality of social order in our communities will determine the health of the body politic. After all, provided that communities are working well even poor government can be tolerated. The converse, however, is not true. It is to the betterment of those primary cells of society that I now propose to turn.

The Primary Cells

Neither Parliament nor local government serve what I will call community democracy. By community is meant the primary cells of society—the neighbourhoods; by democracy is meant the right and duty of all adult persons to participate.

There is nothing new in this. Trial by jury provides a perfect example. A community trusts a group of their neighbours, twelve in number, to determine (with legal advice) the guilt or innocence of alleged offenders. They are not experts in law or government, but are given the important collective responsibility of participating in the criminal justice system of the land. The same principle operates in the magistrates' courts, where people from many walks of life not only adjudicate on the guilt or innocence of minor offenders, but also devise the punishment. If we are looking, therefore, for examples of citizen participation in the making of important decisions, our system of criminal justice provides it. These 'primary cells' with all their human frailty, by general consent work well.

The idea that citizens in a democracy should be enabled to participate in public affairs and political activity is well over two thousand years old. '... for a Greek, citizenship always meant some such participation, much or little.'[10] In Britain today, the growing need and desire for participation requires that it should be much rather than little. The ballot box in parliamentary and local government elections, on the other hand, is little rather than much. We do not always trust or agree with politicians and their officials. Our present government was elected with the support of less than one third of the electorate.

Politicians rate very low in public estimation compared with most of those in the professions and public services. The reform of local government, carried out in 1974, weakened its links with neighbourhood affairs. It is no longer, in the true sense, 'local'. Councillors serve their wards as representatives but cannot guarantee to improve or change neighbourhood facilities nor solve neighbourhood problems. They are not only subject to party political pressures, but may belong to one of the permanent minority parties which are themselves lacking power to effect change. As representatives and not delegates, they are free to ignore the issues troubling their wards. True, they may fail to be re-elected, but the position of their successors would be no different. This at a time when more citizens than ever before have more knowledge, more ability, more information and more inclination to participate. Ironically we have to re-invent local government for tomorrow's society.

The Community Forum

A network of community forums should be provided as a first step to tap the resource of people power. Every adult person should have the right to belong. Each street, housing complex or apartment block would appoint a delegate to represent their views at the forum which would meet in public. Being a delegate and not a representative would require the person nominated to seek and express the views of the residents. As the scope of the forum would be confined to local matters, people would be discussing issues with which they were familiar.

The forum area would cater to some 15,000 to 20,000 inhabitants in urban areas, though fewer in suburbs where the density of population is lower. The parish councils already partly fulfil this function in the rural parts of the country. Local authorities should be made reponsible for drawing up a definitive map, marking our community forum areas, having regard to both the topography and the demography of the district. In most places, even in the seeming anonymity of inner-cities, there are communities which can easily be identified. The Barclay Committee on social work set out useful criteria when they reported, 'What we mean (by community) is best illustrated from the standpoint of an individual person living in a particular locality. He is likely to share things in common with, and to feel some loyalty towards, a number of other people within a particular geographical area—his family, his immediate neighbours, relatives and friends readily accessible, employers and fellow employees if he works in the area, local shopkeepers and school teachers; publicans and others who cater for his leisure. More remote, but important for his peace of mind, are local representatives and officials who determine his rates, clear his rubbish, sweep the roads, and make decisions which affect his environment.' This is a good description of a primary social cell.

As in similar projects under Local Government Acts, the definitive map, once drawn up, would be open to public comment before publication. The implementation of a community forum, should then rest not with government but with the residents. A formula of some kind would be required for this purpose. A petition signed by, say, one hundred residents would suffice for activation.

The community forum would be voluntary in nature and have access to public buildings, including schools, for the purpose of its meetings. The local government authority would be responsible for the provision of a part-time clerk to take and circulate the minutes of the meetings. Meetings of the general forum would be limited to, say, four per year, or, in exceptional circumstances involving a neighbourhood crisis, as the need arose.

The community forum would call for reports from local government committees in matters touching on the social conditions and environment of their area. Where necessary, they would have the authority to call for the attendance of local officials and representatives—indeed, it would be essential for local officials to be designated to community forum areas.

Community forums should be concerned with housing, planning, social services and criminal justice. They should be active in considering neighbourhood problems of youth, the aged, the disabled, the unemployed and the full range of neighbourhood welfare.

The Community forum itself would sponsor active working groups from within the neighbourhood. Such groups would be encouraged to sponsor initiatives to improve neighbourhood services in conjunction with local government. The provision of such services as transport, launderettes, day nurseries, trading posts and exchange marts could all be developed. As well as funds from official sources being carefully allocated for projects for most in need, private capital and local chambers of commerce should be encouraged to help.

Action is now urgent in communities where conditions

continue to deteriorate and where apathy and alienation fester in frozen anger, where crime and disorder grow.

In the 1960s, when I was a senior police officer in the police district covering London's East End, the Borough of Hackney displayed (as it does still) all the signs of an impoverished ghetto, in spite of (or perhaps because of) re-housing on a large scale. The old solidarities and mutual self-help generated by tightly knit communities were broken up when modern tower blocks replaced houses lacking modern conveniences. The best intentions of the planners resulted in the destruction of organic communities. Behavioural patterns deteriorated, as people found themselves cut loose from their social moorings, adrift without the social control of neighbourhoods, relatives and the 'clan'. As always happens, such social ghettos attracted the abject poor, drifters, various immigrants and the socially incompetent. The social order broke down as children brought up in such circumstances were unlikely to experience (other than school) what may be called the normal socialising processes which strength good behaviour. Now Hackney is officially designated as the most deprived of all the urban areas of England. It should surprise no-one that it also has the highest per capita crime rate in London. If we know very little else about crime we know this—that crime and social deprivation go hand in hand.

A recent study by Paul Harrison[11] reveals a social situation reminiscent of Charles Dickens' portrayal of London's twilight world of the late nineteenth century. After 18 months of meticulous and detailed study he makes the comment that: 'The inner-city is a zone of segregated misery, mysterious to outsiders. Yet its destiny should concern us all, morally, and will concern us all directly, whether we like it or not.'

In such areas, the prospect of generating active community forums and extending democracy to them are grim indeed. To do so would require the setting up of teams of helpers, official and voluntary. Once organised, the voices of the demoralised poor could be orchestrated, drawing the attention of government to the urgency of new social priorities. Otherwise crime and anti-social behaviour will flourish and the immediate official response will be the deployment of hard-pressed police with their new tactical riot squads. This in turn will only serve to harden and compound the problem.

There are already signs that in some urban areas the realisation is growing that action along community lines is vital if civilised social order is to be strengthened. In Glasgow, Newcastle and Walsall, and Islington and Hackney in London, there are signs of experiment. This is not enough. We need nothing less than a new network of community action throughout the country; we need to create a communitarian society.

My vision of a communitarian society would, by its nature, lack the efficiency striven for by bureaucrats. It would generate a new dynamism and confidence but, as a 'people's' society, it would be more difficult for public officials (with their own monopolies and spheres of influence) to control.

Where the people living in a community are not organised for effective participation, much can happen to disadvantage them almost without their noticing it. Decisions are made remotely and, before anything can be done to modify their harmful effects on the locality, the government machine grinds on. A good example of this was the subject of editorial comment in the *Sunday Times* of 21 August 1983. 'The threat to 39 acres of recreational land in the London Borough of Ealing involving 30 football pitches and some 500 games players each weekend, is one of the most dramatic instances to date of the growing attack on Britain's playing fields.' This at a time when unemployment and increased leisure time make growing demands on existing facilities.

It highlights the bureaucratic effect of the Land Act of 1981, which was intended to identify unused or derelict lands owned by local authorities and to register them. Much of this land is rightly to be sold off for building purposes, but the net has drawn in recreational land or land with potential for recreational purposes. The Department of the Environment and the Ministry for Sport, operating at the centre, clearly do not always operate in desirable unison. It is in cases such as this that a community forum should raise its voice, seek consultation and thereby act in the interests of its members.

If we are convinced by the potential value of the communitarian society and of its importance in an uncertain economic future, then a start has to be made (or, at the very least, a new impetus created) in the field of education.

This is not to decry the efforts which are presently being made by the more enlightened of our education authorities. But here I am not discussing the preparation for life in the existing social order, valuable as it is, but looking forward to a society in which participation is the norm. As Halsey pointed out, 'In Britain, political fraternity is citizenship.' Commenting on this valuable British tradition and the failure of government to 'nationalise the welfare societies of an exploited class', he regrets that 'the ideal of public service has been diluted in its transformation to an over-powerful bureaucracy. So the political organisation of citizenship, which is democracy, and the social organisation of citizenship, which is community, continue to be thwarted by class interests and bureaucratic subversions,'[12] It is in wresting those political and social traditions from bureaucracy that the communitarian movement should find much of its purpose. Education therefore is a powerful weapon.

Community Education

It is not only in Britain that social education is a priority. The Council of Europe, through its Council for Cultural Co-operation, has embarked upon a major project called *Preparation for Life*. In a recent report following an international synposium of leading educationalists, it was stressed that the future will demand more from the rising generation in the form of 'self-confidence; an ability to question and examine one's environment critically; and experience of participating in decision-making processes'. If educational systems are to develop these faculties in the young, and there is then no social or political outlet for their energies, it would amount to a form of betrayal.

The Swiss experience points to the seriousness of this conflict. In 1980, after widespread and prolonged youth riots in Zurich and other cities, a commission of enquiry was set up; it established, with a considerable degree of certainty, that frustration was the main cause. This frustration arose from the contrast between the high social expectations engendered at school and the reality of a social order which prevented the fulfilment of these expectations.

The communitarian society would not only encourage the

209

young to adopt responsible civic attitudes, but would provide them with opportunities for participation within the framework of the community forum.

The Barclay Report on the youth service in England said, 'It is felt that the community has a legitimate interest in what is taught in schools, and this has focused attention on curriculum matters. An effect of this has been more emphasis on social studies, courses for personal skills, and programmes to help young people prepare for citizenship and other aspects of adulthood.' If disenchantment and cynicism in young people are to be avoided, education should not raise social expectations that cannot be realised. There is a trap which awaits those whose commitment is to community education. As R. W. J. Keeble points out in his excellent commentary on the subject, 'So, link the word "community" with the word "education" and you would arouse a formidable array of expectations—it will not help you to say that you only intended a very limited operation.'[13]

Education always runs the risk of moving ahead of social change, yet this is a risk which has to be taken if desirable social change and progress are to be brought about. Speaking of the expectations of young people following such widening of their understanding, Keeble comments: 'Fortunately for both local and national government, they are seldom expressed to any considerable degree,' and as a parting shot: 'One day they will be.' Perhaps that day will arrive sooner than Mr. Keeble anticipated even as recently as 1981.

The subject of political education in our schools raises eyebrows. But these fears are akin to those, not long ago, when comparative religion was introduced into the school curriculum to supplement the teaching of Christianity. In a multi-religious and liberal society such as we have in Britain, an understanding of other religions is, of course, extremely important. The same emphasis must now be given to comparative politics, if our young people are to play their full part in participatory democracy. To expect them to gain their political education from demagoguery, underground newspapers, rival journals and rival propaganda is to fail to provide them with adequate preparation. The Thompson Report on the Youth Service clearly reflects the concern of that Committee for appropriate political education, while remaining mindful of the difficulties. 'The amount of political education carried on within the Youth Service,' they said, 'seems to be relatively small.' Only five per cent of local units included it at all in their programmes. The majority of local education authorities reported a similar low level of political education in our schools. 'We have to be wary of that,' was among the comments made.

I agree with the Thompson Report that lack of political education was the real danger and not its inclusion in school curricula. Any plan to widen political education would, of course, call for improved teacher training in the subject, and care with the balanced and controlled content of the programmes. 'As it is,' the Report considered, 'too much lip service is paid to the virtues of a democratic society, without enough attention being paid to the risks and hard work involved.' For those of us who have witnessed the political corruption of youth and the attendant consequences for the democratic ideal, any arrangement which provides for the loss of political innocence within a proper educational context can only be welcomed.

Alongside political and social education comes moral education, to complete the armoury of the young citizen's needs. Of course, education in all these areas (social, political and moral) should be continuous throughout life, since change is the only permanent feature of them all. The goal of all genuine morality is personal autonomy and this, when achieved in harmony with the social structure, reduces the need for the intervention of paternalism, authority and the law in human affairs. When popular morality and the law are in conflict, the law is gradually forced to adjust, at least in democracy, but the interim period, when adjustment is taking place, is often a time of social upheaval. The 1960s provide proof of this. As the young in Western society distanced themselves from many contemporary conventions and laws, the phenomenon known as the 'generation gap' became increasingly evident. Cohabitation outside marriage, easier divorce laws, the rights of 'illegitimate' children, women's rights, legalised abortion, homosexual rights and many other areas of social and legal convention were affected by moral changes. Of course, for many this was heady stuff which led them into excesses in drug abuse, sexual crimes and varieties of behaviour regarded as anti-social. But at the same time there were other gains of great social importance. The young were less hypocritical, more tolerant, keen to experiment with communal living, more internationally minded, and most certainly prepared to question all forms of authority, including the police. But a society was being created in which youth was liberated from many earlier social controls, such as religious dogmatism, paternalism and authoritarianism, and was at the same time given many more opportunities (not always legal) for hedonistic licence. Those in authority—from governments to parents—are finding that they can no longer impose their moral values simply by demanding conformity and forbidding deviations from it.

As a society moves towards the strengthening of the communitarian ethic, as is to be hoped it will, better preparation of the rising generation will be among the primary aims at all levels of education. A generation which is socially, politically and morally educated is the first step towards a more civilised and just social order.

The second, equally crucial step would be the creation of a network of thousands of community forums, as earlier described. This would bring together the right and the opportunity of democratic participation as a better foundation for the social order, one in which crime, disorder and anti-social behaviour would be contained and modified at its origins. Such local control would stop the drift towards greater reliance on the formal system of police and the criminal sanction. As our social problems increase, so do the cases coming before the criminal courts. Our prisons now contain more prisoners than at any time in our history. Hardly a triumph.

Community and Criminality

Enough has been said to illustrate the type of environment which most readily breeds crime, but crime, to a greater or lesser extent, can spread like the common weed. All of us have a moral as well as a vested interest in reducing it, whether we live in an orderly community or not. The community forum would naturally, therefore, have strong links with the many community policing consultative groups and neighbourhood watch schemes now springing up all over the country. Their terms of reference should include prevention of crime, treatment of juvenile offenders, imposition of community service orders for offenders, supervision and rehabilitative help for offenders and discharged prisoners, and administration of support for victims of crime.

In all our juvenile court proceedings, a representative from the community forum of the alleged offender should be present. Although probation officers and social workers represent the state's interest in the welfare and punishment of the offender, it is seldom that his or her community is represented. Such representatives could be constructive in a number of ways. In the first place, the community is thereby committed to the protection of its own lawful values. Secondly, it becomes involved in the problems of the criminality existing within its borders. Thirdly, it can be drawn into commitment to the welfare of its own people in the form of both offender and victim. A community forum representative might also take on the role of assessor to the magistrates. By reporting back to the forum, the people would be involved in the scheme of things being done in their name. Consequently, the process should both inform and induce civic responsibility and participation.

I have already commented on the positive socialising influences of the work-place. There are, however, conflicts within industry which from time to time explode into social disorder and in consequence damage both worker/management relationships and efficient productivity. Every police officer who has ever been involved in controlling violence in industrial disputes must wonder whether it really is necessary, or whether there cannot be found new ways of ordering human affairs which stress mutuality of interest and social purpose along with economic realities and social economic justice.

Industrial Democracy

Although a policeman has to recognise the limits of his knowledge of economics, he is at the same time a frequent witness of the social damage caused by the problems of greed and envy and of genuine anxiety concerning injustice and conflict. R. H. Tawney wrote that: 'Both the existing economic order and too many of the projects advanced for reconstructing it break down through their neglect of the truism that, since even quite common men have souls, no increase in material wealth will compensate them for arrangements which insult their self respect and impair their freedom.' In the context of social order, this can be readily understood by any thinking policeman. Further, and more important for this purpose, he considered that: 'A reasonable estimate of economic organisation must allow for the fact that unless industry is to be paralysed by recurrent revolts on the part of outraged human nature, it must satisfy criteria which are not purely economic,' This goes to the heart of the matter.

Any society which attempts to create a communitarian framework within which to achieve a social structure that is both just and workable, without bringing about the kind of revolution predicted in Marxist theory, should address its mind to the values of cooperatives, profit sharing and worker participation in management. The Bullock Report on Industrial Democracy, which came out in January 1977, failed to get backing for its recommendations, but it is a matter of speculation whether, in the industrial climate of 1984, it would be given greater consideration. Growing communitarianism as a political philosophy in action in neighbourhoods will increase the prospects of further development of existing participatory democracy in trade and industry. Co-operation at work and co-operation in communities are mutually reinforcing. They also make for improvement in the social basis for an orderly society.

The demand for the establishment of co-operatives shows a promising though not a surprising increase. The Director of the Cooperative Development Agency reported in August 1983 that, in the five years since the Agency was established in 1978, industrial and service worker cooperatives had increased from 180 to 900. They range from a work-force as small as 12 up to 1,000, and they include participation cooperatives where the workers and management buy out a company, trusts where shares are passing to employees, and 'Phoenix' cooperatives arising out of the ashes of bankrupt

214

companies. Community cooperatives are being established to run pubs, shops and bus services. It is also important to remember that viable community enterprises such as these operate within the legal economy, and taxes and national insurance contributions are paid. The black economy, on the other hand, which deprives the Exchequer and encourages illegal activity, is undoubtedly outpacing cooperatives at the present time.

Order Without Law

Those who speak of the 'war on crime' or cast themselves in the role of 'crime fighters' usually refer to the 'forces of law and order.' The criminal laws, the police, the courts and the penal institutions are thought of as the front-line troops in these enterprises. The front line of the social order is, in fact to be found in the families, the schools, the communities, the work places, the playgrounds—and in the hundreds, even thousands of areas in which people strive to behave in ways which cement and preserve order.

If there is to be a debate on the desirability of order in a liberal democracy, it is in these areas that it should begin. The present concentration on monetarist economic policies as an end almost in themselves, as a kind of supreme virtue, drowns the need for debate on the kind of social order which speaks of fairness and justice. It is no surprise, therefore, that a society which makes gods out of economics, production, competition and the Gross National Product, while paying insufficient attention to the creation of those human values which represent the quality of the social order, will always require more police, bigger prisons, and will generate a boom in the sale of locks, bolts and bars. It is not actually iniquitous to try and better your life in materialistic terms; if more and more people learn to use force (of either information or brutality) to acquire more wealth than their neighbours, only the means are wrong, not the ends. But since the ends represent status and success, more and more people are tempted to use dubious means.

Throughout my experience in the police forces of England, I have continually been impressed by the level of potential for a more orderly, happy and just society. I can think of no better

Appendix A

Evidence Submitted by the Writer to Lord Scarman's Inquiry on the Brixton and Other Disorders—1981

The Crisis in Policing

It has become apparent over recent years that a crisis has been developing concerning some aspects of policing the plural, multi-racial and participatory society which we have wittingly created.

It is not so much that the Police Service has deteriorated. On the contrary, it is larger, better equipped and more selective in its recruiting than ever before. It is rather that the arrangements for policing somehow no longer seem to match the complexity of society. This in turn tends to disorientate the police themselves who at times feel like a misunderstood minority. This is dangerous. If the police become alienated from the public on any wide scale it is likely that the fundamental nature of policing will change from an essentially pro-active to a reactive force. The former, relying as it does on public support will give way to one based on force and repression. The Rubicon will have been crossed. This in turn would have deleterious effects on other aspects of government including disrespect for criminal justice, difficulties in obtaining cooperation with the police from other professional bodies including education, social services, probation and after-care, and the medical profession, all of which are essential to effective policing. Although this condition is at present far from universal (there is still much respect for the police), it is sufficiently virulent to be worthy of correction.

The questions which this trend raises are considerable. Acountability, direction and control, police methods, and the whole ethos of policing are called into debate. The present arrangements put forward by the Royal Commission on the Police in 1962 and enacted by Parliament in the Police Act of 1964 are seen to be out of balance.

Seeking the Balance

Some, in order to redress the balance, advocate political direction and control of the police. There are many and valid objections to this.

Others maintain, with equal enthusiasm, the virtues of the present system, though unwilling or unable to account for the present problem. Others feel that some redress is needed but seek a compromise. It is not so much that Commissioners and Chief Constables have too much authority; their authority is commensurate with their responsibility. It is rather that they carry too much responsibility in the direction and control of police forces. Since the passing of the Police Act in 1964, police forces have increased very considerably in size and complexity. Like many other facets of local government they have moved further away from the people they serve. This in turn creates a feeling of impotence and frustration amongst many sections of society, including those who have the best interests of the police at heart. Those who wish to share in the responsibility of policing our society are excluded as effectively as those who seek to use the power represented by the police for their own ends. The skill is to let in the former but to exclude the latter. This can be achieved.

A New Social Contract for Police

The time has come about, therefore, when steps need to be taken to encourage and facilitate a new ethic of policing suitable to our times. The police function should take a wider orbit in which a new social contract might be developed; one in which both public and police can come together through the institution of community policing.

Community Policing—A Restoration of Balance

Community Policing requires three elements: Community Police Councils, inter-agency cooperation, and community constables appointed to localities, and this arrangement in turn requires committed leadership and wide dissemination of information to the public at large—a truly participatory scheme of things.

The objectives of the system include cooperative action for the prevention of crime, united support in reducing fear of crime, the creation of trust or its reinforcement in neighbourhoods, and the better direction and use of resources. The system should be supported by a battery of initiatives from all components. Since the system is based mainly on better organisation of existing resources it requires minimum finding. Experience indicates however, that reliance on voluntary development of the scheme is unlikely to produce the necessary impetus. Furthermore, cosmetic schemes may be set up to stifle criticism. The force of law is required to bring about necessary radical change.

It is 'pie in the sky' to expect community policing to be brought about by voluntary agreement. Neither the Home Office nor Police Authorities are able to guarantee to bring about change without some form of coercion. The present constitutional arrangements for police inhibit this. In the first place neither the understanding nor the will always exist, and in the second place the concept requires delineation.

Prevention of Crime—Inter-Ministerial Responsibilities

Since community policing is preventive social organisation and a consultative enterprise, it calls for Inter-Ministerial sponsorship. Home affairs, Health and Social Security, Education and Science, and Environment should jointly sponsor the creation of the system. An advisory department for community policing affairs should be formed. This represents the central Government element.

The Department of Health and Social Security has created a system of consultation under the National Health Service Reorganisation Act 1973 which offers a useful guide.

Community Police Councils

At Local Government level, the Police Authorities as at present constituted are required to maintain an adequate and efficient police force. They should be made responsible for setting up District Community Police Councils at District Council level and Neighbourhood Community Police Councils in urban areas. In rural areas existing Parish Councils would fulfil this function. For the District Community Police Councils and Neighbourhood Community Police Councils one third of the members might be nominated by the Police Authority, one third by the County Council or Metropolitan Council, and one third by voluntary bodies.

Function of District Community Police Councils (Provincial)

The basic task of the District Community Police Councils would be to receive information about crime and police problems within the area and to represent the public interest. They would have the right to ask questions concerning police within the area, and to make representations to the Police Authority, e.g. on police cover, closing of police stations, and complaints of general concern. They would receive resolutions from Neighbourhood Police Councils and take them up with the Police Authority. District Community Police Councils would be entitled to send one observer to Police Authority meetings and at least once a year the Police Authority would meet representatives of the District Community Police Councils. Members would serve for three years or less by mutual agreement or removal arising from default.

Metropolitan Police Councils

In London this would mean a Metropolitan Police Council for the Metropolitan Police District. Members might be appointed as to one third by the Secretary of State, one third by the London Boroughs and one third by the Greater London Council, or by some similar formula. Each London Borough would be served by a Borough Community Police Council, with one third of the members nominated by the Secretary of State (as Police Authority), one third by the Borough Council and one third by voluntary bodies. Arrangements similar to those for the provinces would provide for the conduct and business of meetings. This would fill a very important gap in the policing arrangements for London since the people otherwise have very little say in the matter, save through their local MP, on issues usually of complaint. This of course does not apply to the City of London whose inhabitants are very privileged in this connection.

The funding of these Councils would be the responsibility of Police Authorities who would also hold responsibility for reconciling conflict. In serious issues the Secretary of State would have power to intervene.

In this way the police would be made more accountable to the public, and in turn could expect more public support. In addition, political control of police operations would be avoided.

District Police Commanders

Just as Police Authorities are required by the Police Act 1964 to appoint senior officers at Force level, so District Community Police Councils should have a say in the appointment of their local police commander. This could be done from a short-list provided by the Chief Police Officer and the Police Authority. Promotions, however, should continue to rest with Chief Officers.

The Community Police Council structure would be served by the police commander for the area who would be expected to know the nature of police operations being conducted in his area. Only in very exceptional circumstances should another department carry out a major operation in a commander's area without his knowledge. To do so would disadvantage him considerably in his dealings with Community Police Councils.

Community Policing—Other Agencies

Representatives from other major statutory agencies might from time to time be involved with Community Police arrangements since the prevention of crime is one of its main purposes. Social work, education, youth, community welfare, probation, health, planning and housing are just some of the services whose cooperation is essential for effective community policing. Voluntary bodies should also be drawn into the scheme.

Community Police Constable

Police officers chosen for this role should be mature personalities with the correct attitudes. They would certainly hold no prejudice against those amongst whom they are to work and, ideally, they should be left in post to develop knowledge and understanding. In addition to serving an identifiable community they would provide an effective sounding board for the police organisation. They would know when things are going wrong! They should be fully supported in their work by senior officers who would need to respect the role. This kind of work can only prosper if the police organisation as a whole is fully committed to its success.

Community Police provide the roots for the sound growth of healthy policing. The trunk and branches are represented by the more familiar police functions of patrols, public order maintenance and criminal investigation.

Keeping the Peace or Enforcing the Law?

It is repeatedly proclaimed that the task of the police is to keep the Queen's Peace, that state of tranquillity in which our daily lives can carry on reasonably free from interference. It is not the same thing as law enforcement. Law enforcement is part of the concept of keeping the peace but by no means is exclusively so.

To put it simply, if in order to enforce laws methods are used which in themselves result in widespread disorder, then the Queen's Peace has been disproportionately broken. Thus, in striving to enforce laws police have to do so in a manner which would not be disproportionate in the social damage caused by police law enforcement activity. In practice this can mean achieving objectives

221

by prevention and pro-activity rather than solely by reaction; by summons instead of arrest; and by caution instead of prosecution. Where relations between police and public are sound and stable the tolerance levels (to offences) will be known and each will check the other's excesses. This is likely to happen in a middle-class neighbourhood. Where police and public are estranged, this relationship will not exist nor will understanding of tolerance levels. It is in this situation that police action might breach the Queen's Peace to a greater extent than offences themselves. The remedy becomes worse than the disease. Community policing is designed to reduce these possibilities to a minimum. The issue highlights the difference between police efficiency and police effectiveness.

Efficient or Effective

The Police Act 1964 (section 4) requires a Police Authority to maintain an 'efficient' (and adequate) police force and the Secretary of State to ensure police efficiency generally (section 28). The concept of 'effectiveness' is not considered. The distinction is very important.

The measurements for an efficient police force centre upon the tangible—things capable of ready measurements. Criminal statistics are most widely regarded as a mark of efficiency. When crimes reported fall, this is often claimed for police efficiency. Certainly when crimes detected rise this is so. And yet neither phenomenon may necessarily reflect a rise or fall in efficiency, but of other factors outside police control. Crimes are more likely to be reported to the police where they have effective public relationships and, conversely, less where relationships are ineffective.

Response times, i.e. the time lapse between a call for police and their attendance, are also a measurement of police efficiency though not necessarily of effectiveness. By that is meant that effective policing may reduce the need for some response requests by, for example, better community policing. A strategically placed foot patrol would prevent street crime and be effective, whereas an 'efficient', high-powered radio car would react to a victim's call.

It may be possible to have a police force regarded as efficient by internal measurements such as these, but regarded by the public with indifference and even hostility. It is generally a fact that the public prefer human contact with police before conflict to impersonal mobile police afterwards.

Thus, pursuing police efficiency without at the same time considering police effectiveness is to miss the meaning of peace keeping. Whether the public feel properly policed is the aim of effectiveness. Control of criminal excesses and disturbances is as important to effectiveness as it is to efficiency but whether the public respect, trust and support the police accrues to their effectiveness as does the general tranquillity of a neighbourhood.

Community policing goes towards establishing effectiveness as does proper use of police discretion. In seeking a more effective style of policing, the wise commander will balance the use of his resources to provide community policing, backed up by response capabilities.

It should be said, however, that to base police operations entirely on the evidence of raw and unrefined criminal statistics may lead to creating unrealistic policing policies, particularly where the accent is placed on detection as opposed to prevention.

By selective preventive measures aimed at specific problems, e.g. street crime, a different climate in a neighbourhood will be created from that where the hunt for offenders provides the main emphasis. The former will accrue towards keeping the peace, whereas the latter may lead to the disruption of daily life and the creation of hostility from law abiding people who are unduly disturbed by insensitive and indiscriminate policing methods of that kind. Where this happens, the junior ranks of the police are often disorientated by the seeming paradox, believing, as they have been taught, that the public can be expected to help them prevent and detect crime.

A pilot study carried out to evaluate police and public perceptions of this phenomenon indicates that whilst both police and public believe that the prevention of crime is the primary police objective, only 15% of the public were of the opinion that this should be achieved mainly through prosecution of offenders whereas 33% of police thought this to be the main solution.[1]

There are clearly differences of perception between police and public on issues of policing and a dearth of research does not help. Nevertheless, the availability of Community Police Councils as sounding boards would help to narrow the gap.

Police and Education

The school offers a major opportunity to establish meaningful relations with young people yet they are unlikely to be welcomed into some schools if the police in the area generally have a poor reputation or where ignorance of the police exists. In turn the police can offer much constructive help to schools. Community policing requires that police find resources for this work. This is of crucial importance where there is a tendency towards hostility between youth and police. In some areas, sympathy for the police from youth (and vice versa) is impeded by poverty or cultural differences, and here extra

223

effort and stoical patience will be required.

The objectives of a schools' scheme should include:

1. The creation of sound relationships between the police and the school community, pupils, teachers and parents.

2. Assistance to the school community in its preparation of pupils to cope with life outside the school and in the development of good citizenship.

Officers engaged in this work should be chosen for their aptitude by educational as well as police officials. From time to time they should inform the Community Police Councils of their work.

Policing with Other Agencies

In order to cope with the prevention and containment of juvenile delinquency the setting up of Joint Services Youth Support Teams should be required by Community Police Councils. Such teams could operate at District Council or Borough level to offer advice to parents, teachers, police, social services, probation and youth services. The teams should consist of social workers, selected police officers and probation officers with an educational liaison officer (probably Educational Welfare Service). They would be required to take an interest in children at risk undergoing community treatment as opposed to close confinement.

More and more juvenile offenders are being dealt with in the community through intermediate treatment schemes, community service orders and after-care orders. Before such people are dealt with by magistrates for subsequent offences the Joint Services Youth Support Team should be consulted.

This team also offers a consultative service to other agencies including the police. It arranges cautions and supervision. Its existence influences inter-departmental policies, reduces stereotyping of agencies, and diminishes barriers between the various agencies concerned with youth. A scheme of this kind has been working in Exeter with success for two years and is funded as an experiment by the Urban Aid Programme. Community Police Councils could make it part of their community policing arrangements.

Policing by Consent

Much is heard of the principle of policing by consent, but whose consent one may ask? Is it that of the majority, say 51% of society? What about the other 49%, or the other 30%, 20% or even 10%?

Policing in a multi-cultural society has to be seen to be by general consent in spite of the many differences. Policing by consent has to be permanently negotiated since it is the permanence of change that poses the challenge. Policing has to go with many cultures (if legal, of course) not against some and with others. That is one reason why policing has to be community-based to be effective. It must be sensitive to religious, racial, class and other differences and be prepared to compromise with the monolithic characteristics of a large bureaucracy such as a modern police force, and to learn to serve the people not the organisation. There is a natural tendency to regard 'the Job' as of primary importance rather than service to the people. Community policing redresses this balance as police officers become more community minded.

To keep repeating the phrase that 'we police by consent' is meaningless rhetoric unless that consent is earned by the police. It is more likely to be given if the police respect cultures which differ from their own and are manifestly seen to respect them. It is a question of entering into the culture to mobilise it in support of policing at community level as well as generally.

Where the mass of the people have grown up since the Universal Declaration of Human Rights was promulgated by the United Nations, where they have been educated to expect respect from those in authority and to question their excesses, the police are likely to founder unless the very ethos of policing takes on characteristics compatible with such a society. Therefore, the training and leadership of a police force is critical in achieving such goals.

Community Policing and Leadership

The leader of a police force should set out to create two climates. The first is that within the organisation. This climate should permit the growth of initiative, fulfilment and enterprise. It should strengthen the positive aims of the organisation and weaken the negative. The rhetoric used to describe the police role is very important since it will facilitate desirable change through better understanding or it will reinforce traditional conservatism, prejudice and resistance to change, and create a false, though sincerely held, belief that all is well.

The second climate to demand attention is that between the organisation and the many publics which it serves. Again, the rhetoric used is vital. On the one hand it can create confidence, understanding and trust; on the other, it can create doubt, hostility and even fear.

In order to produce conditions to optimise the prospects of success

225

for community policing a persistent campaign of information has to be undertaken for the benefit of the public.

This has to go beyond mere news reporting. The media should be regarded as the means of policing through enlightenment, for very little police work, experience and understanding is secret or confidential. In addition to using the media, the setting up of evening classes and even day classes during school holidays helps to reinforce the flow of information and thereby to secure understanding. Furthermore, it is not costly in manpower or other resources though the results are of great value.

It is through a well-established system of community policing (as described) that the optimum conditions are likely to be created towards positive and constructive activity. The public, perceiving that the police care for their own group, or culture, are encouraged, and if given information and trust will help the police to achieve their goals through persuasion and, in proper cases, enforcement of laws. It is important that this simple formula becomes part of the general police understanding and that leaders pursue it energetically.

Community Policing and Training

A great deal of improvement in police training has been evident in recent years, particularly for the higher ranks. The basic training of the constable is currently under examination. It is regarded as being too heavily legalistic and is ready for a change of emphasis towards social studies. But good as the general training is, it cannot guarantee to deal with the particular.

Society's plurality and multi-racial make-up call for special training to deal with particular localities. In the first place, officers with the understanding for cultural diversity or with the mind to acquire it have to be chosen specially for duty in particular areas. It is only then that the relevant training can begin. In the second place, this responsibility will fall on the local commander who has himself been chosen for his compatibility with his area. But a contribution to local training can be made by the Community Police Council representing as they do the many elements of the area. This should be a joint police/public training enterprise based on the Community Policing system. This is very important for a variety of reasons.

Conservatism, Dogmatism and Racism in the Police

It is noted that people who join the police force tend to show a higher degree of authoritarian conservatism than others of similar social backgrounds[2]. It has also been noted that there is a tendency for these levels to give way to the liberalising effects of early training. Subsequent police service and cultural exposure tend to increase illiberal/intolerant attitudes generally and sometimes towards coloured people in particular. It is crucial therefore that the police should be exposed to the influence of Community groups as soon and as often as possible in a non-conflict form if they are to reach a better understandng.

Some senior officers are not immune from similar characteristics and a great responsibility lies upon them to provide the correct example and to facilitate the proper training of their junior officers.

The manifestation of racial prejudice in the performance of police duty should be included as an offence under the Police Discipline Code. Not only would this permit racism to be dealt with by internal sanctions but it would also act as a deterrent to those officers who may be inclined towards racial prejudice.

It would also help if the United Nations Code of Police Conduct, and the Code of Ethics of the European Commission on Human Rights were made a personal issue to every police officer and frequently drawn to attention.

When policing is really seen to be a joint enterprise of social contract between the many and varied groups and cultures in our society much of the work of the police will be facilitated.

Recruiting and Minorities

Community policing not only demands that the police seek identification with their many problems but also that the public seek to identify with the police. This question of identification, so long taken for granted and part of folklore, is in danger of disappearing in the plural multi-racial society unless the value of this relationship is brought into focus. This would be better facilitated if there were adequate numbers of police with diverse cultural backgrounds in the area being policed. Not only would such officers be able to interpret their own culture to their police colleagues and thereby diminish misunderstandings, but in turn they could transmit the police point of view to people of their own culture.

When Sir Robert Peel made it a deliberate policy to recruit men 'who had not the rank, habits or station of gentlemen'[3] he was no doubt discriminating in favour of officers who belonged to the bulk of people being policed. It was a conscious decision on class or cultural grounds. A similar rationale has to be considered with regard to ethnic minorities.

So long as the police are seen to represent only (with few exceptions) the majority of white British culture there will be difficulties aongst minorities in achieving better identification.

Although there are objections at present, from within minorities themselves, to joining a police force which rightly or wrongly is often perceived to be unsympathetic, bold steps should be considered to change this.

Many physicaly qualified young coloured people fail to pass the educational standard tests. This is likely to be exacerbated now that whites with very good educational qualifications are available in large numbers, many more with degrees. Unless special provisions are made with regard to coloured youth there is no present hope of improving the position. We should not continue to have a multi-racial society with mono-racial police.

There is at least one possible solution to the problem. An annual quota of places in the police should be reserved for coloured minorities. Recruiting of young men and women at age 16 into the cadet corps might be made through a thorough recruiting drive. These young people of good health, physique, sound character and temperament should be educable. During their cadet training every effort should be made to raise their educational levels before they are absorbed into the Force.

In answer to those who may say that this is discrimination in reverse it may be pointed out that we discriminate at present in favour of graduate entrants (to get our quota) who are given accelerated promotion opportunities over and above other entrants. Discrimination is sometimes made in favour of people with special talents, e.g. sportsmen and musicians.

Nothing less than a determination to change will bring about a multi-racial police. Resistance to any determined proposal of this kind should not be underestimated.

General Comment

In spite of all that might be said in the way of constructive criticism it should be remembered and stressed that the police generally strive to perform one of the most difficult tasks in contemporary affairs. Faced with an ever increasing range of demands upon their skill, impartiality and courage, the police still retain a great deal of respect, even of affection, by the public at large. They are deserving of all the help and support necessary in the proper discharge of their function. Community policing as described is designed to help them in their difficult tasks. By letting in the public to police affairs on a wider and even local scale an insurance against alienation is posited.

Nor should community policing proper be regarded as a substitute for those other and often more dramatic aspects of police work, but rather as a complementary strategy. Dealing with organised crime, violence of the gratuitous kind and outbreaks of public disorder, to say nothing of terrorism, require that the police, supported by the public through a better social contract, are capable of raising their own performance to overcome such difficulties. That, after all, is what the public expect of us, nothing less.

Appendix B

The People's Republic of China: Ministry of Public Security Rules and Regulations (Approved 27.6.52 to commence 11.8.52) (Reaffirmed in 1980)

Para. 1

To aid the Government it is the responsibility of all persons in all areas, to maintain Peace and Public Security. All persons must work together. There must be no rivalry or discrimination between Departments or ranks. To effect this Public Security departments will be established and operate in all communes in all areas.

Para. 2

All Public Security Committees must work together and be responsible to the Party Ministry which itself is directly responsible to the Party Chairman.

Para. 3

Public Security Committees must be established in all Districts and Local areas, Factories, Schools, Farms, Kai Fong (Village Councils) etc. where communes are established. Committees will be responsible for all property in their area and all persons therein will be responsible to the Committee for the security of such property.

District Committees must consist of one Chairman, one Vice-Chairman and at least two other members.

Other Committees must have from 3 to 5 members who will be responsible for the Public Security of the communes they represent. All matters and applications dealt with by these Committees must be referred to the District Committee before a decision is made.

Para. 4

District Committees must change members (no period given).

1. The Chairman must be security checked and his family history examined. He must be a true Party member, capable, honest and hard-working and his character must be without blemish.

2. The Vice-Chairman must be elected by all members of the District People's Committee (commune). He must not be appointed by any single area, party or any other faction. His work must be

examined every half-year and should he be deemed unsuited for the task he must be replaced.

Para. 5
The District Committee Chairman is responsible for:

1. Maintaining the utmost secrecy on all matters. He must make wide enquiries into the running, work, etc. of the Sub-Committee communes and other Associations in his area. He must ensure that firm action is taken against all criminals, law-breakers and dissidents and that any would-be offenders are warned of the consequences of their actions.

2. He must ensure that the people assist the Government at all times and do not transgress or oppose the Laws.

3. He must ensure that all people behave strictly within the Law and that they teach and instruct their young to do likewise. All must be prepared to work for and support the Government in its aims and Laws.

4. He must ensure that all new Laws and Regulations are displayed and brought to the attention of all members of his area community. He must ensure that these Laws and Regulations are taught to and understood by the people; and by his example, encouragement and the generous use of praise, where it is due, he must exhort them to give of their best to the Government.

Para. 6 Local Area Committees

1. The Chairman must be a Party member who must be vigilant in seeking out dissidents and bringing them before the courts of Justice.

2. He must be very diligent in seeking out traitors.

3. The Committee is responsible for the direction and distribution of labour of all persons within its area.

It is responsible for the distribution of films, propaganda, etc. in its area. It is empowered to deal with assaults and can order the punishment of offenders including exile or deportation.

4. It is responsible for the arrest of all traitors, dissidents and their associates and must ensure that all are dealt with and that its area is purged of same.

Para. 7

1. It must ensure that all Government laws are brought to the notice and attention of the people and that they are duly instructed in such Laws.

2. Secrecy must be maintained at all times.

3. Offenders must be arrested, irrespective of their rank, position,

connection with or relation to persons in authority.

Any attempts to bribe or obtain release of offenders must be severely dealt with.

4. All persons must be induced to assist authority by persuasion. Resort to use of force or trickery must not be used.

Para. 8
In Communes of large Factories, Building works, Schools, etc. the chain of responsibility must be maintained.

Public Security Committees must be elected and must be responsible for:

1. Dealing with all offenders.

2. In towns all Laws must be displayed on the streets where the people can read them. They must be read and explained to the people, who must listen to the explanations, etc. and comply with the Laws.

3. The Village Chairman is responsible for Public Security in his village and the instruction of his community re. the Laws.

4. Seamen must listen to and take orders from the Chairman of the Local Area Committee in which they find themselves.

Para. 9 Local Area Committees
Applications for buildings or extension of Party Association must be submitted to the District Committee for approval.

1. Times of work and study by the aged are to be arranged by the Local Committee but such times and work must be agreeable to the persons concerned.

2. All workers must obey local regulations but should the People's Committee or other association object then the Local Committee must refer the matter to the District Committee and not proceed with its intentions until a final decision is reached.

Para. 10 District Committees
Must ensure that all Laws are exhibited prominently (in public places and streets) and that the same are broadcast to the people.

Any person who does not listen or pay attention must be reported.

Para. 11
All Laws must come from Party headquarters from whom prior permission for all District and Local Laws must be obtained and to whom all matters referred to Local and District Councils must be referred to final decision.

Notes

Prologue
1. John Alderson: *Policing Freedom:* Part Four: Macdonald and Evans (1979).

Chapter 1
1. Talcott Parsons: *The Structure of Social Action:* The Free Press (1937): Ch. 3.
2. A. H. Halsey: *Change in British Society:* OPUS 1978: Ch. 8.
3. Bertrand Russell: *History of Western Philosophy:* 2nd Ed: Unwin (1961): Ch. 26.
4. D. J. West and D. P. Farrington: *The Delinquent Way of Life:* Heinemann (1977): Ch. 8.
5. *Families in the Future:* Study Commission on the Family (1983).
6. M. Rutter: *Human Growth and Development:* O.U.P. (1976): Ch. 2.
7. *Ibid.*
8. 'Manifesto for Change': *Times Educational Supplement* (Jan. 30 1981).
9. *The Brixton Disorders: 10–12 April 1981:* H.M.S.O. (Nov. 1981).
10. *Ibid.*
11. Emile Durkheim: *The Division of Labour in Society:* The Free Press (1947).
12. *Royal Commission on Criminal Procedure: Cmnd. 8092:* H.M.S.O. (1981).
13. *Ibid.*
14. *The Vagrancy Act 1824:* sec. 4.
15. Girth and Wright Mills: *From Max Weber:* O.U.P. (1946).
16. 'Final Report of the Working Party in Community/Police Relations in Lambeth': Lambeth Borough Council (1981).
17. Hans Toch: 'Cops and Blacks: Warring Minorities' in *Police and Law Enforcement:* AMS Press NY (1972).
18. Ken Pryce: *Endless Pressure:* Penguin (1979): Conclusion.
19. Norman Fowler: *After the Riots:* Davis-Paynter (1979): Ch. 14.
20. John Alderson: *Policing Freedom:* Macdonald and Evans (1979):

Ch. 27.
21. *The Times:* (23 Sept. 1981).
22. Geoffrey Gorer: *Exploring English Character:* Cresset Press (1955).
23. William A. Belsen: *The Public and the Police:* Harper Law (1975).
24. *Racial Attacks:* Home Office (Nov. 1981).
25. Paul Wilkinson: *The New Fascists:* Grant McIntyre (1981).
26. *Searchlight:* (Jan. 1983).
27. *The Times:* (15th August 1977).
28. Richard Clutterbuck: *Britain in Agony:* Faber and Faber (1978).
29. Helmut Schoek: *Envy—a theory of Social Behaviour:* Secker and Warburg (1969).
30. John Rawls: *A Theory of Justice:* O.U.P. (1973): Ch. 1.
31. Emile Durkheim: *The Rules of Sociological Method:* The Free Press, Ill. (1938).
32. *Report of the Royal Commission on Criminal Procedure:* H.M.S.O. (1981).
33. *Ibid.*
34. *The British Crime Survey:* H.M.S.O. (1983).

Chapter 2
1. John Rawls: *A Theory of Justice:* O.U.P. (1972).
2. 'Race Relations and the "Sus" Law': *Second Report from the Home Affairs Committee: H.C.559:* H.M.S.O. (1980).
3. *Unpublished Paper*—Institute for Criminal Justice Ethics, John Jay College, N.Y. (April 1982).
4. Patrick Devlin: *The Criminal Prosecution in England:* O.U.P. (1960).
5. *Poor Law:* (1983).
6. *The Guardian:* (25 June 1983).
7. Robert Conquest: *The Soviet Police System:* Bodley Head (1968).
8. *Ibid:* Ch. 3.
9. Heinz Hohne: *The Order of the Deaths Head:* Pan (1979): Ch. 1.

Chapter 3
1. *Article 3: European Convention on Human Rights:* Judgment of the European Court of Human Rights (18 Jan. 1978).
2. Jacobo Timerman: *Prisoner Without a Name, Cell Without a Number:* Weidenfeld and Nicolson (1981).
3. Supra (1).
4. *Hansard:* (11 Dec. 1979).

Chapter 4
1. Robert Mark: *In the Office of Constable:* Collins (1978): Ch. 5.

Chapter 5
1. R. v Commissioner of Police of the Metropolis ex parte Blackburn No 3 (1973): Ch. 5.
2. *Royal Commission on the Police, 1962:* H.M.S.O. (1962).
3. *Ibid.*
4. Sir David McNee: *McNee's Law:* Collins (1984).
5. *Political Studies:* Vol. XXIX No. 3.
6. *The Times:* (12 Sept. 1981).
7. *The Guardian:* (20 March 1982).
8. *The Times:* (10 April 1982).
9. Cowell, James, and Young: *Policing the Riots:* Junction Books (1982): Ch. 4.
10. *The Times:* (12 Sept. 1981).
11. Supra 9.
12. *Ibid.*
13. *Daily Telegraph:* (18 March 1982).

Chapter 6
1. E. J. B. Rose: *Colour and Citizenship:* O.U.P. (1968).
2. Ann Blaber: *The Exeter Community Policing Consultative Group:* NACRO (1977).
3. John Alderson: *Policing Freedom:* Macdonald and Evans (1979).

Chapter 8
1. Ken Pryce: *Endless Pressure:* Penguin (1979).
2. *The Observer:* (6 April 1980).
3. *The Challenge of Crime in a Free Society:* U. S. Govt (1967).
4. *McNee's Law:* Collins (1984).
5. *Racial Attacks:* Home Office (Nov. 1981).

Chapter 9
1. P. J. Stead: *Pioneers in Policing:* Patterson and Smith and McGraw-Hill (1977): Article by J. J. Tobins.
2. *Somerset's Case.*
3. T. A. Critchley: *A History of Police in England and Wales:* Constable (1978): Ch. 9.
4. *New Scientist:* (28 Oct. 1982).

Chapter 10
1. *Cmnd. 8193:* H.M.S.O.

Chapter 12
1. David H. Bayley: *Forces of Order:* Ministry of California Press (1976): Ch. 1.

2. *Skeffington Committee Report:* 'People and Planning': H.M.S.O. (1969).
3. Sir Henry Maine: *Ancient Law:* Everyman Edition (1917).
4. Bertrand Russell: *History of Western Philosophy:* George Allen and Unwin (1966): Ch. 14.
5. *Ibid:* Ch. 18.
6. G. H. Sabine: *A History of Political Theory:* Harrap 3rd Ed. (1963): Ch. 5.

Chapter 13

1. Radzinowicz and King: *The Growth of Crime:* Hamish Hamilton (1977).
2. *Ibid.*
3. *Cmnd 8427:* H.M.S.O. (1981).
4. David Donnison: *Urban Policies: a New Approach:* Fabian Society (1983).
5. Bedford Square Press (1982).
6. *Report of the Review Group on the Youth Services in England:* H.M.S.O. (1982).
7. Ralph Dahrendorf: *On Britain:* B.B.C. Pub. (1982).
8. Ann Blaber: *The Exeter Community Policing Consultative Group:* NACRO (1977).
9. R. H. Tawney: *History and Society:* ed. Winter: Routledge and Kegan Paul (1978): Ch. 8.
10. Sabine: *A History of Political Theory:* Harrap (1963): Ch. 1.
11. Paul Harrison: *Inside the Inner City:* Penguin (1983).
12. A. H. Halsey: *Change in British Society:* O.U.P. (1978).
13. R. W. J. Keeble: *Community Education:* National Youth Bureau (1981).

Appendix A

1. Police—Public Relations Survey, Department of Social Administration, University College, Cardiff. March 1981.
2. Colman and Gorman: 'Conservatism, Dogmatism and Authoritarianism in British Police Officers', 1980, unpublished dissertation.
3. Critchley: *History of the Police in England and Wales 900–1966:* p. 52.

INDEX

Alderson, John
  addresses Police Federation on
    crime prevention, 1976 130–4
  becomes Assistant Commissioner
    at New Scotland Yard 126
  Commandant of Police Staff
    College 126
  communitarian ideas, *see*
    Communitarianism
  community policing ideas 135–8,
    152–3, 213
  DAC for Training, Metropolitan
    Police 122
  discusses community policing
    with Alex Lyon 138
  evidence to Scarman Inquiry
    163–4, 217–29
  From Resources to Ideas (paper) 136
  handling of Luxulyan power
    station case 181–9 *passim*
  Policing Freedom 112, 139
  publicises community policing
    139
  reports on police training for
    changing role in society, 1960s
    123–5
  service in East End of London,
    1960s 207
  studies community policing in
    Far East 140, 141–53
Anderton, James 107
  at odds with Jack Straw 103–5
  comments on police committees
    108
  fears attempts to undermine
    police 108
Anti-Semitism 6, 44, 46, 47

Aristotle 197
Association of Chief Police Officers
    (A.C.P.O.) 92, 94, 102, 103,
    110, 127, 128, 129
  evidence to Scarman Inquiry 158,
    159–61
  seeks advice on plastic bullets and
    C.S. gas 172

Barclay Working Party
  defines 'community' 200, 205–6
  on education 210
  Social Workers—their Role and Tasks
    200
Bayley, D. H. 147
  compares police in U.S.A. and
    Japan 193
Belsen, Dr. William
  on police attitudes to immigrants
    45
Bentham, Jeremy 51
Better Execution of the laws of
    Ireland Act, 1814 168–9
Bill of Rights 14
  need for British 7, 11, 87–8, 198
Blaber, Ann 135
Bradley, Chief Inspector 183
Breathalyser
  police discretion and use of 61–2
Bristol
  'Black and White Club, The' 154
  St. Paul's riots, 1981 154–5
  W. Indian problems in, 1980 42
Britain
  cracks in social substructure 199–
    203
  multi-racial society in 121–2